ISSUE 48   n+1   FALL 2024

INSIDE JOB

THE INTELLECTUAL SITUATION

1 **Hollow Man**
Biden, Gaza, and the Democrats

POLITICS

13 **Crow Jane Makes a Modest Proposal** SAIDIYA HARTMAN
A solution to the problem of race relations

21 **Do Border** DANIEL DENVIR
Immigration politics and the nativist cycle

FICTION & POETRY

67 **Trying to Establish Myself as a Young Man** ANGELO HERNANDEZ SIAS
It's college radio, I said, exposure

83 **Girls and Institutions** DARIA SERENKO
I peered into their sympathetic faces and couldn't tell them apart

111 **Two Poems** LAURA KOLBE
Everything winds up everywhere, that's thermodynamics

121 **The Resurrection Appearance at Parque Lítico La Movediza** TOM BUBUL
The pope is reading Erowid

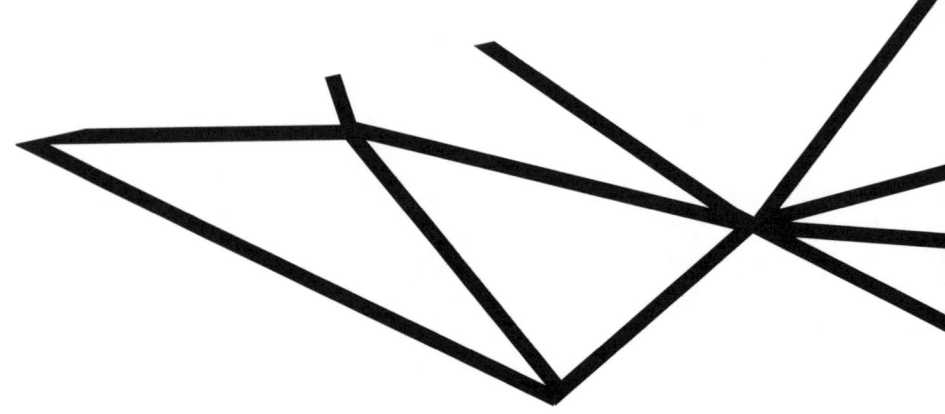

ISSUE 48
FALL 2024

ESSAYS

RAVEN LEILANI **Death of the Party** 37
On grief and writing

LEIGH CLAIRE LA BERGE **The Contingency Contingent** 47
My fake job in Y2K preparedness

RACHEL OSSIP **Eat Poop You Cat** 93
The humanity of GenAI art

REVIEWS

DAN BERGER **On prison organizing** 149
REED MCCONNELL **On Pinocchio** 157
MARK KROTOV **On the New York Auto Show** 167

LETTERS 177

One person's bag of dog hair is another person's treasure

n+1

n+1 is published three times a year by n+1 Foundation, 37 Greenpoint Ave #316, Brooklyn, NY 11222. Single issues are available for $16.95; subscriptions for $45; in Canada and other international, $64. Send correspondence to editors@nplusonemag.com. n+1 is distributed by ANC and Small Changes, Disticor in Canada, and Antenne in the UK and Europe. To place an ad write to ads@nplusonemag.com. n+1, Number Forty-Eight. © 2024 n+1 Foundation, Inc. ISBN 978-1-953813-12-1.

EDITORIAL

Editors
LISA BORST
MARK KROTOV
DAYNA TORTORICI

Senior Editors
TESS EDMONSON
CHAD HARBACH
CHARLES PETERSEN
COLIN VANDERBURG

Associate Editors
LAURA CREMER
CLARE FENTRESS
JANE HU
ELIAS RODRIQUES

Assistant Editor
NICOLE LIPMAN

Contributing Editors
ARI M. BROSTOFF
KEITH GESSEN
MARK GREIF
RACHEL OSSIP
NAUSICAA RENNER
SARAH RESNICK
NIKIL SAVAL
NAMARA SMITH

Founding Editors
KEITH GESSEN
MARK GREIF
CHAD HARBACH
BENJAMIN KUNKEL
ALLISON LORENTZEN
MARCO ROTH

Special Projects
STEPHEN SQUIBB

Senior Writers
RICHARD BECK
KRISTIN DOMBEK

ART AND DESIGN

Design
DAN O. WILLIAMS

Art Editors
TESS EDMONSON
OFURHE IGBINEDION
ZACH NGIN
RACHEL OSSIP
SU WU

WWW.NPLUSONEMAG.COM

THE INTELLECTUAL SITUATION

A Diary

Hollow Man

NOTHING SO POSSESSES THE AMERICAN imagination as presidential elections. Straightforward materialist explanations—the absence of laws limiting the length of campaign seasons; millionaires and billionaires increasingly unbound by campaign finance legislation; a vapid media class fixated on the horse race above all else—can't quite account for our misplaced obsession. Has any other national literature produced a text as deliriously election-pilled as Richard Ben Cramer's *What It Takes*, which devotes a thousand pages to the emotional lives of the 1988 primary contenders? ("Michael [Dukakis] was a man who was never depressed—not for one day in his forty-five years. He never took more than one aspirin!") In other countries, the great writers have better things to focus on.

In this context, the role Joe Biden occupied during the 2020 presidential election was unusual. Campaigning from his basement, the oldest major party nominee in history wasn't going to inspire overwhelming passion among the electorate. But his strange nonpresence would be framed as an upside. Throughout the race, the arguments Biden and his surrogates invoked in his favor were paradoxically the most minimizing: if he was maybe a little visionless, Biden would at least take up less space than his predecessor. He would turn down the temperature. He would restore to the White House the minimal chaos and comparative normalcy associated with an avuncular lifelong politician in his late seventies (rather than a TV-addled sociopath in his mid-seventies). He would only seek a single term and then make room for a new generation of Democratic leaders. Biden would hold the party together by virtue of his age, his whiteness, and his fundamentally reactive orientation; as a veteran Senate operator disposed toward negotiation, he would mediate between the party's various factions, not dogmatically hew to any one agenda—more vessel than steamroller.

In their recent book *The Hollow Parties*, Daniel Schlozman and Sam Rosenfeld describe the Republicans and Democrats as lacking in the internal organization that could, respectively, moderate extremist tendencies and mitigate elite capture. The two parties, they write, are "hard shells, marked with the scars of interparty electoral conflict, [which] cover disordered cores, devoid of concerted action and positive loyalties.... For all their array of activities, [they] demonstrate fundamental incapacities in organizing democracy." What we had in Biden was a hollow President, a figurehead with fundamental incapacity issues and little substance inside the shell. At best, Biden's hollowness contrasted powerfully with the great-man theory of the presidency embodied by Trump, and his reactivity made space for a resurgent electoral left. At worst, these qualities devolved into impotence, and Biden was revealed as a leader who simply couldn't lead.

The Intellectual Situation

THIS TIME LAST YEAR, halfway between the surprisingly undisastrous 2022 midterms and the 2024 presidential election, the upsides and dangers of a hollow President were already apparent. Biden—never, in his thirty-six years in the Senate, an ally for the left, and backed to the hilt by the Democratic donor class—nevertheless came into office buoyed by a wave of left-wing organizing. The Bernie Sanders campaign helped catalyze a progressive resurgence, and a remarkable number of socialists took office in 2020 alongside Biden. The upheavals of the pandemic and the George Floyd rebellion contributed to a collective sense that change on a societal scale was necessary, and, thanks to Biden's lack of vision and tide-drifting passivity, Congress was able to harness the anything-is-possible energy of unprecedented times to pass major legislation. Signed by Biden, the American Rescue Plan temporarily increased the child tax credit, extended unemployment insurance, delivered stimulus checks to families, and raised SNAP benefits, amounting to the largest expansion of US welfare programs in fifty years. There was no nipping and tucking at the behest of Larry Summers, as in Obama's big crisis-mitigating legislation. To Democratic allies across a constellation of think tanks, grassroots organizations, and political advocacy groups, the left-liberal war of position seemed suddenly winnable.

Biden also presided over a series of significant agency appointments early on that bore the left's imprimatur, particularly on labor and antitrust. Writing in the *American Prospect* about LinkedIn billionaire Reid Hoffman's campaign to oust FTC chair Lina Khan, who has waged an aggressive antimonopoly effort against giants like Kroger, Nvidia, and Microsoft (where Hoffman is on the board), David Dayen recently argued that Hoffman's agita is about more than one competent chair of the Federal Trade Commission. There's [Consumer Financial Protection Bureau director Rohit] Chopra and [DOJ Antitrust Division head Jonathan] Kanter and Jennifer Abruzzo at the National Labor Relations Board and Julie Su at the Department of Labor and even Transportation Secretary Pete Buttigieg, who is holding Delta accountable for failing to compensate passengers after the CrowdStrike meltdown. Over the past four years, the fight against corporate power has been embedded into the architecture of Democratic policy.

Biden's openness to the left made itself felt beyond DC's hearing rooms. Franklin Foer's account of the administration's first two years, *The Last Politician*, offers a reminder that even before Biden walked the picket line with UAW workers last year, he recorded a video in support of the RWDSU's unionization campaign at an Amazon warehouse in Bessemer, Alabama. "The White House counsel's office," writes Foer, "with its corporate lawyers and technical objections, questioned the legality of the President using his power to influence a union election." Biden did it anyway. The union lost that drive, but still, here was something new: a transgression against the natural order of things, in which Presidents gesture at labor while inevitably siding with capital.

Within a few months of the American Rescue Plan's passage, however, the activity and energy of the administration's first few months gave way to a new balance of forces—or perhaps an old one. Though Biden continued to advance various redistributive priorities via executive action—on student debt, ACA expansion, prescription drug costs, junk fees, and airline fees—the stimulus marked the legislative high point. *The Last Politician* rightly spends a lot of time on the steady erosion of Build Back

Better and on its nemesis, the deficit-fearing and inequality-loving Shadow President Joe Manchin. Named for the economic specter that had cramped its horizons, the Inflation Reduction Act that resulted from the torturous negotiations with Manchin (and his shiftier, less effectual ally Kyrsten Sinema) took no action on universal pre-K or the care economy more generally. Left behind was the PRO Act—labor's big ask—as well as paid leave. Instead of green jobs, let alone a Green New Deal, we got energy-permitting reform and tax subsidies for American green industry: nipping and tucking. Did the IRA and the related CHIPS Act represent a revival of industrial policy, or did all this constitute little more than what the economist Daniela Gabor has called "derisking," creating more favorable conditions for climate-conscious corporate investment? The robust arguments on the left about this suite of policies suggest that there is at least something here worth arguing about, which hasn't been true of major Democratic legislation in a long time. Even so, the left got less than it wanted, and less than the country needed.

After the slow collapse of Build Back Better, the reactivity that had briefly made Biden a useful ally rendered him a constraint, as he took pains to accommodate the center—defaulting to the Democrats' reflexive move. "For every blue-collar Democrat we lose in Western Pennsylvania, we will pick up two moderate Republicans in the suburbs in Philadelphia," Chuck Schumer said in July 2016, a statement almost sublime in its multivalent wrongheadedness and still somehow an article of faith for Democrats. For the left—whose national program depends on a rural-urban working-class coalition—the party's ongoing suburbanization poses an enormous challenge. Electorally it leads to the defeat of younger progressives like congressman Jamaal Bowman, whose lavishly funded opponent beat him in a district remapped in favor of the wealthier suburbs, and fellow Squad member Cori Bush, whom AIPAC spent $9 million to take down. On policy it points to a return to the punitive mean on immigration and policing after the hollow promises of criminal justice reform—a mean very much in keeping with Biden's own voting record over the past fifty years. The fragile left-liberal alliance that held early in Biden's term now feels like a lifetime ago.

AS BIDEN BEGAN to make his case for reelection last year, he faced difficult headwinds. Though inflation across most sectors had cooled, grocery prices had risen permanently. Housing costs and mortgage rates had soared. Wage growth was strong, especially at the lower end, but how much did this matter when the wages (and the jobs) were so shitty to begin with? The effects of most of the administration's executive actions and much of its legislation won't be felt for years—if they aren't clawed back altogether by a reactionary Supreme Court, as with student debt relief.

Any Democratic opponent would have struggled to land a message of accomplishment against Donald Trump, who takes credit for others' successes, real or unreal, and spins any accountability for his misdeeds as persecution. But Biden was far more vulnerable than the average Democrat. Reading Foer's generally sympathetic book—its reverent and unwittingly ironic final line is "He was a man for his age"—one is struck by the mismatch between activity and rhetoric, between real accomplishments and a story to give them shape. "Biden believes that narrative is the foundation of good politics," Foer writes, with the platitudinous solemnity of the Beltway journalist.

But was Biden even capable of spinning his own narrative?

For years his greatest weakness had been visible to millions of Americans, even if they were urged not to believe what they saw, or at least not to care. (After the June debate, Joy Reid vowed to vote for Biden even if he was "in a coma.") In poll after poll, across all demographics, every kind of voter (registered, likely, independent) expressed deep concern about Biden's age and fitness—what physician Rachael Bedard, in a recent *Times* op-ed, identified as his "frailty." This, Bedard wrote,

> is the most important, all-encompassing geriatric syndrome: it's the framework we use to describe what others sometimes understand as the accumulating burdens of old age.... A shifting ratio of good days and bad days is often how clinical frailty appears. The pattern of decline in frailty is a gradual dwindling of a person's health, a line sloping slowly downward.

Voters may not have diagnosed the problem with such sensitivity, but they knew the difference between a President who was supposed to take up less space and one who was unambiguously diminished.

A *Wall Street Journal* report in early June amplified the sotto voce chatter among Democratic voters and the many stakeholders and insiders unwilling or unable to speak their minds. While loyalists insisted that the Joe Biden whom people saw in meetings was sharper and quicker than the halting, increasingly gaffe-prone public Biden, Annie Linskey and Siobhan Hughes chronicled numerous previously unreported incidents of confusion and slippage. "What you see on TV is what you get," Idaho senator Jim Risch told Linskey and Hughes. "These people who keep talking about what a dynamo he is behind closed doors—they need to get him out from behind closed doors, because I didn't see it."

After the cataclysmic debate later that month, the news media turned up its scrutiny of Biden's frailty—his dropped sentences and flubbed remarks, his vacant squint and shuffling gait—and a strong, clear narrative, the kind that had eluded Biden for three and a half years, took hold: the President was in terminal decline. As the clamor rose for Biden to step aside and let a younger candidate take his place, as he'd once promised, a vocal group of professional and amateur pundits tried, with impressive ingenuity, to paint these demands as an "elite" revolt by millionaire donors, or even a capital strike. The rapid closing of checkbooks in Hollywood and the Hamptons was no doubt crucial to Biden's decision. But to any intellectually honest observer, it was clear, then as now, that the push for Biden to withdraw from the race was a rare example of Democratic near-unanimity. The big tent Biden was supposed to support had been assembled at last—against Biden himself. Calls to drop out came from a cross section of swing-district centrists and progressive insurgents, DC bloggers and socialist activists. For all the concern-trolling about the antidemocratic nature of the process, Biden was probably never closer to the will of the people than when he finally, belatedly, bowed out.

Between the debate and Biden's announcement that he would not seek a second term were three agonizing weeks of indecision, bluster, and inescapable discussion of Biden's fitness for office. How long had this been going on? What did the President not know, and when did he not know it? Published only a few hours after Biden's announcement—but obviously in the works for weeks beforehand—a follow-up article by Linskey, Hughes, and three other

Journal reporters deepened the impression of a code of silence. Full of sobering quotes from White House officials and European diplomats, the article opens with a meeting between Biden and congressional Democrats in which the President "had spoken disjointedly and failed to make a concrete ask of lawmakers." Dean Phillips, the Minnesota congressman who ran a quixotic primary campaign against Biden, told the *Journal* that "it was the first time I remember people pretty jarred by what they had seen." The big reveal is that this meeting took place in October 2021.

If this wasn't a conspiracy to obscure reality as such, it was at least an act of radical recklessness.* For three long weeks, and for months and maybe years before that, numerous pundits, politicians, and sycophants argued that what we saw was not, in fact, what we had seen. Conspiracy or recklessness? Joe Biden and his entourage should be forever grateful that in the end, events moved too fast for Americans to definitively determine the difference. The institutional omertà around the President's condition was the consummation of Democrats' and Biden's hollowness: Biden the symbol had to be protected, at more and more dire costs, from Biden the man. The increasing emptiness of the Democratic Party itself—its big tent long since frayed by class dealignment, deunionization, and plutocratic capture—likewise needed to be shielded from view.

PART THREE of *The Last Politician* is devoted to the US withdrawal from Afghanistan. Here Foer's book, which otherwise delivers the expected pleasures and frustrations of a well-sourced insider report, acquires more momentum and urgency. The descriptions of White House officials' anguish and the heartbreaking scenes at Hamid Karzai International Airport, along with Foer's breathless blow-by-blow narration, are meant to underscore the tragedy of the withdrawal that, Foer writes, "scarred [Biden's] legacy."

For a small but influential coterie of neoconservatives and hawkish liberals, the exit from Afghanistan was a profound national dereliction, in which the US gave up on its mission, its allies, and its responsibilities to the people of a country it helped destroy. (For the eternal cold warrior Anne Applebaum, "the events in Afghanistan" were a blow to "liberal internationalism.") The withdrawal was indeed a defining moment of the Biden presidency, though not in the way neocon saber-rattlers think. It was that rarest accomplishment in modern US politics: a concerted reduction in the footprint of American empire. For a military hegemon whose sprawl and bloat are unequaled in history, it was a modest yet momentous step. (That the withdrawal also fed another cycle of disaster in Afghanistan—with the disintegration of the US-trained army, and the Taliban's near-instant consolidation of its brutal rule over the country—is a terrible irony, but one inseparable from the violence of the American occupation itself.)

For Biden, the administration's greatest triumph abroad was US support for Ukraine. There, Biden believed, American military might was deployed in service of democracy and stability; the moral stakes were

---

* A Politico article published after Biden withdrew revealed that the campaign had done no polling in battleground states for months, as if the entire operation had chosen to stick its head in the sand. This squares with Foer's account of Biden's response to *Dobbs v. Jackson*. Though Alito's opinion had leaked to Politico weeks earlier, "Biden still felt gobsmacked by the moment. . . . He was supposed to have a raft of policies and executive orders ready to unveil in [his] speech. But he hadn't agreed to them yet."

clear and the cause was just. Foer describes the President's meeting with Ukrainian refugees during a March 2022 trip to Warsaw. "It was overwhelming for Biden," he writes. "The visit with the refugees had put him in a passionate frame of mind." So passionate that, a few hours later, Biden remarked in a speech in Warsaw that Vladimir Putin could not be allowed to "remain in power"—an inflammatory off-script blunder that the White House press team spent days trying to walk back.

It's not surprising that Biden—longtime member of the Senate Committee on Foreign Relations, interlocutor with world leaders, international legacy burnisher—would leave his biggest mark in foreign rather than domestic policy. His greatest impact will be felt not in Afghanistan or in Ukraine, however, but in Gaza. Any assessment of Biden's presidency is stained by Gaza, where for almost a year he has supported, defended, armed, and funded Israel's genocide. It is in Gaza that Biden has abandoned his passivity, where he has been least reactive and most active.

IN THE DAYS after October 7, 2023, it was clear that Israel would respond to Hamas's horrific attacks with unprecedented cruelty, and that unspeakable numbers of civilians would pay the price. Less immediately clear was how much cruelty the US would tolerate, let alone actively sponsor.

"I've been a strong, strong supporter of Israel from the time I've entered the United States Senate back in 1973," Biden said at a campaign event late last year. "I am a Zionist." As Branko Marcetic, Jeremy Scahill, and others have documented, Biden's backing of Israel was indeed unwavering during his years in the Senate and in the White House. Writing in the Intercept last fall, Scahill described a 1982 Senate Committee on Foreign Relations meeting with Israeli prime minister Menachem Begin. Then-senator Biden defended Israel's invasion of Lebanon and its right to self-defense in such stark terms ("If attacks were launched from Canada into the United States, everyone here would have said, 'Attack all the cities of Canada, and we don't care if all the civilians get killed'") that even Begin was taken aback. "I said to him: No, sir; attention must be paid," Begin told reporters at the time. "This is a yardstick of human civilization, not to hurt civilians."

The intensity of Biden's passion for Israel has been the great constant of his career—perhaps the only one. When George W. Bush condemned Israel's "targeted killings" of Palestinians in 2001, Biden criticized Bush and defended the policy. During the 2021 Gaza war—the first test of Biden's orientation toward Israel as President—he never wavered. "In [Biden's] view," Foer writes, "the quickest way to end the conflict was to stand squarely with Israel, to smother Netanyahu with love. Then, at the right moment, Biden said that he would take advantage of the trust he had deposited in the bank."

At various points during Biden's term, it was tempting to look back at the primaries and imagine another Democratic President as a superior alternative. Perhaps President Buttigieg might have pushed Manchin further on Build Back Better. Even a President Klobuchar likely would have communicated her administration's accomplishments more effectively. President Sanders—well, that goes without saying. Almost any other candidate would have been more principled; literally anyone would have been more dynamic. But in the immediate aftermath of October 7 it was evident that Biden, already unpopular and diminished, wasn't merely a suboptimal choice whose rapprochement with the left dissipated not long after it began. He was, in fact, the very worst option. The hollow President had a single issue on which he was resolute, on which he would entertain no entreaties or counterarguments from members of his party. On Israel, Biden would be more than a vessel. He would steamroll ahead, no matter where the path took him.

Not that the Democrats were in any position to restrain him. The US-Israel alliance is all-powerful: its roots lie too deep for any one politician, administration, or party to extract. Within the Pentagon, among self-styled "single-issue" donors like Miriam Adelson and Haim Saban, and in the offices of AIPAC and other Zionist lobbying powerhouses, support for Israel is the sine qua non of US politics. Most elected Democrats are seduced, to varying degrees, by the Israel lobby. Even those who avoid complete seduction fall prey to the hegemonic view of Israel as an ally and "her" (always that disturbing feminine possessive pronoun) antagonists as uncivilized hordes and terrorists. Very few Democrats have expressed meaningful criticism of Israel's actions since October 7, and perhaps only one congresswoman, Michigan's Rashida Tlaib, has been a consistent voice of opposition. (For this she has been targeted relentlessly by members of her own party and, it goes without saying, Republican opponents.)

And still, with his calcified commitment to Israel as an emotional beacon rather than a nation-state, his reflexive rejection of all differing perspectives, and his permanent deference to Israeli leadership, Biden was uniquely unsuited for the moment. Even if the differences between him and a more agile median Democrat would have amounted to a slightly longer pause in bomb shipments, or more vocal determination to keep aid flowing, many thousands of lives might have been spared. Not that this would have been anywhere near enough.

In the time between October 7 and October 18, when Biden gave Benjamin Netanyahu a bear hug on the tarmac of Ben Gurion Airport in Tel Aviv, at least 3,000 people were killed and 12,500 injured. That day the head of the World Health Organization, Tedros Adhanom Ghebreyesus, declared that the situation in Gaza was "spiraling out of control." By October 25, at least 7,000 people had been killed and the health-care system in Gaza was in "complete collapse," according to the Gaza Health Ministry, with another 7,000 sick and wounded patients in the territory's hospitals facing death. That day, at a press conference with Australian prime minister Anthony Albanese, Biden said, "I have no notion that the Palestinians are telling the truth about how many people are killed. I'm sure innocents have been killed, and it's the price of waging a war. . . . But I have no confidence in the number that the Palestinians are using." In October alone, the IDF bombed the Jabalia refugee camp five times and would bomb the camp again on November 1. The estimated death toll from these strikes was over three hundred.

By January, Israel had destroyed or damaged at least half of all buildings in Gaza. A week after authorizing airstrikes against the Houthis, Biden was asked outside the White House about the efficacy of those strikes. "Are they stopping the Houthis? No," he said. "Are they going to continue? Yes." In April, Israeli finance minister Bezalel Smotrich called for the "total annihilation" of Gaza. "There are no half measures," he said.

On July 25, forty-five American doctors and nurses who had volunteered in Gaza since October 7 published an open letter to Joe Biden, Jill Biden, and Kamala Harris. Their report was a rare firsthand glimpse into the near impossibility of life under the Israeli assault. "With only marginal exceptions," they wrote, "*everyone* in Gaza is sick, injured, or both. This includes every national aid worker, every international volunteer, and probably every Israeli hostage: every man, woman, and child." They wrote that they had all "treated children in Gaza who suffered violence that *must* have been deliberately directed at them. Specifically, every one of us *on a daily basis* treated preteen children who were shot in the head and chest." "We cannot believe," they wrote, "that anyone would continue arming the country that is deliberately killing these children after seeing what we have seen." But Biden wouldn't—perhaps couldn't—see it.

EVEN FOR A NATION obsessed with presidential politics, the past summer has furnished a shocking density of spectacle. The calamitous debate; the torpor over Biden's decision-making and the internecine drama in the Democratic Party; the surreal assassination attempt against Donald Trump; the Republican National Convention that began two days later, where the hateful and punitive conservative project put itself on full display and coronated its new geriatric-millennial standard-bearer, J. D. Vance; Trump's endless, soul-sucking RNC acceptance speech; Biden's unassuming announcement-via-PDF of his decision to withdraw; the impossibly rapid rise of Kamala Harris in his place.

In the US this was a season of unprecedented political dynamism. In Gaza, it was the tenth month of horror. More than 1,200 people were killed in the tense and hectic weeks between the debate and Harris's ascent, and nearly 4,000 people were injured. On the day of the debate, Congress voted to ban the State Department from citing statistics from the Gaza Health Ministry. By that point, nine in ten people across the Gaza Strip had been internally displaced, some up to ten times. At long last, the UK decided to start funding UNRWA again after a coordinated—and subsequently debunked—Israeli PR campaign that crippled the main humanitarian operation in Gaza, introducing the explicit threat of famine and marking a new phase in the genocide. The Knesset gave preliminary approval to a bill that would declare UNRWA a terrorist organization, while the US, its most important funder, continued to withhold support. The US's much-hyped temporary shipping port on the Gaza coast, which delivered a fraction of the humanitarian aid that could have traveled through the Rafah crossing if Israel hadn't insisted on its closure, was disassembled, and tons of goods were left to rot in the sun. The International Court of Justice declared that Israel's occupation of Palestinian territories is illegal. The *Lancet* estimated that, accounting for famine and disease, the death toll in Gaza could exceed 186,000.

"I've been doing this a long time," Joe Biden said on October 11. "I never really thought that I would see and have confirmed pictures of terrorists beheading children." But as a White House official soon confirmed, Biden hadn't seen those pictures—allegedly from Hamas's October 7 attacks—because their existence has never been verified. Did he think he had seen them? Did he refuse to believe that he hadn't? The *Washington Post* reported that Biden had overruled his staffers' suggestion that he cut a reference to beheaded children from his remarks. He mentioned them again in November.

The consideration of Biden's frailty alongside the war he has championed is an uneasy one. There is still much we don't know about both the nature of Biden's condition and the way US support for the war has been conducted. Are Jake Sullivan and Antony Blinken chiefly responsible for the morally and strategically disastrous regional war they claim is only a possibility (but which has already enfolded Lebanon, Yemen, and Iran)? Or has Biden—increasingly isolated and dependent on prejudice and instinct—continued to call the shots? Has his ability to assimilate new information faltered in recent months? Is life on the ground in Gaza simply unimaginable to him, or does he not care that much? If he encountered a group of Palestinian refugees, would he be capable of the "passion" he felt when he met those Ukrainian kids in Poland? Was he capable once, but no longer? Which answer is worse?

It is safest to remain in the interrogative mode, because nearly any speculation feels obscene. But it is hard not to observe, however tentatively, that Biden's diminishment coincides with his overseeing of the genocide, as if the unceasing violence were an expression of an altogether different kind of hollow President. "I'm the first President in this century to report to the American people that the United States is not at war anywhere in the world," Biden said during an Oval Office address a few days after his announcement. Was this cynicism? Or a sign of Biden's deeper estrangement from the world he has made?

AFTER ITS EARLY PROMISE, Biden's only term as President ends with a blood-choked whimper. The President who entered office on a wave of rage and energy and possibility is now the target of such a wave: more than seven hundred thousand people voted uncommitted in the Democratic primaries to protest Biden's support for Israel. If Biden was a political shell in 2020, he was at least capable of carrying collective potential; now he is merely empty.

The appearance of a new candidate in the presidential race is welcome because Kamala Harris is not Joe Biden. She can campaign with vigor, communicate with relative clarity, and potentially energize an electorate Biden would have left out in the cold. She can win. After a long period in which Trump's return to the White House seemed inevitable, this is novel territory. On Gaza, Harris will be a better President than Donald Trump because the Republican Party operates with total bloodlust, no matter what credulous commentators say about Trump and Vance's "isolationism." But being better than Trump is nowhere near enough.

The incredible upsurge of pro-Palestine protest since October 7 has been a bright spot in the darkness of the past year, a crucial reminder that a real internationalist politics is possible, that new forms of organization can be improvised at breakneck speed, that America's young people see the US's role in the world far more clearly than do their parents or grandparents. But the condemnation of last spring's encampments by many elected Democrats, and their repression by many Democratic mayors, confirms that for all the tentative points of convergence between the left and the Democrats during the Biden presidency, Gaza has marked a fundamental rupture in the party. Behind closed doors—most notably in her recent meeting with Netanyahu—Harris has reportedly voiced more concern for the plight of Gaza's civilians than has her boss; a top vice-presidential prospect for her ticket, Pennsylvania governor Josh Shapiro, was allegedly passed over in part for his staunchly pro-Israel, anti-encampment record. Yet hours after Harris spoke to Uncommitted activists in Dearborn, she responded to pro-Palestine protesters at a rally with the snideness of Democrats past: "If you want Donald Trump to win, say that. Otherwise I'm speaking." As if she weren't addressing a core group of constituents—in Michigan, no less—desperate for a belated shift to American policy that would end the war and end the genocide. The Uncommitted movement doesn't want Trump to win, and neither did the students in the encampments. For her part, Harris will have to face what Trump never will, and Biden never could: that American policy is immoral and unsustainable, and the war in Gaza is the Democrats' war. +

Fall 2024

ROMAN YEAR
A Memoir
André Aciman

SALVAGE
Readings from the Wreck
Dionne Brand

MEDITATIONS FOR MORTALS
Four Weeks to Embrace Your Limitations and Make Time for What Counts
Oliver Burkeman

V13
Chronicle of a Trial
Emmanuel Carrère
Translated by John Lambert

STRANGER THAN FICTION
Lives of the Twentieth-Century Novel
Edwin Frank

THE ULTIMATE HIDDEN TRUTH OF THE WORLD . . .
Essays
David Graeber
Edited and Introduced by Nika Dubrovsky; Foreword by Rebecca Solnit

ANNIHILATION
A Novel
Michel Houellebecq
Translated by Shaun Whiteside

FAR DISTRICT
Poems
Ishion Hutchinson

THE POSITION OF SPOONS
And Other Intimacies
Deborah Levy

IGNORANCE AND BLISS
On Wanting Not to Know
Mark Lilla

MY GOOD BRIGHT WOLF
A Memoir
Sarah Moss

LAZARUS MAN
A Novel
Richard Price

INTERMEZZO
A Novel
Sally Rooney

LINGUAPHILE
A Life of Language Love
Julie Sedivy

MODEL HOME
A Novel
Rivers Solomon

FAMILY ROMANCE
John Singer Sargent and the Wertheimers
Jean Strouse

ABSOLUTION
A Southern Reach Novel
Jeff VanderMeer

FSGBOOKS.COM   MCDBOOKS.COM

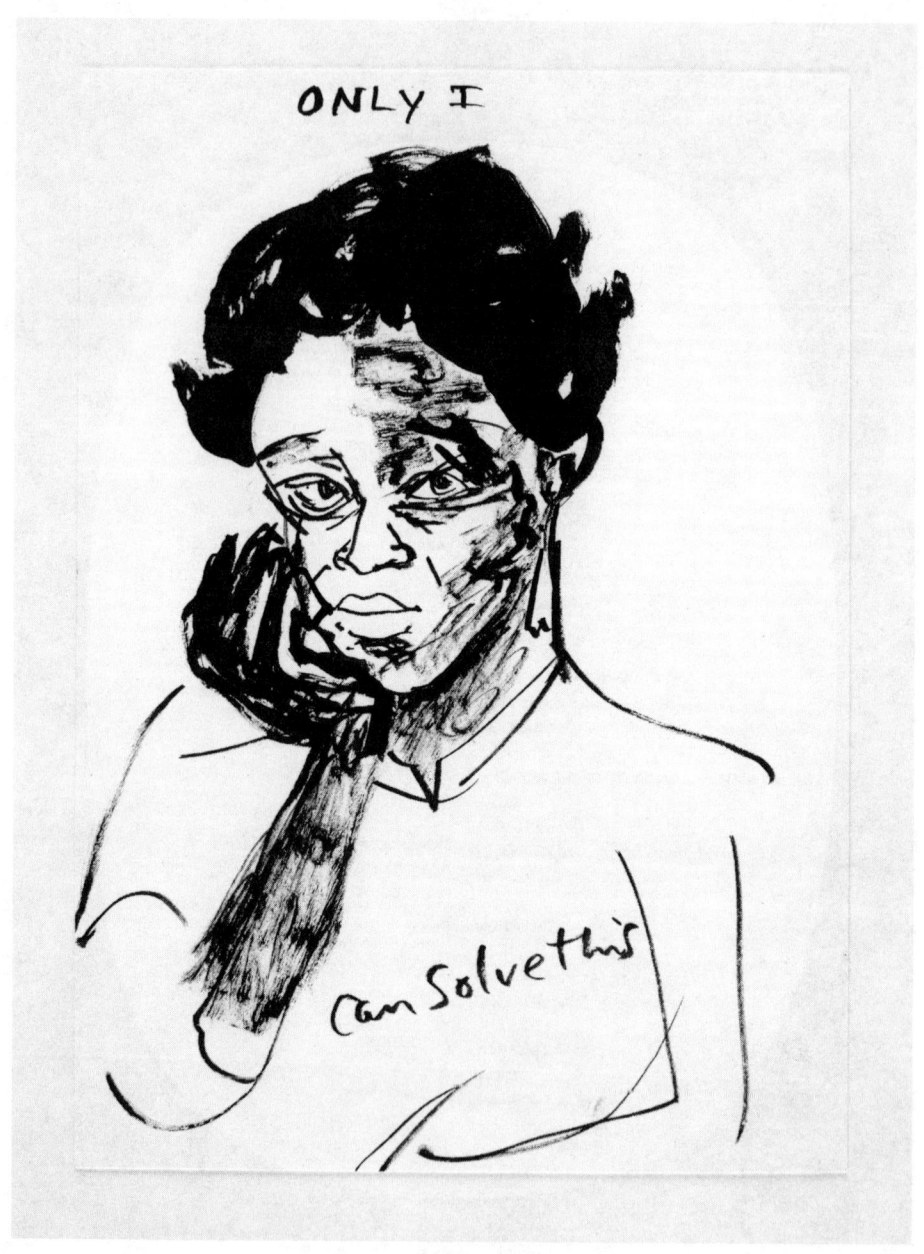

KARA WALKER, *ONLY I CAN SOLVE THIS (THE 2016 ELECTION)* (DETAIL). 2016, INK, WATERCOLOR, AND GRAPHITE ON PAPER. 10 1/4 × 7 1/8". COURTESY OF SIKKEMA JENKINS & CO., NEW YORK, AND SPRÜTH MAGERS. © KARA WALKER.

POLITICS
Memoranda

SAIDIYA HARTMAN
Crow Jane Makes a Modest Proposal

CROW JANE DOESN'T SAY *THE SUN'S GONNA shine in her back door someday* or lament motherless children or keen for those murdered in the streets, but she does assure us that a better day is coming, that the arc of empire bends toward justice. That progress, although sometimes painful, is inevitable. As the crisis unfolds, she *humbly proposes a plan, perhaps not worthy of the attention of our esteemed audience, because it consists only of modest suggestions,* a handful *of her thoughts* and ruminations for saving democracy, a task to which she is selflessly devoted even if it requires her to lick all the pots in sorrow's kitchen. She proffers a remedy for what can't be repaired, exhorts us to be patient. She goads us to believe what we cannot, eschewing everything *we* know and imploring us to forget. With brevity and poise, she insists we pin our hopes to the project. She remains confident that this remarkable journey *we* as Americans have embarked upon will be triumphant. Imperial dreams are as unstoppable as wars without end, as manifest destiny, as lebensraum, as the divine mission of the settler state. An eternal empire hearkens to the future. We are all on the same team, she coaxes, ignoring the fissures and chasms, the divisions between citizens and animals. We stand united until we are not, until the bloodbath, until democracy itself is on trial. She forgets it has always been on trial for some of us, while most of us have never experienced it. Crow Jane finds such rhetoric tedious, crude assertions of the intellectually lazy and the identity extremists, a poor substitute for rigorous thought and incontrovertible evidence.

Optimism is never cruel, she quips, but a requirement for living. It is this good faith that makes our republic exceptional and has propelled us forward since 1619. Even a word as anemic as *justice* doesn't figure in her solution to the problem of race relations, her plan for saving the empire. It is imperative to unify the divided nation (in a more old-fashioned parlance—the Negro or Native problem). She offers threadbare homilies about lesser evils, institutional neutrality, pragmatic actions, realist solutions, rational discourse, the imminent dangers facing the West and menacing its borders. It goes without saying that she abhors the violence of the dispossessed. The goal, repeated ad nauseam, is to rekindle the *American spirit*, which has been tested in recent crises. *Rights* and *reform* are words that portend a brighter future, unlike *abolition* or *reparation* or *sovereignty* or *return*, which stymie and derail the conversation every time. At hand is a trove of facile advice, DIY instructions for averting the disaster and surviving the predation, if only by disavowing it—even as we are knee-deep in it. Glock 43Xs, AR-15s, bunkers, citizen militias, settler confederations, red ribbons, nooses, swastikas, bones and scalps, cherished mammies, redface mascots, and Black lawn jockeys are part of the American spirit too, so we must learn to coexist peacefully with our differences and embrace neighbors who dream of our extermination. Her untiring optimism and dogged innocence are performatives necessary to fortify the nation, our democracy.

America is beautiful, incomparable, and Crow Jane believes she can rescue it. At least 62 percent of white nationalists might still be converted to pluralism or convinced that *human* rights don't threaten or depreciate the value of the Aryan. In the aftermath of the *evil and wicked traffic* and the way of death and the Trail of Tears, she remains steadfast: there is an antidote for the transubstantiation of the poor white into the planter oligarch and state executioner, a corrective for every white citizen who internalizes the power of the police, each day reinforcing the barrier between the governable and the disposable. As if the plot against America *isn't* America, as if fungibility were a shared condition. As if the next time, the president-elect might induce the patriots and supremacists to change their minds and not storm the Capitol or fire on Fort Sumter, not embrace the boogaloo and the bloodbath, and allow us to live; and after the genocide, he might stand heroically against the murder of innocents and proclaim with the necessary gravity: it's *over the top.* As if this is the most we could hope for, or all that we should want.

Crow Jane's lecture is a composition deracinated from the field and choked with the language of the covenant. It is reasoned, measured, never strident, to ensure its reception by those who are not inclined to heed any truths dropped from *sooty* lips, who prefer to talk about the weather as we are dying, who espouse civility as the tanks roll into the city, who demand the exchange of ideas without antagonism or unrest, those for whom conquest is encounter and slavery a training school for Negroes, those who are accustomed to dictating the terms of address, those who possess the power to deaccession your ass in a minute. Yet, in her case, they prove willing to suspend, if only temporarily, the rules of engagement, the visceral disbelief in any worldview but their own, in any standpoint hostile to their *determined chains* of meaning, and cede to the native informant's predictable babble. Fortunately, she has been educated at the most elite schools, so the master's episteme is her own. Like the quiet storm, her modest proposal is easy listening, nothing but legible speech without any discordant tones or ugly feelings; it is assimilable, digestible, delectable as good Negroes are wont to be. The *so articulate* delivery extends the reassuring comfort of the familiar, mammy fascism, statecraft in black- and brownface. No hue and cry. No *fuck it*, no *burn it down*, no *program of complete disorder*, no rebellion, no unrepentant destruction. Just this metaphorical aptitude, this figurative capacity or talent for becoming whatever is required, or nobody at all. Just the tender gift of reproductive labor *in service of* the order, the welcome of her beautiful humiliation, the betrayal of her volition, the dulcet tones of submission, the vow to wait, to keep waiting and waiting until oblivion. The propensity to endure until hardly any of us is left standing, just the appeal, father may I, master may I, man may I, which is so much better than any pledge of allegiance.

Like other realists, Crow Jane wastes no time on imagining a state change, a new set of arrangements, but rather devotes herself to the likely, the probable, the parameters of the given. An Ivy League degree and $100,000 in student debt have translated her forebears' incisive critique—same shit, different day—into her own eloquent holding pattern, a dicty expression of servitude disavowed. Though loath to admit it, in her heart of hearts, she believes the order is eternal. The admission hurts, yet is not without a small consolation—why even try to create something different, why waste the effort? The gift of pragmatism is a profound tolerance of the unlivable. The paradox is that she makes her living as a *changemaker*, analyzing the problem and proposing solutions for transformation, albeit incremental. In crude terms, she nips and tucks the racial order. 2020 was a watershed year. Her client list grew exponentially, as did her investment portfolio. She penned solidarity statements for the Fortune 500, drafted thousands of diversity-and-inclusion pledges, waxed poetic about the compassion of J.P. Morgan, Barclays, HSBC, and Lloyds, about the long history of their investments in the Black community. A feature on white fascists and their love of their Black children earned her a finalist spot for the Pulitzer.

For a robust six figures, she helps institutions navigate the turbulence produced by rabble-rousers and the ungrateful, anarchists and militants, and sometimes, surprisingly, even upstanding citizens. If pushed to the wall, even decent, hardworking folks might relish the sight of a police precinct engulfed in flames, or celebrate the vision of their oppressors quaking in fear. She doesn't permit herself to consider whether her life might be better if she weren't the Associate Director of Diversity and Inclusion or a Title IX officer, especially since most of those she takes to task for intolerance or hate speech are the university's most recent arrivals. Why can't the ethnic studies professors and the DACA students just shut their mouths and do their work? Why can't they uphold the values of the university instead of attacking them?

Sadly, their arrival on campus signals the death of liberal ideals.

This line of work comes naturally to her. Her father had worked his way up from an FBI informer to a big muckety-muck at the Department of Housing and Urban Development; he made his reputation by eliminating more housing units in one year than had been created in the previous two decades. The demise of the Black Panther Party had enabled him to purchase a modest ranch-style home for his family in a less fashionable section of the Oakland Hills. It was a time before influencer mansions and media deals and multimillion-dollar anti-racism centers and BLM hedge funds. Unlike her father, Crow Jane was no Judas goat, at least not at first—she really did intend to make things better, if only by being a positive role model for her race, a star of the flock, the native most fluent in the language of Man.

Crow Jane has mastered the art of appeal and persuasion, regaling audiences with tales of American opportunity, of how she resisted drugs and pregnancy and Afropessimism, advancing by her own merit. Or she enchants them with stories of her unworthiness: she was lazy and received opportunities she didn't deserve, and this hurt her, but eventually she learned to work as hard as her white colleagues. Now (that she got hers), Crow Jane advocates for the end of affirmative action.

Her broad, warm smile opens doors. A bear hug can do the job just as well when her words fail, or the environment is too hostile for speech. She can recite verbatim the chronicle of the four hundred years of transformation from captive to citizen, from tool to worker to felon. She notes key dates when our recognition as human beings was injured if not negated entirely, while gracefully balancing the promise of the world's oldest, greatest democracy against the peril of being permanently marked as commodity and slave. Yet in this terrible history she discerns the working of Providence.

Lavish praise is heaped on the wealthy and powerful, thanked for their generosity and small mercies, the extracted wealth parsimoniously redistributed. She thanks the donors more than Jesus because they have opened the floodgates for her enrichment, allowing her to retire from the Manhattan Institute and create her own firm, Hemings Equity Partners™, guided by the dictum *Nigra libertas, patronatus albus*. Amen to that.

She whets the appetites of the 1 percent, the great soaring predators, the towering figures, the rulers of men, the owners of Earth who still remember the stories whispered by fathers and grandfathers behind closed doors, tales of delectable flesh and rare copies of the collected works of de Sade bound in the hide of a Negress, or who fondly recall their first blue movie, *Gone to the Quarters*, in which Rhett and Mammy get down. Crow Jane, outfitted in her thigh-high patent leather boots, effortlessly conjuring Patsy as ur-Negress and dominatrix until they are frenzied with rage and lust and want to destroy anything with a vagina, or sack and impale a she-male. They beg to feel her stiletto against their throats.

Crow Jane plays the part, the vainglorious servant in the house, shucking and jiving, not putting on ole master, but dissembling before us, trying to teach field Negroes the meaning of hegemony and its possibilities, instilling the idea that the plantation belongs to us too. How one day we might inherit it. How we have the power to make it more humane. Later that evening, she kicks it with the master, downing a glass of his best bourbon in one swallow, her diamond earrings and Gucci Horsebit Chains incongruous with the osnaburg dress and the indigo headscarf covering her plaits, looking every inch the part, a planter's pinup, the bondage-and-domination imago, the role-play: *the frightened, humiliated captive trembling in front of the white master* or the rebellious slave in need of correction. In the moonlight, it can't be denied, how Dark & Lovely, how radiant the exemplary slave.

She narrates the once upon a time from 1619 to the Voting Rights Act, explicating the origin of racism. No, it wasn't stamped from the beginning, progress is inevitable, merit is the best equalizer, how far we have come. Who could have anticipated the day when the name of a Black woman would be inscribed on an oil tanker? Her proposal concludes on the upbeat: as it stands, depeopled, a great nation.

To earn her keep, she learns to spin the problem in new ways and generate new products, from how-to books to a line of apparel. Escrava Anastacia on the new Converse and Solomon Northup on T-shirts and a line of urban sportswear with the slogan *refusal*. Even the Fondazione Prada is doing Black Study, and the Ethnological Museum has incorporated native perspectives in the wall text to contextualize their loot and disarm those demanding the return of human remains. She drafts a statement of restitution, but in the small print the museum and the university assert their rights to the bones. A series of grand pronouncements to do better and try harder masks the new idioms of predation and the same ole routines of theft and destruction.

It feels good to be a role model, she reflects. Young people need examples they can emulate, otherwise they risk nihilism. Melancholy historicism, as has been documented by several big-data projects on the counterintuitive ratio between happiness and hunger in the Global South, is an obstacle to upward mobility and success.

The morality tale about her crackhead sister, her cousin Pookie, and her death-dealing nephew Bar-b-que goes over well with the conservatives. On special occasions, at a Juneteenth celebration or a mass funeral, she might even hum a few bars from "To Be Young, Gifted and Black" or sing off-key "Lift Every Voice and Sing," in homage to her community.

What is to be done? the audiences clamor. She indulges them, knowing they don't want an answer. Just words of comfort, the given arrangement clad in a fresh guise, and vague earnest gestures pointing to a path forward. They leave sated. When called to appear before a congressional body assembled to address the most recent crisis, and after due consideration of the terrible events—the mass killings, the plagues, the immiseration, the war, the camps, the boats—with the obligatory gravity, she advises: The first task is to establish a commission to study the problem. The white paper, released with pomp and circumstance, offers a road map detailing the long course ahead, the slow steady road to change, what will be required of all of us as Americans and citizens. Reform is within reach, and it need not be uncomfortable or jeopardize our way of life.

Crow Jane has become an expert in speaking in a clipped, brisk cadence, in a sonorous tone, with a dusky, enchanting timbre. No slipped *R*s or *G*s, but a sleek technical presentation with PowerPoint, statistical tables, and re(tro)gression analysis, which rouses the audience, inducing satisfied grins and short-lived paradigm shifts. Roses are thrown onto the stage, and the stampede of applause lasts for several minutes. The mob loves her. But even if they booed and threw tomatoes, she would be fine. It's all part of the job. Before each public appearance she rehearses the insults likely to be hurled at her, so now even the N-word doesn't make her flinch. It would be a violation of her professional code to ever say that she was offended or respond heatedly to the most hostile question. The noise of rancor and hate is preferable to the cut of chilly silence and indifference. To her credit, she has never called anyone a racist as an act of self-defense. She knows these are fighting words, and the meekest will go full commando at the merest hint of the charge, so she takes another approach. It is worth it if she can be of service.

The crowd loves this too—her ability to brave the slurs and assaults, yet not fold under pressure. On one or two occasions it backfires and stokes their cruelty, and she narrowly escapes when delight yields to wrath or the need to humiliate, when the hunger for violence overrides the safe word—*democracy*. Most of the time, they applaud her reasonableness, slap her on the back for being a good sport, commend her for not making a big deal of an innocuous exchange, not getting bent out of shape about a poor choice of words or hysterical about the misspelling of *niggardly* in an email from the chair, when clearly, he meant to indict the ungenerous administration, not direct a racial aspersion at junior colleagues and recently hired adjuncts. Lessons she learned from her private life prove useful in the political arena. She never makes anyone feel bad. Her language is neutral. She restricts herself to *some of us* and *we*, letting the audience decide the crude taxonomies of difference, the immutable badges and marks, the heritable indicators of privilege and disadvantage. For a moment, they pretend to almost forget that she isn't one of them. The audience leaves brimming and placated.

Crow Jane delights in the invitation to the table. If you don't have a seat at the table, she quips, then you're the lunch. Her responsibilities have been clearly outlined.

In her presence, people have the same conversation they have had for the last century, but now that she is at the table, it appears as if everything has changed. She bridges the gulf between those of us who are inviolable and sovereign and the some of us who are disposable, fixed on the losing side of the divide between life and not-life. Addressing this assembly of the powerful, the donors, trustees, collectors, board of directors, she is sassy and revanchist, perfectly delivering what they like, getting them off so easily in conversation—service by the hour or the term. She appears devoted, like a martyr for America, like a Dixiecrat's wet dream, like a woman eager to get paid, like she's on the clock for the project, like declaration and allegiance are slave play, like we have all the time we need, like *deliberate speed* is sufficient, like she can change the world—one white mind at a time.

Crow Jane is no innocent. She is diplomat and trickster and has navigated treacherous waters. *No one group has a monopoly on truth* has rescued her from many difficult situations. After a year in her first job as the highest-ranking and most visible diversity officer in the history of the corporation (a real estate company with a university attached), she had an epiphany. A lengthy search process with McKinsey failed to yield one viable candidate despite the handsome fee. The truth struck her like a brick to the head. A solution to the problem was not desired. She was one of a skilled set of personnel required to quiet the volatility of campus life, avoid the embarrassing spectacle of students dragging mattresses across the stage at graduation or placards demanding divestment on alumni weekend. A brilliant young program officer who entered the race-and-racism industry with her had been fired after devising a plan for the return of all the value extracted from the corporation's stolen land and labor. She couldn't find another position; diversity and inclusion had canceled her. Rumors were rampant. Some said she was now a trader on Wall Street, others that she was a minister at a megachurch in Atlanta preaching prosperity consciousness to her struggling flock.

At the Aspen Institute, Crow Jane explains structural inequality to the millionaires. The billionaires opt out; they don't do woke. At the cocktail hour, they seek her out. Sorry I missed your lecture, but if it isn't an imposition, can you teach me to do the stanky leg? Outfitted in the string of pearls and Hermès scarf from her gift bag, she begins the step-by-step instructions: bend the leg and pop the knee. After her second or third glass of Château Lafite Rothschild (2019), she twerks, imitating a respected prison abolitionist. The white boys are hysterical with laughter. They beg for another impersonation. Do Topsy this time.

The lecture circuit is her bread and butter. Crow Jane takes to the podium like a fish to water, like a devoted servant to the back stairs of the great house. She is no Red Peter compelled to account for his appearance before the Academy, offering a personal history of captivity and cruelty, negotiating the chasm between himself and Man. Her speech is devoted to policing the crisis and averting imminent dangers. Impaired citizenship and precarious life are no obstacle to faith in the Founding Fathers, a steadfast belief unshaken by the murder of her sister and the sentencing of her brother; true conviction is unwavering, unperturbed by circumstance. No apostate on her deathbed. No *agree 'em to death and destruction* for Crow Jane. She will continue to hold on for the last benediction.

She is a believer in the exceptional promise. The burning streets and mass shootings and state-sanctioned murders instill no doubt. She never loses heart and assures us—the some of us slain in the streets and murdered in our homes—that we won't have to tarry forever. We are the explicit audience of her address, but beneath the demand that we do better and try harder is the hidden polemic, the chastisement: Avoid outside agitators and get your shit together because the powerful are indifferent to your complaints, your protests and slogans are unheeded. She might as well say *cast down your buckets* as she advises tolerance and fortitude, which are gold, which are better than money in the bank, which are essential to the task of creating a more perfect union. In the 21st century, there is no us and them. She utters the word *responsibility* eleven times and closes with an out-of-context quote from "Of the Faith of the Fathers." Wait—just long enough to get this octogenarian into office; long enough to count the ballots; long enough to quell the riots; long enough to hide the video from the body camera; long enough to extract more from the bottom; long enough to lure the nationalists and patriots, the moms for liberty and the Karens, the gun lovers and the swing voters; long enough to quiet the abolitionists and round up the Marxists; long enough to make peaceful protest a felony; long enough to win the center right; long enough to quash all talk of antifascism, anti-Blackness, and Palestine; long enough to burn and ban books; long enough to subsidize the markets, engorge the rich, and canonize the venture capitalists; long enough for data points to cultivate desire, produce and direct thought; long enough for AI to make scholars and writers superfluous; long enough to exploit want, to exalt and intensify the illusory autonomy of the consumer's *I* and *mine*; long enough to make our cities safer; long enough to reform the police and enlarge their budgets; long enough to maim and eradicate the wretched, to watch the spectacle of our death with an orgy of tears, with sentimental hard-ons. Crow Jane condemns the looters and the rioters, the free issue, los sin papeles, the undocumented, the refugees, the arsonists burning the big-box retailers, the vandals defacing the proclamations and monuments, the revelers heaving Colston into Bristol Harbor. They clearly don't love liberty. When they chant, Reject the manumission papers, dismantle the state, free the land, she advises the governor to call in the National Guard.

The intended audience cheers, the town hall rings with applause and shouts of approval, high fives and awkward fist bumps. The ones clapping and heaping on praise, the members of the assembled body, the convention, the faculty senate, the true objects of her address don't ask *what is it?* when she is within earshot. They bite their lower lips so as not to laugh at the ungainly sight of her in the flesh-colored suit, the body bag so unkind to the darker races. They don't look askance at her large rough hands, thick wrists, and broad shoulders, or joke that there is nothing petite or diminutive about her, no porcelain doll or alluring frailty, *wouldn't want to drown in that hole*, they chuckle and wink behind her back, man-to-man they concede to wanting to do her brother too, discourse on the incitement of pendulous breasts. Steatopygia or no, blond wig or no, like Jefferson they disavow the want of the very thing loathed; orangutans prevaricate in *Notes on the State of Virginia*, making even the deceiver George W. seem less so; the rapturous dalliances are legend; the predator Presidents, great statesmen, Founding Fathers, rapists, despoilers, and rakes lie like hell in the State of the Union; the senators from the heart of the Confederacy deny the monstrous intimacies of Strom Thurmond, the threnodies for dead slave girls recited with friends at the planters' club, swear on their mothers' graves and the pedestal of Aryan womanhood to be loyal to the cause in the anti-miscegenation filibuster.

When they go low, she gets down, making even Uncle Tom's apotheosis seem half-hearted, sluggish. Crow Jane smiles, despite the black eye, the swollen lips, the blood filling her mouth, as she endeavors to subdue her public; yes, boys will be boys. She gives it her best effort, trying to disarm her handlers, escape the battle royal with all her teeth and minimal bruises; exchange pleasantries with her colleagues, her allies, her neighbors; as if a bright smile or choked laughter might provide a solvent against hate, goad loathing into affection, turn negation into recognition, make analogy of antagonism. How might she rearrange their desire? Or change their mind about some of us and let just a few escape their heel? Quell their doubts by touting our accomplishments and how little of it would have been possible without the little lady who started the war, the army of teachers, the philanthropists, and the Society to Protect and Care for the Darker Races? She rewrites the history of slavery as a story of interracial cooperation and friendship, insisting the slave has no heir, and Black radicalism no future.

This abject groveling doesn't shield her from enmity or the blunt force of contempt and derision. A pit of doubt opens in her solar plexus. Has she been wrong about everything? In a moment of panic before the sea of Anglo-Saxon faces, she wants to retract everything. A voice in her head pleads, get me out of this now. But how? She could bolt from the podium, but there is nowhere to run and hide; she wouldn't get far before her hosts blocked the path and asked, what the hell are you doing? They didn't pay her for this nonsense. She counts to ten, catches her breath, composes herself, and proceeds. She is exhausted before she opens her mouth, humbled with gratitude, flushed with shame. Incorporated by the structure, puffed up with the little power they have deigned to give or concede, she laughs at herself, as she ventriloquizes the language of state and empire. She laughs exquisitely. She goes for the language of the mountaintop when they reach for the tiki torches. She reiterates the pledge: *I am not trying to reconstruct anything.*

When Crow Jane explains the scheme, the plan for our obliteration sounds like a promise to do right by us, like a proclamation of *eventually, in due time, except as punishment for crime.* She has been listening to them for so long that she thinks as they do, rationalizing death, evenly apportioning blame, imploring us to do better, berating the slags, the unhoused, and the impoverished for not carrying our weight, explaining away each tragedy until the last of us disappears. A quiet extinction, like bees and whales and insects and polar bears. A slow death. It is a tragedy, Crow Jane concedes, but *we can't save everyone.* We too are culpable. Aren't we the agent and executioner? Why love a hood rat, why hook up with a drug dealer? We are at fault, she contends, because of whom we love and how we live. Guilty because the decent embrace the criminal. The parallel societies must be extirpated. Crow Jane cautions us to be reasonable, pleads with us not to rush out, not to burn, loot, and destroy, not to terrorize others with our scarves and slogans. She cries on the jumbotron and asks us to weigh it carefully—the legal facts of the new regime versus our threadbare narrative. To make the choice—the state or our sister, civilization or barbarism? When Crow Jane concludes her chronicle, we are attentive but silent, unsure whether to laugh or hiss. +

DANIEL DENVIR
Do Border

"IF THAT BILL WERE THE LAW TODAY, I'D shut down the border right now and fix it quickly." These were the words not of Donald Trump, but of President Joe Biden, speaking in January in support of a bipartisan immigration deal then being negotiated in the Senate. As often happens, Biden's impolitic pronouncement captured the larger dynamics at play. The Democrats are defending themselves against Republican attacks on immigration by going on offense—but for the most part, they're doing so on Republican terms.

The legislation Biden was promoting, the Emergency National Security Supplemental Appropriations Act, included a host of border security measures. It would have significantly expanded ICE capacity for detention, made it harder to win asylum, and effectively blocked asylum seekers who had crossed the border irregularly (that is, without authorization between ports of entry)—all Republican priorities. The bill would have also sent military aid to Ukraine (as Democrats and the remaining national security traditionalists on the Republican side wanted) and to Israel (as everyone but a depressingly small number of left-wingers in Congress wanted), and sent humanitarian aid to several regions, including Gaza (as Democrats looking to differentiate themselves from Republicans wanted). For migrants, the bill promised increases in the allocation of employment- and family-based visas, and protections for certain youth green-card applicants and Afghan evacuees—good things, but not nearly enough to make the rest palatable.

This border security crackdown was designed to either placate or set a trap for MAGA border restrictionists, whose obsessions inspired much of the bill's content. Biden's grand overtures did not win over former President Trump, who urged Republicans in Congress to vote it down, thereby torpedoing its chances. Trump has no incentive to let Democrats take credit for the anti-immigrant agenda that—as he emphasized with sick repetition in the first 2024 presidential debate—he plans to ride back into the White House. For Trump's allies in Congress, the choice to oppose a bill tailored to their wishes was no contradiction; it was pure political logic. Meanwhile, Democrats sincerely believe that Republicans' opportunistic obstruction of a serious border-security package is one of their tickets to victory in November. "We had an epiphany," Senate majority leader Chuck Schumer told the *New York Times* in February. "Do border. If we did it right and were tough about it, it's a win for us."

Months after the bill's failure, Democrats continue to make immigration central to their 2024 campaign. In June, with an eye toward the November election, the Biden Administration announced two executive actions on immigration, the first gutting basic asylum protections at the border and the second providing a potential path to citizenship. Between the aborted Senate deal and Biden's executive actions, a reasonably complete picture of the Democrats' approach to immigration has emerged. The juxtaposition of the two executive actions—a massive border security "win" to appeal to the right, a substantive but partial action on legalization to appease progressives—is only the latest in a classic pattern: given the choice to pander to reactionaries or shore up the party's left wing, Democrats tend to prioritize the former. The result is a dangerous asymmetric polarization: Republicans radicalize on immigration, while Democratic elites chase after them. The "normal" position on immigration moves ever rightward.

This is the state of American immigration politics: a dangerous competition over who can do border better. But, as the unholy linking of foreign military aid to domestic border defense attests, this gross spectacle distracts from a far wider web of issues. Who has a right to migrate to the US and make their home here? Who gets to drop US-made bombs, and who is expected to silently suffer them? Because a Democratic President is punishing refugees at the US-Mexico border while also sponsoring the genocide of refugees in Gaza, these are not unrelated questions.

THE BIDEN Administration's attempted agreement on immigration was, in part, a gambit to win support for Ukraine from Republicans on terms they might find congenial; yet as Biden's executive action curbing asylum rights made clear, cracking down on immigration is an important Democratic objective in its own right. Until recently, unauthorized crossings at the US-Mexico border were at record highs, as masses of people were pushed from their homes and toward the US by overlapping political, economic, and ecological crises—crises whose causes are complex, but often substantially American in origin. Many migrants quickly move on to cities farther from the border in search of family and social networks. Republican governors Greg Abbott of Texas and Ron DeSantis of Florida have exacerbated this trend, paying to bus or fly migrants north to Democratic cities in an elaborate stunt to expose liberal hypocrisy. The Democratic response has frequently been to turn MAGA-inflected border delirium into bipartisan common sense. New York Mayor Eric Adams—like Biden, an expert at squandering public goodwill—responded by warning that migration "will destroy New York City." His police commissioner Edward A. Caban declared, with no basis in reality, that "a migrant crime wave is washing over our city."

Announced on June 4, the first of Biden's two executive actions on immigration all but halts new asylum requests for those entering irregularly at the US-Mexico border if "there has been a seven-consecutive-calendar-day average of 2,500 encounters or more" between migrants and US border personnel—as there had been throughout Biden's presidency. The action also makes it harder for migrants to win other forms of protection against deportation once that threshold is reached. Drawn from the foiled bipartisan Senate deal, the plan also recalls an order promulgated by Trump in 2018 (ultimately halted by the courts) that preemptively denied asylum to migrants crossing irregularly. And like Trump's most draconian border crackdowns, Biden's action looks for authority to Section 212(f) of the Immigration and Nationality Act, which allows the President to "impose ... any restrictions" on or "suspend the entry of all aliens or any class of aliens." Given the current flow of migrants to the border, the 2,500-encounter threshold is likely to effectively shut down the ordinary asylum system for the foreseeable future. Even though rates of border crossings have dropped sharply since Biden's action—likely already below the 2,500 daily-encounter trigger—they remain far above the 1,500-encounter threshold required to end the asylum suspension.

n+1

n + 1 Foundation
37 Greenpoint Ave #316, Mailbox 18
Brooklyn, NY 11222

PLACE STAMP HERE

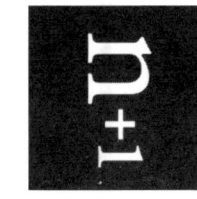

Dear Reader,

Has life brought you money? Have you ever thought of doing something unusual, like backing a literary-political-cultural magazine? Now's the time. *n+1* is in need of supporters: people to help us be really ambitious, to encourage us to fight the forces of reaction in politics and the arts, and to publish the best new and unknown writers.

If you'd like to support n+1, please visit nplusonemag.com/donate or write to us at editors@nplusonemag.com. We have much to talk about, and so much more to do.

—The Editors

Not that long ago, Democrats were speaking the language of migrant rights. Negatively polarized against Donald Trump's "big, beautiful wall" and the separation of migrant children from their parents at the border, the party appeared, in the Trump years, to coalesce around a more liberal immigration politics after years of reflexive rightward movement. At the time, this could seem like a hopeful sign that Trump's extremism had permanently broken the bipartisan anti-migrant consensus that first consolidated under President Bill Clinton. I for one argued that this might be the case. But this humanitarian spirit would prove an aberration: the party's nativist impulses were simply too entrenched, whatever the pro-migrant position of the Democratic base.

Nativism in American politics long predates the Clinton Administration. But it did not begin as a blanket rejection of immigration. Nativism's historical precursor was instead a racially selective pro-migration program: the project of settler colonialism demanded that certain types of European migrants "advanc[e] compactly as we multiply" across the North American continent, as Thomas Jefferson wrote. Enslaved Africans, of course, were transported by force. It was the sort of demographic regime of ethnic cleansing and replacement that governs other settler-colonial projects—including the one still unfolding today in Palestine.

As Indigenous people were killed, dispossessed, and displaced across an expanding United States, settlers came to identify as natives—and, in turn, as nativists. Calls inevitably arose to exclude would-be immigrants who didn't fit the white-settler racial ideal. Since the early 19th century, the racist demand for immigration exclusion—anti-Irish, anti-Chinese, anti-Japanese, anti-Jewish, anti-Italian, anti-Filipino, anti-Mexican, anti-Latino, anti-Arab, and anti-Muslim—has been a key motif in American history.

Today's nativist politics owes much to that lineage, but also to more contemporary inputs: overpopulation hysteria beginning in the late 1960s; the eruption of anxiety about border security since the 1970s, when a stagflated economy spawned the initial neoliberal counterrevolution; and, in the 1990s, the hardening of vehement anti–Mexican migrant sentiment into a bedrock of Republican and conservative-movement politics, which promptly began pulling Democrats to the right.

Starting in the early 2000s, against this rising tide, responsible liberals and conservatives sought a solution to please all sides: "comprehensive immigration reform." Time and again, Democrats and self-styled Republican moderates proposed increased border security as a part of larger packages that would also legalize undocumented immigrants and supply American business with guest workers. These negotiations became major priorities for Presidents George W. Bush and Barack Obama, who each spent significant political capital trying to pass legislation. Yet they failed every time, stymied by conservative nativists who, riled by Fox News and talk radio, insisted on border security alone, with no accommodation for undocumented immigrants.

In response, Democrats and Republicans serially capitulated to the right, strengthening enforcement with no pro-immigrant measures attached—all in order to prove their "seriousness." Since 1992, the Border Patrol ranks have grown by nearly 400 percent, from 4,139 agents to roughly 20,000 today. The number of miles of border fencing—Trump's "wall" in all but name—grew from just 14 in 1990 to 654 at the time of Trump's inauguration. Democrats have likewise expanded and accelerated the federal deportation pipeline by linking it to the gargantuan US criminal justice system. Both Clinton's Illegal Immigration Reform and Immigrant Responsibility Act and the Secure Communities program, piloted under Bush but rolled out under Obama, made cops, courts, prisons, and jails a powerful force in immigration incarceration and deportation. All in exchange for nothing.

When these escalating crackdowns on so-called "illegal immigration" inevitably fail to achieve their goals, they only reaffirm the nativist claim that the border is "insecure," further raising the bar for tougher enforcement. In his 2000 book *Border Games*, Peter Andreas identified this perverse dynamic at the border itself: the wave of crackdowns in the 1990s on long-standing unauthorized crossing points created spectacles of an "illegal" invasion, which inflamed rather than tamed nativist sentiment, prompting ever more border militarization. Trump's wall obsession was a logical outcome. The determination to "secure the border," after all, is as quixotic a mission as "eliminating Hamas." Both are maximalist, racist political fantasies that rationalize any and every cruelty enacted in the process. The border is too long, the terrain too complex, and the number of people desperate to enter the US too consistently great for border security to be anything but a metaphor. But it is a metaphor that both parties treat as a plausible aspiration.

The dysfunctional US asylum system is a crucial context for today's anti-immigrant politics; it is also the scene of another cycle of backlash and escalation. Interminable backlogs push people away from official points of entry and toward dangerous desert crossings. The law denies migrants work permits for at least six months from the time they apply for asylum, leaving them destitute; it then takes years to receive an asylum hearing in understaffed immigration courts. Meanwhile, Republican governors send buses of migrants to cities where they may not know anyone, and the federal government does nothing to coordinate their settlement, for fear of being implicated in the problem.

DOMESTIC IMMIGRATION politics has always depended on the conflicts and accords of American empire. In the early 20th century, the US opted not to formally restrict Japanese immigration—as they had Chinese immigration in 1882—for fear of provoking a rising imperial power. (This "Gentlemen's Agreement," in which Japan informally pledged to stop laborers from emigrating, lasted until the 1920s, when their nationals, too, were formally banned.) The Philippines won independence from the United States in 1946 in part because congressional nativists wanted an end to the migration rights Filipinos had enjoyed as US nationals. The 1965 repeal of explicitly racist immigration quotas in place since the 1920s was spurred in part by cold war rivalry. After the end of the Vietnam War, in 1975, more than one million refugees and immigrants from Vietnam, Laos, and Cambodia came to the United States as Southeast Asia was wrecked by imperial violence. Reagan welcomed refugees fleeing Khomeini's Iran and socialist Nicaragua and persecuted those fleeing US-backed right-wing death squads in El Salvador and Guatemala. Most recently, the US took in more than five hundred thousand Ukrainians in two years. (In contrast to the uproar over Latin American migrants, no one really noticed.)

That colonial and neocolonial subjects of Western liberal empires often end up as citizens in the metropole is an ironic contradiction. (Thus, for example, the Biden campaign's incomprehension that there are enough Arabs in Michigan furious enough about Gaza that they might have cost him the election.) Everywhere this postcolonial boomerang leads to fantastic flights of projection: the specter of a Mexican "Reconquista" of the American Southwest, or a France menaced by a "great replacement" at the hands of Muslims. It's revealing that anti-migrant rhetoric so often portrays migrants as colonialists, which of course has everything backward: Trump's infamous call for a "total and complete shutdown of Muslims entering the United States until our country's representatives can figure out what the hell is going on" was a calculated way to mystify what the hell was actually going on. In the US today, nativism is inseparable from this deeper dread over decaying imperial power and white Western decline. Trump, as usual, makes this tendency explicit, constantly invoking both the United States' place in the world and its demographic makeup. "On January 6, we had a great border, nobody coming through, very few," Trump said during the presidential debate. "On January 6, we were respected all over the world. All over the world, we were respected. And then he comes in and we're now laughed at."

This perceived threat of racial-imperial collapse has also been inflated by the very real economic dislocations of globalization. NAFTA stoked fears of what Ross Perot warned would be the "giant sucking sound" of American jobs siphoned into Mexico. It was during this intense debate over free trade that resurgent nativist organizing secured passage of California's radically anti-migrant Proposition 187, which the Republican governor Pete Wilson made the centerpiece of his successful 1994 reelection campaign. That same year, the Clinton Administration rolled out its marquee border-militarization campaigns, Operation Hold the Line in El Paso and Operation Gatekeeper in San Diego. The border became the site of mass anxieties over the mobility of both people and capital; the bipartisan elite did all it could to keep the voting public fixated only on the former.

The September 11 attacks only amplified these trends. To wage the war on terror, the US government built a new national security state, for which border security became a renewed and lavishly funded obsession. In 2004, the newly created US Customs and Border Protection agency, part of the likewise novel Department of Homeland Security (DHS), announced that "preventing terrorists and terrorist weapons" was its "priority mission": "We cannot reduce or eliminate illegal entry by potential terrorists without also dramatically reducing illegal migration." The conflation of border insecurity and terrorism has remained mostly unchallenged throughout the war on terror and its afterlife.

Nevertheless, September 11 did not at first provoke a rise in xenophobic public opinion. A Pew survey in December 2001 showed that Republican favorability toward Muslim Americans *rose* from 35 to 64 percent in the months after the attacks. Bush had declared that "Islam is peace," and promoted the wars in Iraq and Afghanistan in part on liberal paternalistic grounds: it was the United States' imperial burden to rescue Muslims everywhere suffering under backward regimes. Remarkably, many Americans believed it. Only later would the wars' collapsing legitimacy trigger a hard turn toward racist exclusion.

Bush's wars were sold as an unstable compound of emancipatory nation building and merciless patriotic retribution, liberal universalism and vengeful jingoism. The US invaded Afghanistan and Iraq both to promote democracy and to "put a boot in [their] ass," as Toby Keith sang in 2002. The refusal of Iraqis and Afghans to greet their occupiers as liberators, and the US's failure to establish thriving liberal market democracies in those countries, brought Bush's freedom agenda crashing down to earth. By the mid-2000s, public support for the war on terror had collapsed, while hostility toward Muslims and Mexicans soared. With the rise of a powerful right-wing anti-immigrant movement, the racist revenge fantasies of the war on terror coursed through the body politic more strongly than ever, now untempered by any liberal apologia.

This helps explain why, in his second term, Bush's call for comprehensive immigration reform was met with a fiery right-wing reaction. The news media was enraptured by the Minutemen border vigilantes, while the House of Representatives approved a draconian anti-immigrant bill that would have criminalized the mere status of being undocumented. The Sensenbrenner bill never passed the Senate, and instead sparked the millions-strong pro-immigrant street protests of 2006, culminating in massive May Day immigrant-worker marches. As comprehensive reform continued to flounder in Congress, a bipartisan coalition handily passed a bill, duly signed by Bush, that led to the construction of hundreds of miles of border fencing; meanwhile, ICE orchestrated giant workplace raids. In an interview years later, DHS Secretary Michael Chertoff confirmed that the raids were intended "to establish credibility with respect to enforcement, which would then enable reforms in a more comprehensive way."

The 2008 financial crisis brought insurgent conservative xenophobia to a fever pitch. The Tea Party, founded amid the Great Recession as a right-wing fiscal-populist movement, soon became overwhelmingly fixated on opposition to "illegal" immigrants. Among their priorities was Arizona's infamous SB 1070, the "show me your papers" law, championed by Phoenix's infamous Sheriff Joe Arpaio, whose deputies scoured the city on the hunt for "illegals." President Obama, who like Bush called for comprehensive immigration reform, bowed to the right by overseeing record numbers of deportations. (He eventually backtracked under relentless activist pressure, led by undocumented youth, who won measures like DACA, a rare major victory for immigrant rights.) Meanwhile, Trump launched his political career with an absurd campaign to prove that Obama himself was an "illegal" of sorts, and hysteria exploded over an imagined epidemic of immigrant crime—embodied by Kathryn Steinle, a young white woman shot dead in San Francisco by an undocumented immigrant with schizophrenia. Trump referred to Steinle as "beautiful Kate in San Francisco."

With unprecedented vulgarity, savvy, and scale, Trump represented not just nativism, but its potent fusion with existing anxieties of imperial decline and lost economic might. "I've always said—shouldn't be there," Trump once said of the US occupation of Iraq. "But if we're going to get out, take the oil." The same blend of racism and economism inflected his entire agenda: keep the jobs in and the migrants out. He attacked "a leadership class that worships globalism" and profits from deindustrialization, which leaves "millions of our workers with nothing but poverty and heartache." Launching his first campaign at Trump Tower, he warned that "Mexico [was] not sending their best" across the border, but instead "rapists" who were "bringing drugs" and "crime."

In repugnant, reactionary form, these sentiments voice a real, popular critique of

American empire. After rampant pillaging of national wealth by the 1 percent and two failed foreign invasions, many Americans have loudly declared themselves the victims of another kind of foreign invasion—of immigrants who take jobs at home while globalist CEOs move jobs abroad, all through the same, seemingly porous border. The contradictions of turbocharged capitalist globalization, post–September 11 imperial quagmires, and financial crisis have rallied a critical mass of disaffected voters around the Trumpian vision of a Fortress America governed by an entertaining CEO.

MOST MEDIA COVERAGE of this year's Senate bill described it as a border crackdown paired with military aid to Ukraine. Often downplayed was that, alongside $60 billion in aid for Ukraine, the bill would also have provided $14 billion in military aid for Israel. Uncritical support for Israel—the bipartisan tentpole of US foreign policy—is barely newsworthy, but the spectacle of so many Republicans souring on NATO and even favoring Russia over Ukraine was startling enough to make headlines.

For Democratic leaders, American primacy rests on a set of bedrock alliances—with NATO, Ukraine, Israel, Saudi Arabia, Japan, South Korea, Taiwan, and others—that contain and counter rival forces led by Russia, China, and Iran. Democrats support a liberal order on the premise that investments of capital and military aid are necessary to sustain a multilateral global system that ultimately underwrites American hegemony. For a growing number of Republicans, however, this primacy is the product of raw American power and military might—and little else. Republicans under Trump are closer to mercantilist-militarists who will gladly bomb other countries when necessary, but regard globalization, multilateralism, and boots-on-the-ground intervention as a waste of resources; their American ideal is enclosed and essentially autarkic. As the forever wars continue to wend their way back home, *support our troops* turns to *back the blue* and *build the wall*.

None of this, however, has diminished Republicans' support for Israel, since for them, as for most American supporters of Israel, the war on Gaza is itself a form of border security. Israel is less a regional ally than an extension of the US, part of the minority of nations with a capacity for self-governance, against the many others that must be governed. "The civilized world," Benjamin Netanyahu told Americans in October 2023, must unite to "fight the barbarians." Those with the power to exclude the racially undesirable are the same people who can legitimately use violence; the legitimate targets of that violence are also subject to exclusion at the border, whether it lies at Laredo or Erez.

After the border deal fell apart in February, the Senate moved forward with a separate vote on the bill's foreign and military aid. In a blistering floor speech, the Democrat Chris Van Hollen denounced the assault on Gaza, describing Israel's withholding of food as a "war crime" and its leaders as "war criminals." He then voted yes, alongside every other member of the Democratic caucus, save for Bernie Sanders, Peter Welch, and Jeff Merkley. Pressed by a reporter, Senator Elizabeth Warren voiced her opposition to the Israeli military's threatened invasion of Rafah, by then the most crowded place on Earth—yet she too supported the deal and voted for military aid for Israel. "Right now," she said, "the security package is about getting money to Ukraine." That Palestinians would suffer and die—this was worth the deal, which ultimately came together in April, without any immigration component.

On the ground, however, Biden's backing of Israel has jeopardized every part of the Democratic agenda. The Democrats have hemorrhaged support from much of their base—young, progressive, Black, Arab, Muslim, Latino—because they insist on funding and equipping Israel's genocide, as made clear by the hundreds of thousands of voters marking their ballots "uncommitted" in Democratic primaries. At the debate in June, Biden insisted that "the only thing I've denied Israel was two-thousand-pound bombs. They don't work very well in populated areas. They kill a lot of innocent people." He then continued: "We are providing Israel with all the weapons they need and when they need them. . . . We are the biggest producer of support for Israel of anyone in the world."

WHERE BIDEN'S reflexive support for Israel has reinforced the racialized, militarist border logic of modern US foreign policy, his economic agenda did at least begin to break with the neoliberal model that has helped drive nativist resentment. For all the shortcomings of laws like the Inflation Reduction Act, Biden's was the first Democratic administration since the neoliberal turn to recognize that free-market fanaticism had critically undermined the material foundation of Democratic political allegiances and identities. The IRA and other policies have channeled federal subsidies to green industries and modestly encouraged unionization, while Biden himself walked a picket line with members of the United Auto Workers, who have led a national upsurge in labor militancy. Democrats finally seemed to recognize the need to wrest the promise of reindustrialization from the nationalist right and defuse nativist reaction.

But it's clear that Bidenomics is not enough. Social democratic reform in the US cannot succeed politically without anti-imperialist reform abroad and at the border. Nor can domestic reforms mobilize on a mass scale without stronger mediating institutions—namely unions—to interpret and promote them. The genocide in Gaza is tearing the Democratic coalition apart even as bipartisan nativism stitches together a broad coalition on the right. For all Biden's and the Democrats' hand-wringing over the existential threat posed by Trump, the preservation of American empire has outranked saving the remnants of our democracy. Immigrants and refugees will be the first to pay the price.

Up to the moment Biden finally dropped out of the presidential race, it seemed as though his political ego likewise outranked Democratic political prospects and the terrifying implications of a second Trump presidency. Now the candidate has changed, but on immigration, Democratic strategy so far remains the same. "Donald Trump has been talking a big game about securing our border," Kamala Harris declaimed at one of her first campaign rallies since becoming the nominee, "but . . . he does not walk it like he talks it. Our administration worked on the most significant border security bill in decades." For now, a collective sigh of Democratic relief at Biden's departure still fills Harris's electoral sails; but the honeymoon will be short if she continues to follow Biden in getting "tough" on the border and slandering student protesters as antisemitic. Meanwhile, Trump's campaign has decided to attack Harris as Biden's failed "border czar." Harris must decide whether to respond on Trump's terms or establish new terms of her own. On immigration as on Gaza, she must choose between conventional pundit wisdom and Democratic public opinion.

If Donald Trump is reelected, his second term will be even more horrific than the first. With Supreme Court justices already doing his bidding, Trump will have no real guardrails. His cadre will be equipped to enact their most reactionary designs, nowhere more so than on immigration policy. Stephen Miller has been busy drawing up plans for actual mass deportations. His nightmarish blueprint can hardly be overstated: rounding up millions of immigrants each year and detaining them in massive, purpose-built prisons in Texas; deputizing cops and National Guard troops from red states to enlarge the deportation force; invoking the Insurrection Act to allow the military to detain migrants; barring pro-Palestine international student activists from the country, expelling tens of thousands of Afghan refugees, and once again targeting Muslim-majority countries for travel bans. On the campaign trail, Trump's rhetoric has grown more nakedly fascistic than ever. Migrants are "poisoning the blood of our country"; more recently, he has called them "not people, in my opinion," but "animals."* When a 20-year-old would-be assassin came within inches of killing the former President, Trump had just turned his head toward a giant chart on "illegal" border crossings. A week later at the Republican National Convention, Trump, his ear iconically bandaged, declared, "that was the chart that saved my life . . . one of the greatest charts I've ever seen. . . . Without that chart, I would not be here today."

THE US ELECTORATE is fractured over immigration, but in an uneven way. While nativist policies are a fixation for Republican voters, pro-migrant politics receives far less attention from the left. This is not a knock on immigrant-rights organizers: the issue is simply not that consequential for most left-leaning Americans. A major national poll in late 2023 found that even Latinos, for whom immigration is often an important concern, tended to rank it behind inflation, jobs, and health care. Despite eruptions of protest against the most egregious anti-immigrant politics, the imagined "sleeping giant" of Latino voters who would one day demand immigration reform and punish its enemies never materialized. Unlike many white MAGA supporters, most Latinos have never been single-issue immigration voters.

Democratic leaders have also done little to encourage mass enthusiasm for immigrant rights. Today one hears less romantic rhetoric about the US as a "nation of immigrants" or about the global pull of American universities, and fewer blunt discussions of immigrants as cheap and exploitable labor for American industry; that old liberal case for immigration now rings hollow in the ruins of neoliberalism. Yet these arguments still inform the status quo politics of immigration reform. Democratic politicians' long-standing willingness to exchange more "good immigrants" (expanded legal immigration) for crackdowns on "bad immigrants" (deportations and border enforcement against "illegal" immigrants) was evident in this year's doomed Senate bill and in Biden's executive actions.

The commentator Matthew Yglesias is a symptomatic case of today's liberal confusion on the subject. A veteran blogger who has drifted right since the Bush years, Yglesias considers immigration so critical to

---

* "I know nothing about Hitler," Trump said by way of a disclaimer in an interview with the right-wing radio host Hugh Hewitt. "I have no idea what Hitler said other than [what] I've seen on the news. And that's a very, entirely different thing than what I'm saying."

a second "American century" that the solution is *One Billion Americans*, the title of his 2020 book. And yet Yglesias proposed limiting mass immigration into the US to "Canada, Australia, the Anglophone Caribbean, America's NATO allies, or some other subset of countries that seems popular"—whatever it takes to assuage nativists. In February, assessing Biden's border policy, Yglesias wrote that he had resigned himself to a narrowly "patriotic, interest-based case for immigration" because "most Americans are clannish and nationalistic and don't care about the humane treatment of people from elsewhere." A principled stand for immigrant rights or expanded immigration, he argued, was akin to "cut[ting] Social Security benefits and giv[ing] the money to poor people in Africa": ethically meritorious but politically impossible. Yglesias dispassionately discards liberal arguments for desired liberal policy outcomes and pragmatically adopts a racist form of persuasion in their place.

Yglesias relies on the so-called popularist fetish for current public opinion to justify his position (and to flatter his own, no doubt non-clannish seriousness). But he neglects historical trends that are far more complex than his desultory interpretation suggests. Overall support for restricting legal immigration fell from the peak of the mid-1990s bipartisan nativist consensus through Trump's final year in office; that year, however, support for *increasing* legal immigration surpassed support for restriction for the first time on record. While it's true that under Biden restrictionism is again on the rise, over the past decade the American public has generally possessed a deeper and wider well of pro-migrant sentiment than ever before, as seen in the protests against the Muslim ban and family separation in the early Trump years. Public opinion is neither timeless nor transcendent, but instead historical and contextual. It is not given but made—including by political tastemakers like Yglesias, who cite a static, reified "public opinion" as the basis for their own nativism-normalizing punditry. The politics of immigration could be made otherwise. Bernie Sanders's decisive wins among working-class Latinos in the 2020 Nevada caucus and California primary point toward a social democratic politics that promotes migrant rights not as either an abstract liberal value or a narrow sectional interest, but as a core part of a larger working-class struggle.

Instead, the popularist narrative has increasingly taken hold in the Democratic mainstream. In February, after the Democrat Tom Suozzi beat his Republican opponent in a special election to replace the disgraced Long Island congressman George Santos, the media seized on Suozzi's border security platform as the key to his success. That Suozzi had previously held the same seat for three terms, that he ran a well-organized and well-funded campaign, that the local Republican Party was fatally weakened by Santos's shenanigans—none of this seemed notable. Instead Democratic leaders and the *New York Times* eagerly concluded, without evidence, that Suozzi's anti-migrant politics had won the day.

Promoting the border deal in February, Biden went so far as to ask Trump to join him in some sort of national-unity push to secure the border. "Instead of playing policy with the issue," Biden said on a visit to Brownsville, Texas, "join me, or I'll join you, in telling the Congress to pass this bipartisan border security bill. We can do it together. You know and I know it's the toughest, most efficient, most effective border-security bill this country's ever seen." In his State of the Union address, Biden further mimicked Republican rhetoric, using the word *illegal* to describe a Venezuelan man charged with killing a student in Georgia—a case that attracted rabid right-wing attention. ("I shouldn't have used *illegal*," Biden admitted a few days later. "It's *undocumented*.") More recently, in the June debate with Trump, Biden answered a straightforward question on abortion by referencing an American woman who was murdered by an undocumented immigrant. It was a baffling and self-wounding non sequitur—and an accidentally perfect reflection of the party's pathological insecurity about immigrants and immigration.

BIDEN'S EXECUTIVE action on asylum seekers was described by the *New York Times*—hardly a hostile publication—as "the most restrictive border policy instituted by Mr. Biden, or any other modern Democrat," one that "echoes an effort in 2018 by President Donald J. Trump to cut off migration that was blocked in federal court." Driven by the same wish fulfillment voiced by Schumer and media observers of Suozzi's victory, Biden's June 4 action on asylum sought yet again to rob the Republican Party of its reactionary authority on immigration—and, by doing so, to protect immigration as a liberal ideal. "To protect America as a land that welcomes immigrants," Biden said, "we must first secure the border and secure it now."

As it turned out, the action seemed to please no one. The Republican Speaker of the House and MAGA hard-liner Mike Johnson panned it as "window dressing" and "too little, too late." From the left, immigrant-rights groups were outraged, as was the ACLU, which quickly challenged the order in court. Even numerous elected Democrats pushed back. The Congressional Progressive Caucus chair, Representative Pramila Jayapal, called it a "deeply disappointing" and "dangerous step"; the California senator Alex Padilla said that Biden had "undermined American values and abandoned our nation's obligations to provide people fleeing persecution, violence, and authoritarianism with an opportunity to seek refuge in the US." The Biden Administration clearly anticipated such a response. Two weeks later, on June 18, the President took action to shield undocumented spouses of American citizens from deportation and provide them with a path to citizenship. Johnson and other congressional Republicans predictably pounced on the policy as an "amnesty plan" for "illegal" immigrants. By now it should be obvious that nothing Biden could say or do on immigration would be sufficient to win over nativist firebrands on the right.

In his shambling, roundabout way, Biden has returned to the well-worn framework of comprehensive immigration reform, pairing enforcement crackdowns with legalization measures to try to rally a diverse majority behind him. That he could do so only through executive actions, though, suggests why the strategy is doomed to fail. The majority of Republican legislators have never supported comprehensive-reform legislation, and neither have Republican voters: they won't be won over to Biden's executive-action version today. If it survives expected right-wing legal challenges, the parole measure granted to spouses of US citizens could be transformative for a real but small fraction of undocumented Americans, as the Temporary Protected Status protections extended for undocumented migrants from Haiti, Venezuela, and other countries have been. And Biden's marquee policy, the gutting of asylum protections, will simply reaffirm Republican talking points on border insecurity, making the case for his opponents' agenda—all while life grows ever more hellish for untold numbers of migrants.

One other key facet of Biden's immigration record has been almost totally ignored in the media. In January 2023, the administration quietly piloted a new policy that has since protected more than a thousand undocumented workers from deportation after they spoke out against workplace abuses: Deferred Action for Labor Enforcement, or DALE. The policy posed strengthening worker solidarity as the solution to economic crises facing immigrant and nativeborn workers alike—a path illuminated by Sanders's wins in California and Nevada. Yet while Biden has traveled the country talking up his get-tough border policy, DALE was implemented almost in secret, without fanfare; there wasn't even a press conference.

Thus the same President has implemented an innovative policy fusing labor and immigrant struggles, which no one heard about; a widely touted executive action destroying asylum rights that tries to outflank Republicans from the right; and a progressive executive action that seeks to mitigate the political damage of the previous one, and make a play for Latino voters who are increasingly drawn to Donald Trump for reasons that often have little to do with immigration. Biden criticized Trump's obstruction of the Senate deal as "an extremely cynical political move and a complete disservice to the American people who are looking for us . . . not to weaponize the border, but to fix it." But Biden and the Democrats have clearly made peace with a cynical calculus: sacrifice the immigrants who aren't here yet to win over the center, and reward those who are to solidify your base. Democratic leaders aren't merely responding to nativist public opinion; alongside Republicans, they are more than ever its coauthors and instigators.

FOR FAR TOO LONG, the politics of immigration has been decoupled from the material reality of human movement across national borders. There *is* an immigration crisis, just not the kind that the phrase tends to evoke. Migrants themselves are not the crisis, but they are in crisis, and their predicament and movement are the result of crisis. Republican instrumentalization of vulnerable migrants is revolting, but also exposes liberals' failure to embrace a full-throated pro-migrant politics, even after years of periodic sanctimony. Democratic leaders might claim it's hard if not impossible to defeat nativism with a pro-migrant agenda. Winning durable majorities with a pro-migrant agenda will no doubt be daunting. But the Democratic Party has never really tried, and it is no less clear that countering nativist politics with more nativism is a surefire loser. Those Americans who want a sweeping border and immigration crackdown will always look to Republicans to carry it out.

Much more than domestic political scorecards are at stake. The immigration crisis is global, combining at least three forms of domination: the denial of people's right to remain in their homes, the denial of their right to move, and the imposition of punitive social and economic discipline, particularly in the workplace. The political crisis over immigration obscures, as it is designed to, the deeper crises pushing people from their homes across the hemisphere and the world; yet it also obscures the causes of intensifying feelings of insecurity within the United States. Nativism's trick is to cast racialized foreign others as concrete explanations for problems with otherwise abstract causes. At root, it is sheer scapegoating. In December, Colombian President Gustavo Petro connected the dots: "The unleashing of genocide and barbarism on the Palestinian people is what awaits the exodus of the peoples of the South unleashed by the climate crisis.... What we are seeing in Gaza is a rehearsal of the future." We must either embrace radical new forms of solidarity or normalize the mass death of surplus populations.

These deeper conflicts are basic to American politics: the ordinary citizens of a liberal democracy that dominates the world are also, often, dominated. We supposedly govern the world, but discover with horror that we do not govern ourselves. The contradiction is typically resolved through imperial expansion abroad, escalating oppression of racialized others at home, or a poisonous combination of both. How we approach and overcome this conflict is the crux of political struggle in the United States today.

At the national legislative level, Biden's dismal, futile triangulation on immigration can suggest that this struggle is merely grinding through the same old cycles. Yet beneath the official surface, something has begun to change. Israel's horrific war on Gaza has reoriented what was often a domestic social democratic struggle toward internationalist horizons. The implications of this momentous shift aren't yet clear, but they point toward a politics that can imagine justice not only at the border but beyond it, a politics that demands a new economic and ecological order that equally protects people's right to move—for safety, for opportunity, and to return—and also to stay put, free from immiserating poverty, rising waters, or falling bombs. +

FOR EVERY SET OF EYES
the new album from
J. Mamana

LP out August 23rd, 2024 via

HOLY FAMILY

"If Mamana is borrowing ideas liberally, he is doing so to feed the massive furnace of his prodigious musical gifts." - Jayson Greene, *Pitchfork*

jmamana.net | holyfamily.site | @jrmamana

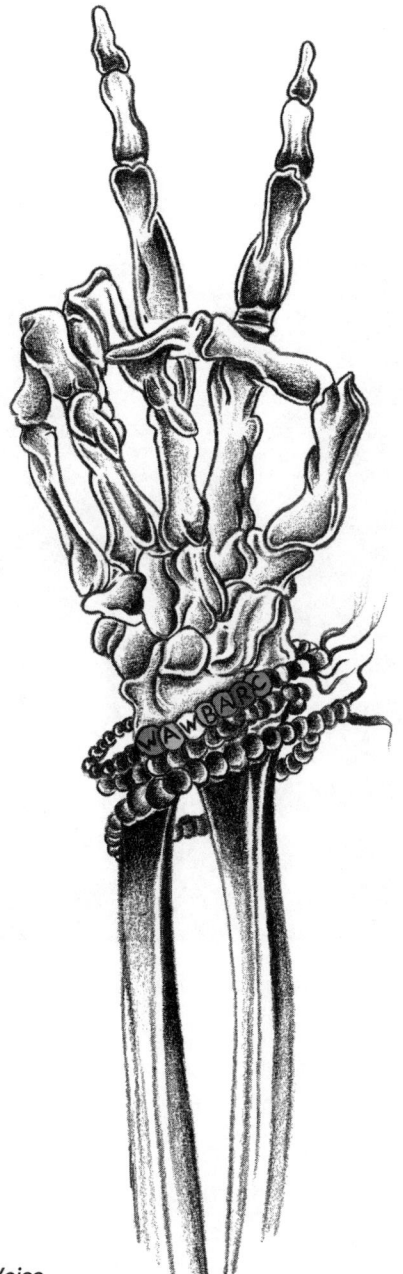

FYEAR
FYEAR

KEE AVIL
Spine

ERIC CHENAUX TRIO
Delights Of My Life

ERIKA ANGELL
The Obsession With Her Voice

WE ARE WINTER'S BLUE AND RADIANT CHILDREN
"NO MORE APOCALYPSE FATHER"

ILLUSTRATION BY CHRISTOPHER RIVERA

All titles in 180gram vinyl art editions,
on compact disc, and as digital files.

Bandcamp digital subscription
includes 25% off all physical.

Constellation
cstrecords.com

EBB BAYLEY, *SOUL -AS MOTH- DEPARTS VIA MOUTH TO DELVE IN THE GROUND*. 2024, CHARCOAL AND PASTEL ON PAPER. 27 1/2 × 39". PHOTO BY EBB BAYLEY.

DEATH OF THE PARTY

Raven Leilani

IN 2020, THE YEAR my father and brother died, I discovered a new genre of laughter. It was a kind of laughter that happened to me. Nothing was funny, though it was the year I published my first novel, and the novel had a lot of jokes. Humor, like grief, like poetry, is occasionally a language of dissonance: dissimilar things side by side reflect back on each other some surprise or shared meaning. But there was no apparent meaning in the adjacency of my mourning and erratic, often ill-timed laughter. It happened when I talked about my father, and because of the professional requirements of that year, it happened with journalists as I talked with them about my book.

I was embarrassed. To be grieving incorrectly, to be doing it publicly, to be preoccupied with whether I was doing it well. Dissonance was everywhere. The blunted, abject language of bereavement, and the responsibility I had, which I had worked for and wanted, to speak clearly about my own sentences. Troubleshooting Zoom for a digital tour in the midst of a pandemic after my father died of Covid, alone in a different state. That I could be talking about him, and hear, as if I hadn't participated in it, my own laughter. In *The Year of Magical Thinking,* Joan Didion writes about the tonal discrepancies endemic to our most acute horrors. The ships that are sunk on Sunday mornings, the clear skies from which planes fall. She writes about the audacity of ordinariness, how it isn't asynchronous with the fact of grief but inherent to it. For a while, I struggled to reconcile both realities, the one in which we buried my brother some months after my father and the other in which my book had changed my life so radically that the weirder manifestations of my grief were sometimes happening on air. I struggled especially with how those experiences changed my relationship to language, and naturally, to writing.

Writing through or about grief is a confrontation with containment, both in the self and on the page. It sanctions an inclination to digress, not only because revisiting is an organic and necessary part of the experience, but because it is an unstable state and subject, prone to a volatility that resists attempts to find forward motion or shape. There can be a holiness about the parenthetical, the cadence of interruption that affords you the scaffolding to approach a subject that feels dangerous. However, if you're a writer and so obligated to the work of exclusion that brings an end into sight, it is a terrible crisis to be lost in that digressive purgatory. That shapelessness can be chronic, in part because it can feel, when there is no beginning, middle, or end, that there is no way out. Bereavement makes a mockery of borders and by extension narrative. It's somewhat of a paradox, too, in that to engage with it is to engage with permanence—the foreverness of death, of grief—but also with what happens after death, whether those questions are spiritual or the practical problems of being the person who is still alive and tasked with the quotidian, like showering or deciding whether or not to stay alive. So it should be noted that grief is sometimes this, grappling with your own desire to die.

This is a good time to be explicit in my biases. I resent the idea of grief as pathology—pathology negatively connoted as failure, as disease, rather than its valid classification as a mental and physical phenomenon that depresses the body's processes, and lacks tidy parameters that might permit a person to, within a reasonable amount of time, Get Over It. I don't believe in getting over it. I believe in weathering it badly, in nursing the grudge, and tending pathologically to the archive of people you have loved. This essay is for people who don't get over things. That is not to diminish the real and desperate feeling of wanting not to be in pain, but to affirm it as a way of being that you have a right to, and that has to be acknowledged if you want to examine how it has remade you and, potentially, your craft. Grief alters your relationship to your tools. Being able to write again meant acknowledging how my process had changed. A revelation I resisted, as my writing practice had developed around jobs, cohabitation, and formative periods of loneliness, until it was nearly circadian, a practice that graduated into something I simply had to do. It's a lucky thing when the work feels like a primal imperative. This was overwhelmingly my experience: pleasure, ease, which is almost as impolite to talk about as the ugly shape of your grief. How good it feels when you are taken up by a project and everything is going so well.

Bereavement changed this experience. I couldn't think, and those failures of thinking were evident on the page. Foiled sentences; the opaque, ironic language of fear. Imperatives began to feel like work. In *A Grief Observed* by C. S. Lewis, a collection of entries drawn from the notebooks he kept after the death of his wife, Lewis writes: "For the first time I have looked back and read these notes. They appall me." In *The Cancer Journals*, an account of Audre Lorde's experience with breast cancer and life post mastectomy, she writes about not being able to think, about the necessity of articulation and the problem of language under the pressure of grief. She writes about not being able to write, and how in that silence "each of us draws the face of her own fear." She describes a loss of control, wanting to write about anger and finding sadness instead.

In *Notes on Grief*, Chimamanda Ngozi Adichie writes about the failures of language made apparent by the awkward vocabulary of condolences. The bright platitudes of other people. Attempts to manage the unmanageable that make obvious the paltriness of words and the ancient horror of death. Meaning absolutely everyone is freaked out by it, and no one knows what to say. After her father's death, Adichie noted the strangeness of people's remarks, the frequency with which her father's death was referred to as his *demise*. In *The Art of Death*, Edwidge Danticat's examination of death across literature and of her own grief after the loss of her mother, she writes that the word *mass* was more palatable than *tumor*. Danticat also writes about the pivotal scene in Toni Morrison's *Beloved* in which Sethe, an enslaved woman, kills her baby, Beloved. This scene has "some of the most deliberately unadorned language in an otherwise densely lyrical novel," she observes, and notes how quietly the killing is conveyed through "the arc of its mother's swing." Danticat refers to an interview where Morrison explains that choice:

> For me, in the process of writing, it is just not authentic or legitimate enough to look at it from the outside. I always tell my students, it's not *a* Black father; it's yours. The one you know? The one. So if I'm going to imagine what it takes to kill your baby, then I have to put in my arms, my baby. And when that happens—and

it's difficult—then the language just pares down. You don't get ornamental with that, you get very still, very clean-limbed, and very quiet, because the event itself is bigger than language.

I feel a debt to these writers for articulating the hairy business of bereaved articulation. The way language becomes truncated. The not being able to think. The debasement of seeing on the page how severely you are not thinking. The infiltration of grief into your prose when you have not made a conscious effort to write toward it, or even when you have made a conscious effort to write away from it. The animate quality of a draft and the submission it requires of its writer is beautiful. The improvisational magic of writing and all it dredges up from the unconscious means you will often surprise yourself. But it has a different resonance when everything you make feels suddenly governed by your dead. If your primary experience of writing was one of pleasure, it's difficult to adjust to the hostility of this kind of haunting. Writing toward it intentionally presents its own difficulties. The complication of momentum and linearity when grief collapses time and compels you to return. Digressions, born of the need to create safety and make sense of what happened, undermine an attempt to find structure, borderlessness being both an impediment to narrative and a result of the fluidity of grief. It's hard to paint a subject that is moving, and even harder when processing grief requires you to be still and to be able to look at it head-on. Adichie aptly calls this problem of looking "the catastrophe of a direct, unswerving stare."

For the grieving person, stillness can be unthinkable and movement the preferred medication. Busyness, blunting one's feelings with the manic activity that is the hallmark of the bereaved and newly single, avoiding yourself and your work—anything is preferable to committing the words to the page, because to go on about your life at the same cadence is to disrespect what has been upended and affirm that what happened is real. After my father and brother died, there was a period when I was given to these activities. They died five months apart, my father in March of Covid and my brother in September of ALS, and in between those events my debut novel was published. Publishing a first book, while an active undertaking, was not an activity in which I could lose myself. It was too new, too public, too high-stakes. The activities I found to blunt my grief I found off-duty and outside of that universe, all the usual means of obliteration that use the body against itself. I was dead to myself and my art, which in some circumstances is a totally reasonable way to be. Life is hard, and it should be permissible to find no art in its tyranny.

However, it's possible to establish a pattern of diversion that, once you and your work want to be alive, gets in the way. Lewis writes about that period of unavailability that has "the fatal power of making everything else in the world seem uninteresting," and makes you unavailable to the wonder you need to work. You need to be interested, available to look, and I was stuck, in part because I was afraid to court the catastrophe of looking directly. No art comes from an averted gaze. After the death of his wife, Lewis writes about feeling like a leper and an advertisement for marital death, seeing on the faces of other married couples a fear that they would end up like him. In *Stay True*, Hua Hsu writes about feeling like the "death of the party" after the murder of a close friend. And after her mastectomy, Lorde took issue with the idea that not wearing a prosthetic breast was bad for the morale of the women in her ward, writing, "however well-meaning and under whatever guise, it must be seen as damaging, for it keeps the post-mastectomy woman in a position of perpetual and secret insufficiency, infantilized and dependent for her identity upon an external definition by appearance." Hiding prioritizes comfort over truth, a false sense of order over the messiness of self-revelation. My period of avoidance was a way to dull and busy myself, to feel in control, but being still was a necessary concession to all that was out of my control—deadly systemic failures and acts of God, and my feelings about those things, which could not be tidied or expedited and surprised me in their lawlessness. Grief is constantly evolving. Documents of it quickly become artifacts. Its resistance to containment, which troubles the boundaries of where it begins and ends, creates a kind of anti-closure, a necessity to get good with not getting over things. Being able to embrace that possibility frees you from the constraints of ordered grieving à la Kübler-Ross, and from designating some discrete, future moment as the moment you should rejoin the world and make things again.

There is some merit in accepting that for some indeterminate time, you may be fucked up, and that is as fine a time as any to do the work. Lorde writes about the importance of not waiting until she wasn't afraid anymore to write about her experience, in part because she felt it was likely she might die first. This is not to romanticize the idea of suffering well or the material forged from that suffering. Enduring a traumatic experience is plenty. It does not have to be productive. It's OK to be inert, useless, or agnostic about the value we ascribe to perseverance. Being unable to persevere, or being stuck, can be a directive from your body to slow down or stop. Lorde's account of not waiting to do the work is not about a denial of that condition, but an acknowledgment that it could go on indefinitely. It embraces a philosophy of anti-closure and imbues that endlessness with urgency. It complicates the framing of grief and death by liberating it from the past tense.

This revelation feels particular to a person grappling with a deadly illness. Dying, or being terminal, is not a discrete form of grief. Its borders are strange. The terminal person never truly sees its end. To mourn a person whose death is certain is to be suspended in mourning, grieving not only after it has happened but while it is happening. In 2014, my brother was diagnosed with ALS, a neurodegenerative disease that results in progressive atrophy and in nearly all cases death. He was a painter, and the disease began with his hands. A season before we knew he was sick, his wrist was tender. It seemed innocuous and not unrelated to his drawing jags. We carpooled to our mother's house for Thanksgiving and the drive was terrifying. I ascribed that to his masculinity. The provocative showboating that the open road seems to inspire in men. In hindsight, he was struggling with the steering wheel. There was the normal bargaining, some hope that the disease might stop, though there was a threshold at which too much had been taken and there was little function to preserve. It destroyed his emotional regulation and his bodily autonomy. He was more prone to tears, and I return, often, to the last time I saw him climb stairs: 2015, Pittsburgh, some months before he moved back in with our mother, who took care of him until he died. For six years he was dying, and every interaction was a confrontation with that certainty. It was evident in his communications, which were mediated through software that allowed him to spell with his eyes, and in his body, all the major and minor bones newly explicit.

When my father died, the parameters of grief were blurred partly by that early moment in the pandemic when people with Covid died in isolation. I could not see him or attend his funeral, and the news of his death came in a phone call from an estranged relative who felt the occasion was worthy of a détente. Closure can be complicated by those protracted or incomplete iterations of grief, but that untidiness can be a kind of freedom from the rigid taxonomies in which a person can be stuck.

Naturally, an examination like this essay also comes up against the caveats born of that fluidity. As I wrote this and my novel, I came up against it myself—how the instability of grief leaves you always changing your mind and having to reckon with iterations of yourself that feel disparate. The sentence you wrote a few months before feels alien and a little stupid. Anti-closure is about recontextualizing grief as a continuum and also as a set of diverse, specific, occasionally self-alienating feelings. Being awake to the diversity of your feelings can be one way to address a creative bottleneck, which includes dealing with the ways you are suddenly unfamiliar to yourself. The mores of grief are too varied and culturally specific to talk in absolute terms about what constitutes a legible or appropriate response. However, writing through and about grief intersects with your relationship to control. That relationship is subject to artistic binaries. Coldness, sentiment; distance, intimacy. Knowing what you think and all you feel. Often when we are talking about sentiment, we are talking about a contamination of feeling. A closeness to the subject that precludes your ability to see it honestly. A loss of control. Anxieties about self-pity and subjecting others to the arcane nostalgia of remembrance, about whether your subject, especially one like death with which everyone has intimacy, can be rendered in a way that is particular and liberated from private baggage that only matters to you.

The question of whether anyone will care is more fraught when you are in the state of supreme caring that is grief. Lorde writes that the subject of illness was well-trodden territory, but she embraced being part of a creative continuum and set forward to be specific in her contribution. That question of specificity is hugely important to the grief narrative, not just because of the commonality of the subject, but because everyone's experience with it is hyperspecific—as any bereaved person, besieged by other people's generalized or hyperspecific advice, can tell you. Lorde's specificity in rendering the mourning of her health and breasts is a harnessing of feeling, of craft, and a surrender to that aforementioned unswerving stare. Her story is not a general one. It's a document of a woman with breast cancer, and she is explicit in how that illness intersects with her Blackness, queerness, and relationship to art.

More specifics result—how those facts inform her thoughts about and interactions with straight and non-Black people; how they inform her relationships to the institutions where she is meant to receive help.

It is worth noting who is afforded enough humanity to grieve. Whose grief we affirm and whose carnage we are immune to. Grief narratives of marginalized people often intersect with the violence of the state. On the day my father died, it was not just a confrontation with that death, but with my government; with history and its resonance in the reporting, and in the tenor of the conversations about the reporting, that Black and elderly people were especially vulnerable. On that day, I took the phone call and went promptly to check the Covid map for my mother's neighborhood.

To insist on specificity can be an insistence on personhood, an act of preservation by embracing the way sentiment orients you toward noticing, or toward the sentimental business of lingering. Across these texts, writers linger and take notes, spurred on by the porousness of memory. Didion notes the tactfulness of the conversation in which she was asked to sign off on donating her husband's eyes. Lorrie Moore, in "People Like That Are the Only People Here," depicts a mother beset by directives to "take notes" as she is grappling with her baby's cancer. Danticat notes the contours of her mother's body as the coroners took her away. The morning my brother was to be collected, I also noticed the coroners. They came as a pair and were cartoonishly opposite, one young and nervous, the other old and unflappable and unmoved when my mother said in a numb voice, "1970," my brother's birth year. Noticing in this way sometimes opens you up to the strangeness of things. Those moments around death that are nearly too symmetrical for any credible narrative. Moments that feel magical in their coincidence. A year to the day after my father passed from Covid, I caught it myself, alone in a hotel in London, where I had too much time to wonder what it meant.

There is also, of course, a current of utter mundanity running alongside that magic: normal rhythms that resist mythmaking, details that are boring or potentially unflattering, whose omission or inclusion poses ethical or aesthetic questions. Hsu writes about this in *Stay True*, contemplating the influence of his grief on his inclination to "flatter the narrator" and force "grace and intention onto every stray meaning." In my own writing, I've thought about these questions and the responsibility not just to represent the story of a life truthfully, but my narrator's place in it. I mourn my father and also engage with those complexities of his character that rebuke any attempt at hagiography. His life as a con man, for instance, and the three-year estrangement I count as the first time I buried him. I mourn my brother and remember those moments where his imminent death was not so sacred that we couldn't every now and then have petty fights. I revisit these facts knowing I too am compromised by grief, ego, and a desire to assign to narrative. Narrative itself is compromised by the nature of grief, the self-absorption and incurious behaviors that make a person (and the things they make) deeply limited.

What feels true is the wildness of the cumulative. The planes that fall when the sky is clear. Laughing when you are mourning. The process of grieving and dying is often a primal confusion that moves you inevitably toward contradiction. Fixedness and fluidity. Specificity and universality. Terror, magic, and mundanity. Setting out to represent it in all its complexity is a way to honor it, to acknowledge what is gone and what of you is gone with it, to give that loss life by coming with clear eyes to the ways you are changed. +

SARAH MORRIS, *MIDTOWN - CROWNE PLAZA HOTEL*. 1999, HOUSEHOLD GLOSS PAINT ON CANVAS. 84 1/4 × 84 1/4". PHOTO BY TOM POWELL. COURTESY OF THE ARTIST AND PETZEL, NEW YORK. © SARAH MORRIS.

THE CONTINGENCY CONTINGENT

Leigh Claire La Berge

IN RARE MOMENTS within the history of capitalism, too few workers exist. Not as an absolute, of course: in total, workers always outnumber paid possibilities for work; that's how our economy functions. But in a specific industry, a shortage may emerge, if only for a brief time. In 1998, on my first day of work as an analyst with the accounting and consulting firm Arthur Andersen LLP, it was clear that some aberration in accumulation had placed me in the twenty-fourth-floor conference room of a Manhattan skyscraper, overlooking the Museum of Modern Art's sculpture garden, staring at a PowerPoint presentation for new hires. On one slide was a cartoon duck, bespectacled and presented in profile, standing on the tiptoes of its webbed feet. In its hands was a sledgehammer, held overhead, ready to smash a desktop computer.

I would learn soon enough that this—my first professional and only corporate work experience—was a fake job. It was fake because although I worked with Arthur Andersen, I never worked *for* them. (Their shade of blue-chip firm would never have hired the likes of me: they recruited from places like Harvard; I'd recently graduated from Hampshire College. They required new hires to have impeccable GPAs; my school didn't confer grades.) Instead, I was employed by a global advertising conglomerate that had hired Andersen on a consultancy project and then placed me alongside the Andersen team—the result of a confluence of staffing shortages.

It was, moreover, a fake job because Andersen was faking it. The firm spent the late 1990s certifying fraudulent financial statements from Enron, the Texas-based energy company that made *financial derivatives* a household phrase, until that company went bankrupt in a cloud of scandal and suicide and Andersen was convicted of obstruction of justice, surrendered its accounting licenses, and shuttered. But that was later.

Finally, it was a fake job because the problem that the Conglomerate had hired Andersen to solve was not real, at least not in the sense that it needed to be solved or that Andersen could solve it. The problem was known variously as Y2K, or the Year 2000, or the Y2K Bug, and it prophesied that on January 1, 2000, computers the world over would be unable to process the thousandth-digit change from 19 to 20 as 1999 rolled into 2000 and would crash, taking with them whatever technology they were operating, from email to television to air-traffic control to, really, the entire technological infrastructure of global modernity. Hospitals might have emergency power generators to stave off the worst effects (unless the generators, too, succumbed to the Y2K Bug), but not advertising firms.

With a world-ending scenario on the horizon, employment standards were being relaxed. The end of the millennium had produced a tight labor market in knowledge workers, and new kinds of companies, called dot-coms, were angling to dominate the emergent world of e-commerce. Flush with cash, these companies were hoovering up any possessors of knowledge they could find. Friends from my gradeless college whose only experience in business had been parking-lot drug deals were talking stock options.

The employment agency through which I got my fake job made no epistemological distinction between knowing something and knowing about something. JavaScript, for example, a computer programming language: I knew about it but did not know it. Fine. Was I aware that the modern world might go on a catastrophic hiatus of unknown duration at the end of 1999? I had heard of something to that effect, although if pressed I couldn't have explained. The Conglomerate was not much more stringent. My interview consisted of about twelve minutes with a laconic, mustachioed, middle-aged Arthur Andersen manager named Dick. (One of the services Andersen had been asked to provide was to help hire the Conglomerate's Y2K team.) "On a scale of one to ten, what's your knowledge of computer software?" he began. I paused for a moment, unsure of whether our interview would include a demonstrative component, as had so many previous interviews for jobs I had not gotten. But his office was empty. I couldn't see how he would test me. I said *eight*.

"And what's your knowledge of computer hardware, on a scale of one to ten?" Dick continued. The moment called for both boldness and modesty. I felt committed to eight, a number I had long appreciated for its intimations of infinity when turned sideways. So I repeated myself: "Eight." It was true that one of my campus work-study jobs had been as a computer lab monitor. I could restart a PC or refill a printer's paper tray if the situation demanded it, although it rarely did. I'd had the weekend evening shifts.

Dick's next question would determine the development of my nascent career. "And what's your level of problem-solving, on a scale of one to ten?" I sensed, suddenly, an opportunity to pass through a corporate loophole, to surmount my lack of credentials, training, and touch-typing skills and lean into my historical moment. "Nine," I replied.

"That was it?" my girlfriend chirped when I reported to her the climax of my interview. The Conglomerate had hired me on the spot.

I WAS PLACED ON the quality assurance team, assisting with work the Conglomerate had contracted to be carried out exclusively by the Arthur Andersen contingent. They weren't called "a contingent" around the Y2K office. The consultants were referred to as the Andersen people, a term that exaggerated the partition between them and other Conglomerate employees, from whom they commanded both bewilderment and respect and, as often follows from the first two, a certain amount of resentment. These contradictory feelings stemmed from the fact that management consultants constituted then—and still do now—the vanguard of corporate work. They flit between companies and industries, parachuting in to diagnose problems and suggest, although rarely implement, "best-practice" solutions. It's management consulting lingo, *best-practice*, and it indicates that the good is not enough: this isn't Winnicott's consulting room. Instead, management consultants aim for superlatives. They hire the best. They practice the best. They claim Pete Buttigieg among their alumni ranks. At the Conglomerate they had their own offices, their own meetings, their own schedules. They worked from the Conglomerate's office space while they were on its project, but when they "rolled off" (they had their own terminology, too) they would take up residence within the ambit of another Andersen client.

"You've been selected because you're Andersen quality but not Andersen price," explained Cindy, the chipper data-warehousing expert who served as the quality assurance team's Andersen-employed leader, on my second day of work. I felt like a piece of organic fruit found in the conventional produce bin. Cindy also told me that, as with wolves, pack solidarity was intense within Andersen groupings. So was a wariness toward intruders.

In the first meeting with my lupine team, I did stand out, though not for lack of credentials. In fact I was the only person not massaging a fistful of Play-Doh. The Conglomerate's office was beige, the carpet beige, the people beige, too. But from each of the four quality assurance team members' hands exploded a most brilliant collection of colors: neon greens and yellows, hot pink, siren red, an almost psychedelic scene. Team members twirled and juggled their own handfuls, separated their globs and recombined them. "It's a new management technique," Cindy said, before I could ask. "It helps relieve stress."

Cindy herself did not seem stressed, but the situation she laid out for our team was certainly overwhelming. The Conglomerate held more than a thousand advertising, public relations, and communication companies worldwide, with possessions in both emerging markets and well-established ones. These cumulatively raked in billions of dollars per year. But any or all of these "shops," in industry lexicon, might collapse as one millennium ended and another began, preventing the Conglomerate from executing its global advertising operations and compromising its earnings and thus its stock price. Perhaps a radio station in Finland would go haywire and be unable to run a Conglomerate-booked spot; conceivably, a television station in Western Australia could disappear and, along with it, a Conglomerate-produced commercial; maybe a billboard would tumble off a highway in Rio de Janeiro amid social chaos, destroying a Conglomerate-created visual. If such events were to transpire, revenue loss would be a best-case scenario; one could imagine far worse. There had been a slide in the new-hire presentation, the one with the duck, that spelled out the possibilities: a stick figure with a thought bubble hovering above its perfectly circular head wondered: "On Jan. 1, 2000 will I still have: electricity, food, telephone, transportation . . . ?" Each life-sustaining noun was contained in its own thought bubble, and the final thought bubble offered only a series of anxiety-producing question marks ("?????").

That same tremulous atmosphere permeated the office, where a thumbtacked photocopy of a *Computerworld* article entitled "Economist Predicts Y2K-Based Recession" greeted team members on their daily arrival at the elevator bay. In the windowless kitchenette, several copies of the book *Time Bomb 2000* were available for employees to peruse while they warmed their instant coffee or selected a Pepsi product—Pepsi being a client—from the mini fridge. Most team members had their own Y2K doomsday clock on their desk, tracking the years, months, days, hours, minutes, seconds, and milliseconds until techno-rapture.

The first segment of the Conglomerate's Y2K project, "Phase I: Inventory," involved retrieving technological inventories from the Conglomerate's various agencies and recording them in a database. The lesser, non-Andersen network analysts entered data about the number of PCs, routers, fax machines, and printers any given Conglomerate shop had in its possession, copying the material from a spreadsheet said shop had emailed them. The superior Andersen quality assurance analysts (and I) provided the oversight, identifying the mistakes our colleagues had made. Someone had hit the *o* instead of its keyboard neighbor, the *9*; another team member, her mind wandering perhaps, had neglected to check the "entry completed" box. Little errors, but the general sense was that history would not judge them kindly. My team set out to rectify them before it had the chance.

The verb under whose sign the quality assurance team labored was a new one for me: to *QA*, past tense *QAed*. All mistakes our QAing located were recorded by hand; all handwritten records of our QAing were photocopied; the copies were kept in Cindy's office while the originals were bound for a secure document warehouse in New Jersey. Necessarily, our records would be kept on paper. If the predicted Doomsday 2000 did arrive, the digital world would be inaccessible, maybe gone forever. Computer technology had gotten us into this millennial quagmire and could not be trusted to extricate us from it. Perhaps that's why my problem-solving abilities had mattered more than my knowledge of computer software and hardware on Dick's scale of one to ten. The fact that the scale itself remained undefined, and that neither interviewer nor interviewee agreed to its coordinates, suggested both the fake nature of the whole endeavor as well as the desperation the Conglomerate felt, its keen awareness that it was running out of time.

THE ANDERSEN POSITION was that "Y2K is a documentation problem, not a technology problem." One could not know the magnitude of the technical problems we would face on January 1, 2000, with complete certainty until that revelatory day arrived, and so 1/1/2000 functioned as a kind of horizon of contingency: would we all be launched, *Back to the Future*–like, into a new stone age, or would a few rest-area vending machines conk out and everyone get on with it? To contend with this range of possible futures, we focused on the past. Instead of fixing things with the hope that they would function later, we would document the anti-Y2K efforts the Conglomerate had already undertaken, necessarily more knowable than those events not yet in existence. We would not, for legal reasons, promise things to come; we would certify that things that had already transpired had been appropriately recorded. To the alarming claim of the Y2K town criers—modern life after 12/31/1999 cannot be guaranteed—the quality assurance team responded retrospectively: whatever happened yesterday would be consigned to a database. At a certain point all that had happened yesterday was our documenting, so then we documented that. Then, exponentially, we had to document ourselves documenting our own documentation.

These efforts—designed to avoid the liabilities of selling a project that offered a Y2K fix, because what if Y2K wasn't "fixable"?—were part of a floating corporate-compliance rubric referred to only as the Process. Proprietary, capitalized, and always prefaced with that exclusive definite article, the Process could only be implemented by Arthur Andersen LLP. When a business engaged Andersen in a consultancy project, they purchased the Process. The Process seemed to have no printed home. To the extent that it existed, it passed between the minds and speech of Cindy and Dick. It was both accessible enough to be constantly appealed to—"the Process says," "How would we apply the Process here?" "I'm not sure this syncs with the Process"—and inaccessible enough never to be grasped with Play-Doh–like tangibility. In keeping with the Process, the quality assurance team scoured hundreds of thousands, millions even, of Excel spreadsheet lines. My day began and ended with comparing database entry to inventory spreadsheet and writing in my own script *Column 4, row 14: "18 routers" should be corrected to read "8 routers." Column 9, row 10, empty. Indicate yes or no.* This was dissociative, diminutive work, and time passed vertiginously, minutes and seconds overlapping on my teammates' unsynchronized doomsday clocks until the day concluded with a final collective effort at preservation. All quality assurance analysts—not Cindy, for hierarchical reasons—would convene in the photocopy room to ensure that, come what may on December 31, 1999, the deliverables from our day's labor would be archived, in print, in perpetuity. The only times we really spoke to each other in an uncurated fashion were over the blinding flashes and tray clicks of the Minolta copy machine. There we would discuss our commuting woes, roommate dramas, awkward dates, student loan repayment plans, as well as a rather unarticulated feeling of: What?

WHO MANAGED the management consultants? Cindy, shepherd of the Process, conducted random checks of all QAed spreadsheets and kept the results in her own spreadsheet. Dick and an elusive cabal of Andersen upper-tier management QAed Cindy. Once a rotund Andersen partner named Benjamin, outfitted in a yarmulke, a three-piece suit, and those unfortunate slipper-like Merrell suede shoes just making their way into the world in the late 1990s, spent an hour in the office, presumably to QA Dick.

The Conglomerate's Y2K managing director, Justin, had constructed a makeshift smoking lounge in the utility closet across the hall from my cubicle. It was there that Justin and Dick would liaise and swap status updates, and Justin often hosted other visitors in his windowless, walk-in humidor. Invariably these were older, suited white men, a world of Dicks. I'd try to eavesdrop, to pry bits of information from the clouds of secondhand smoke that escaped under the door and hovered momentarily about my cubicle before being absorbed into the carpet. A few gems did waft out. I learned, for example, that I wasn't the only team member to whom Cindy had described Arthur Andersen LLP as a pack of wolves: slender, agile, fangs bared, lips curled, marking their territory with urine (complimentary). When Justin heard this interspecies analogy, he balked. "More like bloodsucking leeches. They overcharge. Bullshit their billable hours. They want my employees to fuck up so I'll fire them and they can bring in more Andersen people.... Of course they're part of our team."

But what, really, was there to hear? That the Process was vertically integrated apocrypha? That Dick had knowledge of his firm's various fraudulent endeavors at Enron and was up to something similar here? In fact, Dick and Cindy could not have been more devoted, insistent as they were on evangelizing the Process to the Conglomerate's office. "Y2K is a documentation problem, not a technology problem," Cindy repeated at our weekly analyst meetings, and she invited us to say it with her.

Several months into my employment, in November 1998, a group of Andersen and Conglomerate elite visited our Y2K office to see what the $4 million Andersen project had produced in terms of Y2K preparedness. CEOs, COOs, CFOs, CTOs, an alphabet of executives, all men and some with aides-de-camp, filed through our office into a closed meeting. After their departure, Justin invited all team members into the conference room, where a Roman banquet of muffins and fruit pyramids, a well-appointed coffee cart, and the usual assortment of Pepsi products greeted us. None of these provisions had been touched, and team members were invited to pick through the refuse. "We just had over one hundred million dollars' worth of executives in here," Justin began. "They wanted updates."

We were encouraged to review for ourselves a paper copy of the executive council presentation, many of which lay scattered about the oblong conference table. I was perplexed to see that it was essentially a rehash of the new-hire presentation. The cartoon duck holding the sledgehammer. The stick figure wondering, "On Jan. 1, 2000 will I still have . . . ?" The floating text box, conceptual art–like in display, "Y2K is a documentation" et cetera. But the mood in the conference room was ebullient and self-assured. Even the always starched and monogrammed Dick looked pleased. The man seldom spoke outside of closed-door klatches, but as a measure of the morning's importance, he was invited by Justin to address the team. He rose and delivered a brief, litigious soliloquy:

"When January first of the year 2000 hits and a floodgate of Y2K lawsuits descends, and [we're] being sued by everyone, and the firms who aren't suing us, we're suing, the indemnification issues, the claims of fiduciary responsibility and accusations of abandonment thereof. What are we going to need? Proof. They're going to want to know what we did and how we did it. So that's what this Council is concerned with, proof, paper, documentation. And that's why our battle plan is simple: keep documenting, team."

M ONTHS OF READING and populating spreadsheets turned me spreadsheet-like myself: capacious but conceptless, able to record, to list, and to organize and sort, but according to an unthought, unthinkable orientation. After six weeks or so, and without much consideration, I began producing my own documentation, a kind of casual corporate ethnography. I noted the distribution of titles and nicknames at the Conglomerate. All the managers were men; all the analysts were women. Cindy was referred to as "the den mother." Dick had an alliterative title that recognized his central place: "Dick, the documentation expert." Justin, our commander, was hailed as "the general." I, along with another young woman and quality assurance analyst, an engineer by training who shared my hair color, were given the clunky moniker "the blond QA twins."

My favorite team member was a Viennese network analyst named Magdalena, who went by the German diminutive Leni. Tall and thin, accented and bespectacled, she hailed from fallen Austrian nobility. Her family had lost seven-eighths of their estate in World War I, but they nonetheless remained comfortable enough not to have to concern themselves with bourgeois trifles like work or mortgages. Had her father been a Nazi? Indeed, he had. Imagine a Captain von Trapp–like personality who had never softened under the melodious ensorcellment of a Fraulein Maria. Leni had fled her father's eastern Reich not by yodeling her way over the Alps but through an American husband who got her a green card, then a transnational law firm that got her experience, and then, finally, an analyst position at the Conglomerate. When she interviewed with Dick, she had been asked to rate her foreign language abilities on his mysterious scale. Fluent in German, English, and French, proficient in Spanish, she had given herself a ten.

Each Wednesday we gathered for a general meeting with all team members: the database programmers, who never spoke; the disheveled but crucial IT coterie; all the Andersen people; Conglomerate managers; Dick. Sometimes the receptionist even set the phone to an automated answer function and popped by. By January 1999, after five months on the job, I'd come to find some comfort in the routine coordinates of the general meeting. At 2 PM, everyone except Justin would be seated in the conference room, Pepsi product in one hand, Cindy-authored agenda in the other, waiting for the meeting's commencement, at which point Justin would announce through the all-office intercom that the meeting would begin five minutes late. Those minutes would pass and he would trudge in, a cloud of smoke all but trailing him.

General meetings involved an anonymous all-team exercise called "What's Good? What Needs Improving?" Team members were instructed to rip a piece off some desolate corner of their 8 x 11 agenda and compose two reflections on these stated questions. The compositions were then passed to the table's head for Justin to read.

Justin read aloud one Wednesday from the shrinking pile of anonymous comments. "What's good: getting a lot done. Needs improving: kitchen out of Sweet'n Low." And then: "What's good: enjoyed my office Secret Santa gift. Needs improving: I don't understand what the media team does and I will not accept 'ask a member of the media team' for an answer." As he read, Justin's countenance shifted from curiosity to uncertain disdain. He became aware—as did all team members—that his managerial style, his habit of punting, was being subtly mocked. Not only that: his antagonist was sitting among us. With a sly smile, somewhere between intrigued and embarrassed, he asked: "Who wrote this?" This query caused a swift reaction in Cindy, who responded, "This is an anonymous exercise." Justin interrupted with *Thank you, Cindy*, who, so chastened, let Justin continue: "I asked—who wrote this?"

Dead silence of the urban kind only a skyscraper can provide, where a soft machinic din emits from the building itself. Team members, careful to avoid potentially implicating eye contact with each other, fixed their downcast stares on their Pepsi beverages. "You don't want to tell me?" said Justin. "Fine. We'll sit here all goddamn day. We'll sit here till Y2K. Because I'm going to find out who wrote this fucking note."

Sitting to the right of Cindy, an Andersen analyst named Tracy reached over, took the offending paper scrap, and meekly announced to the nervous audience, "It's a girl's handwriting." I couldn't have felt more relieved. My script is scraggly and angular, the furthest thing from that of a girl. Tracy too must have felt some relief, having just exculpated herself. And Cindy—who would suspect her? As team members began scanning the conference table, privately searching for someone whose handwriting was bubbly and who menstruated, the silence broke.

"I did it—I wrote the note." Leni! Daughter of a Nazi. "It's just that you never answer questions and I thought—well, I thought: You're the boss, you will know."

Justin ended the meeting by ordering her to stay alone with him in the conference room. Later I asked what Justin had said to her in private. "That I'm 'on his shit list,'" she told me. And what did she say? "Fine."

The Contingency Contingent

IN FEBRUARY, with ten months left until the possible techno-finale of modernity, the Conglomerate decided to expand its Y2K preparedness operations and bring more Andersen people into the office. The new consultants also seemed to be wondering what the media team did. Located in an office directly behind my cubicle, they appeared to occupy themselves in the same way we did: printing spreadsheets, photocopying them, faxing them, and placing them in binders. Where the media team distinguished itself was in its leadership: it was the one team in the Conglomerate's Y2K shop run by a manager of color. Perhaps the only bit of knowledge I had of this manager was that he had somehow managed to board a plane to Brazil without having secured the necessary entrance visa. When he arrived in São Paulo he was detained, denied passage, and put on a flight back to NYC. He'd blamed the corporate travel agent, the gay and moody Carlos, and demanded his firing.

Instead, the Andersen axe fell on him. In a presentation to the Conglomerate higher-ups, Dick and a group of Andersen top brass declared that the media team was floundering. Their recommendation: the Conglomerate should fire its one Black Y2K manager, clear out any of his remaining loyalists on what came to be known as the old media team, bring yet more Andersen consultants into the office, and let them staff a new media team. Heather, the Andersen person who had conceived this coup de grâce, naturally took the reins. Her first move was into the old media team's office; her second charge was to populate her team. She needed someone familiar with the Process, someone of Andersen quality but not Andersen price. "You'd actually be helping with critical management considerations," Cindy said, after she'd invited me, for the first time since my hiring, into her office. "Think of it as a promotion."

I didn't know what the media team did, and Leni had been placed on a private shit list for even asking. And the quality assurance team was almost finished with our QA of the inventory database—we had located around 6,700 typos, many of which had been remediated and all of which had been documented as the result of our efforts. After such a collective accomplishment, it felt like an odd time to jump ship. In talking to Cindy, however, I realized that just as the offer to join the media team was to be *thought of* as a promotion, it was also to be *thought of* as a choice.

Changing teams meant learning the ways of a new Cindy, namely a Heather, whose ward I became and whose office I now shared. In contrast to Cindy's genuine enthusiasm for everything about management consulting, from the Play-Doh to the Process, Heather had a hardened corporate cynicism about her. She daily took calls from her interior decorator, Yves, who always seemed to be fifteen blocks away selecting upholstery and end-table pairings at Upper East Side boutiques. In those days before smartphone image-sharing, Yves would engage in elaborate ekphrastic descriptions of this piece or that. Heather put these conversations on speakerphone so she could continue typing with both hands, her manicured nails dancing above the keyboard with such intensity that often she had to ask Yves to repeat himself.

She overheard me, too, of course. Leni had learned that our Y2K office had a toll-free number that, in the case of an advertising-oriented Y2K emergency, Conglomerate employees could call to solicit expert advice: 1-800-Y2K-SAVE. But it was March—hardly time for the world's advertisers to panic about a Time Bomb 2000 detonation—and the line was usually quiet. In the meantime, team members in the know had begun giving out the office 800 number. Friends anywhere in the world could chat with any team member toll free. For me, free long-distance telephony was an enjoyable extracurricular perk, a way to talk to my girlfriend in Massachusetts, ideally when Heather wasn't around to listen.

The objective of the media team was to inquire into the state of Y2K preparedness for the radio stations, television stations, and newspapers that were the Conglomerate's most important global media vending partners. We would do this by mailing them a Y2K questionnaire. Within a few weeks of our dour partnership, Heather had condensed our team's trajectory into a single PowerPoint slide featuring so many capitalized common nouns that, looking back over my notes from the time today, I get the anachronistic sense of reading late-18th-century English.

New Media Team:
   -Media is Y2K mission critical
   -Is designing Y2K Questionnaire
   -Will be contacting Media Vendors
   -Will suggest Y2K Contingency Guidelines

The first bullet point was a bit of a non sequitur, more atmospheric than definitional, and I'm surprised it won Dick's approval. The second? An outright fabrication—Heather downloaded our team's generic questionnaire from a fly-by-night website called Y2K.com. The third bullet point, at least, was not entirely fake. The new media team had inherited from the old media team a bulging, imposing binder full of vendors' mailing addresses. A data dump would transfer those addresses from the binder to a database, and those addresses would be used to send the questionnaire—but first, a QA of the media vendor database was required. Someone needed to identify the bugs and infelicities, the doubles and deletions, that even the cleanest data always seems to include. That someone would be me.

It fell to Leni to reveal what I should have already known: that mine had been a fake promotion. Perhaps I had been moved laterally, or perhaps even that was too optimistic of an assessment. Some clues were obvious: I hadn't received a raise, for example. Others, more subtle. *Quality assurance analyst* has a certain corporate gravitas to it, but what would *media vendor analyst* mean on my resume if I wanted to leverage my Conglomerate time into a future Fortune 500 life or defect to Deloitte? She observed my simmering angst and provided a German term: *Weltschmerz*, or world-weariness. Leni said I was suffering from it. She advised me to open an E*TRADE account and to orient my portfolio toward biotech. She had staked out a position in Amgen and had, within some months, doubled her money.

I T'S A TRICKY risk proposition to mail unsolicited and legally implicating requests to corporate partners all over the world, but the Process demanded it. What, the questionnaire asked, were they doing to prepare for Y2K? For example, were they contacting third-party suppliers to inquire about their Y2K readiness? We knew very well that those five thousand media vendors wouldn't respond to our questionnaire, because the Conglomerate itself didn't respond to the thousands of questionnaires it received from its own business partners asking basically the same question. Heather explained that the Process wouldn't allow a response, due to the legal vulnerability created by the disclosure of such information to another company.

By summer, perhaps our final one, the Andersen people decided that in addition to documentation, personal contact with the Conglomerate agencies was needed to stress the importance of Y2K. Many team members began trotting the globe to conduct Y2K site visits, and the office took on a transient, desolate quality. The speckled dropped ceiling seemed to sag under the weight of the HVAC infrastructure. The

Diet Pepsi began to leave a sour aftertaste. Leni decamped to Asia for two weeks to support a series of Y2K regional meetings. Cindy headed for Vancouver to instruct the Conglomerate's Pacific Rim shops in the ways of the Process. Even Justin left his smoking lounge to take a pre-millennial working tour of Paris, Brussels, and London.

"This is your chance, LC," Cindy informed me at the commencement of my own Y2K grand tour. My ambitious itinerary included cities I had long fantasized about visiting: Tokyo, Hong Kong, urban constellations along the eastern coast of Australia. There would be time for surreptitious tourism, too: the café in Buenos Aires where Marcel Duchamp played chess, the Zócalo and its murals in Mexico City. None of this is what Cindy meant, however. She told me of one team member who "earned so many frequent flier miles, he took his whole family to Sydney business class. They got a club-level suite at the harbor Hyatt." Other team members had redeemed miles for Hawaii junkets, or converted them into points for cruise bookings, vouchers for rental-car upgrades, discounts on duty-free alcohol and tobacco purchases. Around me, I realized, had whirred an opaque economy whose currency was only now becoming apparent. Suddenly, the number of mission-critical Y2K situations throughout the Asia-Pacific region made sense: first-class tickets generate triple frequent flier miles. So did team members' preoccupation with South Africa, a fourteen-hour flight from NYC, and not just Johannesburg: Durban and Cape Town, too, had become improbable locations of Y2K concern. Meanwhile, Canada, our proximal neighbor and English-speaking sibling, home to multiple Conglomerate shops but no long-haul flights, was judged to be fairly Y2K-prepared.

I became as greedy a reward accumulator as the next team member. But during many of my international media site visits, I felt the reliable tug of impostor syndrome. On a trip to Tokyo, in place of the usual audience of one or two media-vendor colleagues in a dingy conference room, two analysts and I were led into the agency's unexpected auditorium to find that a sea of suited businessmen awaited us. Perhaps they had taken our intra-Conglomerate communications seriously: we had after all sent word that the world—or at least the advertising industry—might be ending in short order.

I had always taken some comfort in knowing I was speaking to people whose fluency in English could not be guaranteed. That distance in communication, real or perceived, had been crucial for me as I asked my series of absurd questions. If global technology ceased 1/1/2000, how would your agency continue its operations? The Tokyo shop, however, had arranged for a translator. In an English accent, she asked me to enunciate slowly so she could select her words with the kind of care a world-ending situation demanded.

"On January 1, 2000, will you still have . . ." I began. Concerns were shared about the Tokyo media market: "No Japanese media vendors responded to our Y2K preparedness questionnaire." It was one of those out-of-body, disassociated experiences, so often provoked by trauma but here provoked by management consulting. As Leigh Claire the media-vendor analyst held forth, paused for translation, and then continued, a second, depersonalized Leigh Claire wandered off the stage, collected herself, and took notes. I was disturbed at my own ability to make millenarian pronouncements. Exponentially, like a QAer documenting her own documentation, I began to doubt my own self-doubt.

Many of my Japanese colleagues' responses to my presentation concerned my appearance. My Conglomerate confrères noted how unusual it was to have a young woman with blond hair in their presence, the translator, a brunette woman herself, seemed somewhat embarrassed to convey. "It's exciting for them," she editorialized, "you know, the difference." My blond hair color, the highlights—were these a naturally occurring phenomenon, they wondered. One male media hand after another went up: How old was I and what was my marital status? How long would I be in Tokyo and what were my plans? What were my recreational interests?

This attention to my person was not without benefit: it did distract from Y2K. If someone had asked about servers, routers, why the response rates to our questionnaire mailing in Japan were so low, what advice I had for Y2K compliance, I would have likely taken recourse to my own contingency plan, one developed just then—I would have spoken about the contingency of knowledge itself. Perhaps I had become a convert to the Process: the future could not be known until its moment arrived, and at that point it was no longer the future.

Late in that anxious August of 1999, a freak midnight flood struck New York City. Small puddles dotted the paving stones of Brooklyn's sidewalks and the asphalt had that technicolor, water-mixed-with-gasoline slickness about it. The trains were delayed enough that I didn't leave for Midtown until 10:30. I emerged from the damp morning into a transformed corporate world.

Cindy was perched with hawklike intensity inside a kind of bivouac she'd created between the office door and the elevator. She had a clipboard in one hand and a pen in the other. I had barely crossed the threshold when she broadcast clear across the stand of cubicles: "LC made it!" A different voice rang back: "Check." Cindy had meant to affect a tone of relief at my arrival, but her excitement won out. The woman had spent more than a year preparing the office for a crisis, and now we had one: a flash flood. She herself had walked to work, she said. From the Upper West Side! She said this as though reporting on an alpine trek. A swift and unexpected nocturnal rain had swept through the city, Cindy related. "Some team members won't make it," she said, and, without any sense of her own drama, let a pause take hold before finishing her sentence: "into the office today."

At Wednesday's general meeting, Justin gave Cindy all kinds of commendations for her swift crisis management. The phone tree she had set up practically out of the ether. A collection of alternate transportation routes she'd compiled that team members could consult to solicit guidance on getting into the office in the event of a natural or—dare one say it—technological disaster. A buddy system she organized in which team members could locate a partner, alphabetically or by neighborhood. Already she had initiated the process of assembling the materials into a binder. Dick, her mentor and her boss, gave off a silent but approving glow. Cindy had saved the office, but the flood had exposed a striking irony: the Y2K office, so busy advising others on contingency plans, hadn't developed its own.

"We all knew to expect the unexpected," said Justin. It seemed like he might verge into contemplation and consider the idea of contingency in and of itself: can one really plan for something truly unknown? Instead, he took a more imperative course. "It's balls to the wall from here on out. We've got four months." His charge occasioned a flurry of activity, as team members sought to seize the day while it still existed to be seized. We had lived through a flash flood, and things had gone berserk in a dozen different ways. What would an actual millennial meltdown occasion?

B Y DECEMBER 1999, the feeling at the Conglomerate's Y2K office was that nothing more could really be done. This is a common enough cliché on the approach of any moment of finality, but was particularly apt in our case, since nothing really *had* been done. The travel diminished, and colleagues I'd last seen lounging under a shaded terrace in Milan were again denizens whom I passed in the office kitchenette, Pepsi product in hand. To mark the progress of the calendar and to demarcate our work, team members did what we did best: preside over the expenditure of large sums of corporate cash. With most air travel suspended, we trained our focus on accruing hotel reward points. A series of suites were booked at hotels around Midtown so team members could monitor the developing Y2K situation across the collection of global time zones with which so many of us had become familiar. These graveyard shifts did not require remaining awake, only sleeping within a several-block radius of the office—and with whomever one pleased. Christmas and New Year's vacations were revoked, of course, but that meant that team members could enjoy a series of multicourse dinners on the Conglomerate's tab, including those inflated prix fixe menus that always seem to pop up around the holidays.

Limited time remained, certainly in the office and possibly in the world. But the mood around Midtown seemed the furthest thing from that of end times, unless end times are distinguished by towering Christmas stockings and holiday wreaths the size of tractor tires. At a holiday party, we drank drinks named after 1980s financial instruments: a Poison Pill, an LBO, a Killer Bees, a Bear Hug. Not that those dated terms of corporate chicanery concerned team members: the Conglomerate's stock price was as buoyant as the atmosphere, and team members who had taken some of their salary in options were feeling festive indeed.

Then, as in a modernist novel whose conclusion one knows will not provide an ending, our mission-critical moment, our finale—composed of the scaffolded segments of temporality that team members took such pleasure in delineating: second, minute, hour, day, week, month, year, decade, century, and, yes, millennium—came and went, as any other had and many others would. It seems both necessary and anticlimactic to state what everyone now knows: we survived, with minimal difficulties. Cindy dutifully reported that some automatic toilets in Singapore hadn't flushed properly, stuck as they were in an expired world order. Other team members scoured news sources for tales of Y2K glitches and compiled a modest list. There was an electric garage door opener whose open and close buttons had become reversed; a selection of already-odd Sharper Image gadgets that had no discernible clock control but that had nonetheless broken down somewhere on the momentary midnight bridge between 12/31/1999 and 1/1/2000; and an industrial blender at a cattle-culling facility in Alberta whose whirl wouldn't cease even when unplugged from a power source.

By the time team members reconvened in the conference room on the bright, crisp morning of Monday, January 3, 2000, even these millennial malfunctions seemed little more than a set of curious examples, representatives of a larger case of something whose dimensions had already begun to recede from the Conglomerate's collective consciousness. The sensation of collapse would return, of course, with the two scandalous bankruptcies that would signal the end of the '90s economy, the first great financial bubble of our era. Both Enron and WorldCom had had Andersen as their auditor, and on both projects, it turned out, Andersen had been operating far short of best practices. It had been systematically shredding records for Enron and faking others entirely at WorldCom—documentation problems for the ages. But in the first days of the millennium, I was surprised by how quickly Y2K disappeared from office discourse as though censored, and by how team members adopted an almost amnesiac approach to a period so many of us had let so eventfully structure our lives. There was no self-consciousness: Why did we do that? More one felt a sense of process: This happened. +

ARCHTOBER FESTIVAL TRACING THE FUTURE
OCTOBER 1-31, 2024

Discover all things architecture and design in New York City through events, activities, and experiences for all.

Start exploring at **archtober.org**

Archtober

BEN SCHUMACHER, *SPIKY YELLOW*. 2022, OIL ON CANVAS. 79 × 79". COURTESY OF THE ARTIST AND GRAHAM VUNDERINK GALLERY, PITTSFIELD, MASSACHUSETTS.

TRYING TO ESTABLISH MYSELF AS A YOUNG MAN

Angelo Hernandez Sias

Y<small>ADI AND I</small> have agreed: friends. Last night post-Brujx she held me a birthday party, surprise! Crew left and we should have said good night. Instead we walked through Riverside. Cool quiet night. A man asleep on the slide. Swing set wet. Puddles lamplit. She stopped me, hugged me. Just like in my dream. I squeezed round her waist, bare. Felt her heart. She buried her face in my shoulder. When we came apart she was bleeding. Nose ring.

O<small>BIE SPENT THE NIGHT.</small> Yadi lent me her mattress topper and some blankets, and I set a pallet for him on the floor. We talked like a middle school sleepover. He lives in a building with a sleek website. I had to fill out an application, he said. I thought I would be living with young professionals. It was a quad with four bums. Literal bums, bro. I thought I would be with high-quality people.

M<small>EANT TO GO</small> with Yadi for groceries, overslept. Lunch with Obie. What kind of man are you, he said, looking at my Harvest Bowl. What's with you and Yadi. Saw him off, made a beat, worked on submission (Felton). Dear Committee, I wrote, at Unmasking Historical Legacies I will further develop a creative-critical praxis.

In the evening I FaceTimed Papa. No answer. Deja FaceTimed. Hot there too. She glugged from a large jug of tea. Said she went shopping with her parents today. They want her to have things in Chicago. Rubber spatulas, nonstick pans, eggware. For themselves they bought a stair-climbing trolley dolly. Wheels like fidget spinners. It won't be used, she said.

Re: recurring phone charges
Hello Julio,

We have identified several lines which we believe remain essential (green), though the status of some lines remains unknown (yellow). The attachment lists telephone charges billed to the station. Please review the cells and let me know which lines may be cut. Thank you.

Best,

Trent Kramer

Director of Broadcasting

PS—What's the word on the remote broadcast?

This electronic message is intended only for the named recipient and may contain information that is confidential or privileged. If you are not the intended recipient, you are hereby notified that any disclosure, copying, distribution, or use of the contents of this message is strictly prohibited. If you have received this message in error or are not the named recipient, please notify us immediately by contacting the sender at the electronic mail address above, and delete and destroy all copies.

Slept in, hard to get up. Café, read with Yadi. She was wiping tears from her book. Left, 0.5 hours at library. Harvest Bowl, made a beat, worked on submission (Marshall). Walked through park, stepped on pile of burrito, phone with Papa. Your mama's friends are coming over for dinner, he said, to pretend like they're my friends too. Ran into Francisco, invited me to Kenneth's show. After walk, past dark, returned to café alone, worked more on beat. Irina, former classmate, present employee of café, brought me Viennese coffee. So good to see you! she said, what are you working on can I listen here's my number. FaceTimed Deja before bed. Said she liked the beat. Text from Irina: Can't wait to listen to your stuff. ♥ Could not sleep. Renounce Viennese coffee. Late-night dumplings, organic Cup of Calm in lounge with Yadi, talked music. Found out she went on same walk at same time this afternoon, parallel, ahead.

Chicken apple almond sweet potato goat cheese rice balsamic kale consumed in the student center, where someone disgraced Nocturne in B-flat minor, Op. 9, No. 1, on the lounge piano. Someone here is disrespecting you, I texted Deja, along with a recording. No reply. Ah, she would have said, in my absence they dethrone me. Rest assured, I shall return with a vengeance.

Yadi's room: wine and bachata with Brujx crew before Kenneth's show. Jackson, bashful as usual, sat cross-legged on Yadi's braided cotton rug and drank from a bottle. Francisco, bachata god, danced with Sara asexually, or parodically sexually, liberated by his gayness. Sara fretted about last night, when she accidentally swore on air, then crawled under the board and curled into a fetal ball. I stood organically by Yadi, sipping and saying I would like to delete my "discography" and renounce music. Angst o'clock, she said removing the drink from my hand and taking my hand in hers and pulling. Do not delete your music OK it is an inspiration to some of us you have no right. And it's just a dance chamaco but suit yourself. Oh all right, I said. It felt good to touch her waist again, warm and swaying under my palm. Not so stiff, she said squeezing the back of my neck. I've been taking lessons in Dominican masculinity from Francisco but I'm a slow learner, I said, forgive me. Dominican men don't ask forgiveness, she said. We must be reading different Junots, I said. You're still reading Junot, she said. She pinched my nose and set her head on my shoulder for a slow song, like she did for the long train to Kenneth's show. When we got off the lower sky was visible in the absence of high rise.

I FEEL LIKE ROGAINE / I feel like grow up / I feel like propane / I feel like blow up

TALKED TO KENNETH after his set. He gave me a big hug and said, It's been years bro! Like I was an old friend. How's it been, I asked. I can't lie, he said, been busy, trying to establish myself as a young man, get this bread, plus I'm going through some personal stuff, I'm twenty, you? Twenty-one, I said. He set a hand on my shoulder. Come out to the stu sometime, he said, we should hang.

I should invite him onto Brujx.

RE: KENNETH'S SHOW
Dear Deja,
Last night I went with the Brujx crew to a show by Kenneth, that rapper I met freshman year, the one with the Pikachu track, remember? He opened, which was sad, because the audience was sparse for his set and he was the best of the night. You should have seen him. Like a Super Saiyan in old lady sunglasses. His fro exploding, his skin washed in blue

light. A tucked-in T-shirt with his name etched on it in faux crayon. The whole whimsy thing. Capris, long socks with muffins. Could barely make them out with his legs moving all crazy. He was unfazed by the size of the crowd, maybe twenty of us in a room for two hundred. Could have felt intimate but he seemed dead set on an MSG kind of thing. I imagined him from the nosebleeds. Like we saw Gambino. And Tyler. He'd be better that way. Anyway, I know you had a rough day. I wish I was there to give you a hug, a kiss, so on. UA3631 can't come soon enough.

Yours,

J

I UNDRESSED, brushed my teeth, ate a slice of turkey, lay down, propped my book on my chest, and my phone dinged. No-show. Can you cover?

YADI CAME BY the station to hang while I stayed up all night programming Akousmatikoi. Asked me to sit beside her, rubbed my shoulders. Rubbed, then I lay in her lap and looked up at her while she played with my hair.

RE: RECURRING phone charges
 Dear Trent,
 I checked the fourteen lines under the green PLEDGE column. None of them appear to be owned by the station. My hunch is all these lines are moot. Happy to discuss.
 Best,
 Julio
 Student Director of Engineering.
 PS—Remote broadcast is coming along swimmingly. Yadi and I plan to visit Governor's Island next Monday (after my week away, during which she will cover for me) to test viability of connection.

HAVE TO BE ON UA3631 in some hours and cannot sleep. Probably because I have to be on UA3631 in some hours. Plus what's been going on. Week away will be good. Being here, not good. Too close to Yadi. Together: Brujx, prep for remote broadcast, cataloguing vault—just to name work, small part of life since job is fake but pays well. Plus time at work, not working: listening sessions, production tutorials, recording sessions, cleanups, live sets. Plus time *not* at work, working: library, café, room, lounge. Marshall, Fulbright, Felton. Central Park, Riverside, Morningside, Sunset: skating, walking, smoking. Picnics (goat cheese, crackers, figs). Film nights: one blanket, two tallboys. Good night hug too short. Staff bonding all right—station must be pleased.

Deja however.

YADI CAME OVER. We talked and talked. If you knew me you would be disgusted, I said. My heart, she said, hearing you speak of yourself like that. She thinks if I eat a granola bar I will love myself. Cup of Calm should do it. Brought to me in the night, a note too: I am really grateful for the love we hold for each other as we witness this time of change moving through us, I have appreciated our insomnia solidarity, fly safe, be brave, big hugs, Y. Yes. Big ones. Like earlier today at the station. Didn't want to let go, lingered, feeling foolish.

DEJA PICKED ME UP from Dulles with her brother in the backseat. We went to a Mexican restaurant and talked about plane crashes. He showed a simulation of the deadliest crash in history, which occurred on a runway. In thick fog one plane gains speed. Another enters its path. The first lifts its nose but is too slow. The tail drags on the runway, sparks. Its belly grazes the other. Both light up. 537 dead, he said beaming. Kevin wants to be a pilot, Deja said. He has a flight simulator. I'm flying from DC to Taipei right now, he said. It makes you feel like you're going somewhere.

STRANGE HOW so long apart feels like nothing now that we are together again. I forget life before her. As for after—won't think about it.

LAST NIGHT AFTER her brother left we made love a long time, then lay there cuddling and discussing ancient civilizations, hip-hop, etc. In the morning we went to a café. Forgot her laptop so I lent her mine and read book until the end. Then went across the street to the bookstore with the cat in the sill and got another. When I got back she was wiping tears. What's wrong, I said. Do you feel that, she said. I did, in my eyes. I sat across from her and rubbed my eyes. God, I said, it hurts. Look, she said, pointing at the guy next to us, who was pouring his water bottle onto his eye. Oh my God, the guy said to no one. Let's get out of here, Deja said.

We went to the Portrait Gallery and looked at Frederick Douglass. I was initially excited to be there, but soon got bored and anxious and wanted to leave, plus my eyes kept burning. Am wiping at them now.

Today I asked Kevin how his flight ended. He laughed. Turns out I forgot to set the autopilot, he said. Many hours in the wrong direction. Somewhere in Africa.

Drove west all day yesterday. Stopped for air first thing. Struggled with tires. Ate even though we weren't hungry (too much trail mix). Bad storm last night. D was driving, thank God. We turned the music down. I realized I don't like Aminé as much as I thought I did.

Asparagus festival. Midwestern headassery, Deja said. Hey why won't you hold my hand. Wrapped my sweaty hand around hers and she recoiled. Clammy boi, she said. Then reached for it and our fingers locked, palms damp and pressed together. Walked a while that way. Big sunny morning, supposed to rain in the afternoon, didn't. Guitar somewhere. Dirt road crunching at our feet, dust kicked up and coating our sneakers, legs. Slid her thumb free and tickled my palm. I've really missed you, she said. I missed her too, I said. Kissed her on her cheek, bulging chipmunk-like. My sweet. Good to be with her again. Away, forget how much you like to look at her lips while she speaks, rub your fingers along her biceps, her forehead, snatch it! The frown of her laugh. Her smile when you are kissing her, her teeth on your lips. Remember this next time you are away, feeling foolish.

You're the prayer I'm the pew / You're the AK I'm the pew / You're a blessing like achoo / Hope you never say adieu

Re: "consumame"
yadi, this BANGS! love the filters on the different vocal layers, especially the chopped & screwed stuff at the end (step aside, james blake). goosebumps at 2:40 when you cut to single vocal track and beat drops out. pad that follows the bass on the eighth note motif—can you bring it up, bring bass down a bit in beatless parts? vocals blend well but generally sit on top of beat—bring them all down a few db? ending feels like the sweet spot vocals-wise, with the single vocal track and the beat

banging, but make sure overall vocal levels don't overwhelm when you add back the other layers. really tho, you could drop it as is and it would crush, so take this all with a pinch of salt and trust your gut.

warmly,

j.

ps—the lyrics were very touching

Mushroom benedict at hipster joint with sun window, light on Deja's sundress. Two mimosas though she vowed one. Patted her "food baby." Long wait for the bill brought a silence neither of us knew what to do with. Silence even as we talked. You seem, she said, off. How so, I said. A lot going on up here, she said, finger to temple. My submission, I said. It's weighing on me. Which one. Marshall. You don't have to do it, you know. I know, I said. I want to. I'm sorry, she said. I just don't like seeing you like this. Like what, I said. Exactly.

Big industrial fan in my old room now. Turned it on last night, hot strong wind could have pinned us to the wall. Like sticking your head out the window on the freeway, too much air to breathe. Parents upstairs asleep. Still we wanted the wall of sound. Maybe why they put it there. Some things they prefer not to hear, I understand. Lying there in the dark, moon grainy through the curtain, clasped damply to each other, still, quiet. The old ruts, too deep to forget, too familiar to name, dare not here. I'm on my thing, she said, our one week together and it comes, surprise, the universe hates me. We put down a towel. The first night was too long: took time to remember her, shake off what I thought I might confess. Ensuing nights too short: no stamina. Last night, our last night: just right, despite the universe. Arrived together. Only afterward in the harsh bright bathroom did I feel the scratches, and for the darkened latex a weak repulsion. Wrapped it in toilet paper before disposal. Let a hot wind loose, silent but deadly. Returned to bed. Did you poot, she said. A while ago, I said, in the bathroom like a gent. Ohmygod it trailed you, she said with plugged nose. Then shot up and dragged the sliding door and stuck her head out and laughed. I basked in it. I don't want you to go back, she said. I don't want to go back.

Am back. FaceTime with Deja. She's back in lab and sad about it. Evening in the café, reading with Yadi and Francisco. Irina waited on us. I focused on my book. You still haven't sent me that song, Irina said. I'm sorry, I said. What song, Yadi said. Francisco focused on his book.

TONIGHT I SHOWED Yadi how to ollie in the park. Try a trick, she said. When I half-kickflipped she blurted, That's my husband! Francisco was recording and said, Straight to Deja! We all laughed.

LAST NIGHT UP LATE with Yadi before the storm. We walked through the park, sat on the swing set. She stood on hers and pumped hard, then curled into the seat. She recited one of her mother's proverbs in Spanish. The plant of friendship must be watered, the plant of romance need only believe it is being watered. We are staying friends, she said. She loves me, she said. I love her, I said.

SUBMARINES at the bottom of the sea / Underneath / Only spot where you & me / Get to breathe

KENNETH DROPPED a new single, "Sac On Ur Neck." Played it for Yadi yesterday while we catalogued the vault, our shirts still drenched from the storm. Sac on your neck / Fat, sac on your neck, yuh / Set this sac on your neck. Thought she might laugh at me. Genius, she said. Why haven't you invited him onto the show. I keep forgetting, I said. Do you smell that, she said. Maybe someone blew the bathroom up, I said. She plugged her nose. One person is not capable of such horrors, she said. God, I said pulling damp shirt to face. So sharp it was almost smokey. Francisco entered into the vault and said, Oh my God who farted. Did you blow the bathroom up, I said. I think I might puke, Yadi said. Let's get out of here. She and I went to my room and did email, then made a beat together. Dear Kenneth, I wrote, would you like to do a set on Brujx. U guys pay, he replied. It's college radio, I said, exposure. Bet, he said. Friday, I said. Bet bet, he said. Yadi and I showed each other our new songs and there was some wiping of tears. Let's draft up that release form for our loved ones, she said. Any and all interactions may be used for creative exploits.

RE: FOR THE LOVE of god stop w the Harvest Bowls dude

J,

As promised, instructions for bibimbap: buy cucumber, bean sprouts, spinach, carrots, mushrooms, ground beef, sesame oil, gochujang, egg. And a link to the recipe I use. I love you.

D

Re: rancid smell in station

Dear Trent,

Just giving a "nose" up that there's a rancid smell in the station. I called Public Safety and they determined the cause is sewage, which has been adversely affected by the flash flood. The stench is coursing through the station's vents. It's especially bad in the bathroom and vault. If you notice the sewage smell worsens during your visit to the station today, feel free to let me know so I can get in touch with Public Safety again.

Thank you,

J

Kenneth came onto the show. Came onto Yadi. She wore a thin gold chain, black crop top no bra. Usually I like. But Kenneth stared. But she liked. Blushed how I thought only I could make her, toyed with the chain while she spoke. Spoke soft into the microphone, and when he spoke, laughed as I did not know she could. Veins on her forehead. Sweat. Master control was hot and stunk. We had prepared questions as usual, some mine, some hers. The questions she asked were off script and Kenneth answered steady like the whole thing was rehearsed. I accepted my role as techie, checked their levels, kept them from the red. Kenneth, at ease in English, switched to Spanish. She met him there. I could not. Was so resigned to my superfluousness that I didn't believe her when she asked me afterward to play my own stuff for him. Oh, I said, it's nothing worth. He's humble, she said. Show him! I caught Kenneth's eye. Something buried beneath the sheen of hype. Show me, he said, I would love to hear, this one has good taste. Yadi beamed at him. I pulled a file on my laptop. Played. Yeah, man, Kenneth said, bobbing his head, this is great, I like the beat (vocals bad?!?), will you make me one? Do you pay, I said. Exposure, he said. Bet, I said. We're doing a remote broadcast in a few weeks at Governor's Island, Yadi said. Join us for a set.

HEADPHONES DIED as I walked into the café. Irina was off. The string hanging from the bell above the counter grazed a piece of cake. I found a seat. A couple sat at the table beside me and talked. The Viennese coffee brought to me was overflowing. A ring formed around the bottom of the mug. I burned my tongue and set the mug down. Tried to scoot seat back but pushed table forward instead, spilling further Viennese coffee onto saucer. The couple looked at me. On second sip the Viennese coffee pooled under the mug dripped onto my shorts, then onto bare leg. I set the mug down. Bladder calling. Before I stood another man beat me to it. Several parties entered and laughed.

Spent the night reading an old journal.

STAYED UP UNTIL 5:30 working on submission (Fulbright). Woke up late. Caught the train to the park, where I ate tacos with Obie. Being single sucks, Obie said. I wake up with someone I slept with the night before and want them to leave as soon as possible. This makes me depressed. You like something but don't know if you'd like something else more.

We went to see Yadi perform son jarocho. Kenneth was there. His head was . . . globular. I wanted to punch it. I walked to a café down there. Ten-dollar minimum, ninety-minute maximum. Can I help you, the hostess said. I worked on my submission.

I went to a sunset concert in the park. Got there late and went to the back of a long line. My favorite act warped by the distance. Beside me a girl in a dress read *Sister Outsider*. I pulled out my book and pretended to read. She put away her book and I put mine away and we stood mute without our phones, without moving. Then the line lost integrity. Hundreds rushed toward the front. At first I walked, then, seeing her running along with everyone else, I ran. I lost her and found her again. We stood there without moving. But around us all moved, and moved us gently. What happened, I said. An L, she said. We should finesse our way back in. We joined the mass and talked about music and college and phone numbers and does it matter. We got in for the final act. I pulled out my phone to record and saw that Yadi had texted: I'm too late, I can't get in, stay. I obeyed. I danced with the girl. Afterward I walked her to the train and said good night and goodbye.

YESTERDAY WOKE UP still dark. Remote broadcast prep work. Long journey there and back. Ferry to the island. Heavy equipment.

Back pain. Kenneth only there to perform, still helped me carry what I couldn't. He killed it. Pity Yadi couldn't come. Sara in her place. Poor reception. Trent Kramer thought he was recording the whole thing, found out after he'd forgotten to start. Kenneth said not to worry, the beauty of a show is you had to be there. Trent pulled on his hair. Looked ready to shoot himself, Sara said to me. We laughed. Head hurts. Had a ticket for Little Simz in the evening, too pooped. Gave to Yadi. Went instead to hang with Obie at his new spot. Low-rise neighborhood: bagel shops and makeup boutiques. Thai. We crossed a low bridge over the canal, brown-black and goopy, changing color in the sunset. Would you jump in for ten grand, I asked him. My hair might fall out, he said. Train ride home. I lay in bed sweating, awake in the dark. This morning I walked to the pharmacy and bought ear plugs.

D EJA'S BIRTHDAY yesterday. Forgot to call. Called today. She cried. Weak happy birthday an apology makes. Read in the library with Yadi. Harvest Bowl for lunch. Did email in the station. Francisco saw me and asked if I was all right. Worked on submission (Marshall), or tried to.

S ESSION AT KENNETH'S. Way uptown, lost myself between trains. Rang him, no buzz, texted, no reply—was relieved at the prospect of his flaking. Outside in the heat, visions of his face comporting itself at my art. A woman in sweats keyed in and held the door. I thanked her and entered, caught the elevator, one of those ones with cage-like gate. Hall: dank, damp. Knocked softly, was turning to leave when he opened, smiled, dapped me up, led me in, asked that I take off my shoes and leave all negative energy at the door.

He offered a glass of ice water—sorry, no AC. In the living room: a breathing mass on the couch, a guitar case, loose rancid socks, stench of loud. A pig, he said, but a very good bassist. Down a dark hallway to his room: cramped, bed unmade, desk cluttered, a chair he sat on, trayed roaches, crusty laptop, turntable with cracked husk, two monitors, a stool for me, an MPC, a mic, a journal. I write too you know, he said, helps me see clear, increase my vibrations, manifest light. Journals never bring clarity, I said, we lie to them and they lie back. My guy, he said, what did we say about negative energy. Right, I said, sorry.

He leaned over and squeezed my shoulders. Knots, he said. Breathe with me. In. Out. I do this with Yadi all the time. Better isn't it. Check it.

Made this the other day while tripping acid and enjoying the vastness of my spirit. He played the track. Stutter hat, glide 808s, arpeggiated pads, a Splice loop, still very good. Heavy vocal fry, like recorded after heavy sleep, hook in drag triplets, verse in double time.

Session went well enough, must have—sent me the track afterward and asked me to hop on. Spent the evening lying facedown across the middle of my bed, listening.

SHE THE BEST PART like key lime crust / Where did God go in we I trust / Doing my best to be like tough / She always calls my bluff / But I get soft when she hugs me / Don't nobody love like she loves me / Universe behind us

RE: SOUTH AFRICA program?
Hi Julio,
Did you submit an application to Unmasking Historical Legacies? Pablo mentioned that you had, but I don't see an email from you.
Best,
Naomi

Naomi Lopez, PhD | Director of Undergraduate Research and Fellowships

YADI OFFERED TO celebrate my submission (Marshall). We went to a quiet bar. Our first time not on campus, not in the dining hall or in the lounge, not at a concert with friends, just us two, sitting across from each other in the dumb light, sipping beers, her treat. I bet widows masturbate to dead people, she said. Yeah, I said, ghosts. I used to be a desert, she said. I didn't like anybody and it got so bad I couldn't get off because no one came to mind, no names or images, at least none I was comfortable with. What happened, I said. Kenneth, she said. I felt my head on my neck, heavy. Lightweight, she said. I wobbled to the bar, where the bartender ignored me, then went back to our table and asked if she wanted to leave. In her room we sat on her bed and played music. Do you love him, I said. No, she said. I put my head in her lap and she played with my hair, then vice versa. I lay on my back and she lay beside me. Soon we were on our sides, facing each other. Can I kiss you, she said. I looked at her lips. Only if this has the same integrity as what you do with her, she said. Integrity, I said. I don't want you to feel bad, or for things to be weird with us, she said. I don't feel bad, I said. I feel good.

Grace in town for fancy hedge fund dinner recruiting her. We met over Viennese coffee and talked about writing and Deja, back next week, and Yadi. I feel bad, I said. She (Grace) doesn't want to cast doubt on my relationship, she said, but I should have a real conversation with her (Deja). She (Deja) might be feeling some of the same things. She (Grace) is right about a lot. But she is also nostalgic. I was reading an old diary the other day, she said. My eyelid tape got caught on the bottom of your chin and left a gray mark. Do you remember that? No, I said. Neither did I, she said.

Re: key lime crust yo Julio just checking whether u still wanna hop on this one? Lmk bro -k

Emma's show last night with Deja. Afterward, backstage, the actors remembered themselves. We walked out with Emma. Everybody cheered for her. We bid her farewell. Midtown dinner, Harvest Bowls. The 1 was fucked and we caught a car. A girl sitting shotgun, our age, a classmate apparently. Are you dating? she said. Three years, Deja said. Good luck, the girl said. Why good luck? I asked Deja when we got out. Because senior year is when things crumble, Deja said.

Late start with Deja. Got up first, floated about. Spoke with old Spanish prof for Fulbright language eval (bombed). Heated pasta labeled COMMUNAL in Deja's fridge. Went to EcoReps sale in search of bookshelves. One for each of us. Found two. One finessed by the girl ahead of me. Deja had one bookshelf in her hands, asked me, in front of other girl (thief), Do you want that one too or are you good with this? Good with this, I guess, I said. You put me in an awkward position, I said afterward, having to say I want two bookshelves while that girl takes none. You could have claimed it, Deja said. I'd have looked like an asshole. It's whatever. Have this one.

Dinner with Pablo. Dig Inn, LaCroix, IPAs. I made confession to his roommate, O'Connor, at their party last night. We are disgraceful, we agreed. Pablo tells me you're applying to a Fulbright in Colombia, his friend José said, best country in the world, for a hundred bucks you'll have the night of your life. You say that like it's cheap, Pablo said. José glanced at Deja, who was sitting on the other couch talking to José's girlfriend, also named Deja, then leaned in and lowered his voice: No, man, I'm talking drinks, food, hookers, everything. Just don't fuck the underage.

I TOLD DEJA I got nominated for Marshall. You're going to find a British girl and forget about me, she said.

LAST NIGHT I got to her place at 10:30. We hung in her living room and spoke with her roommate. We sat on her couch and watched Brockhampton. We unpacked her room. I discovered a fidget spinner in one of her suitcases and drove her crazy. We readied for bed at 3. Bathroom, brushed our teeth, she moisturized, I rinsed my mouth guard. We lay down. She wanted to but I felt weird. We were hungry. Or I was hungry and she was willing to eat. We got up, boiled lasagna, fried eggs, heated sauce. Ate and brushed our teeth and lay down again. Now I wanted to and she felt tired. It did not take us long to sleep, we did not sleep long.

INTERVIEW FOR MARSHALL (internal). Dean Lopez of Research and Fellowships and Dean Fritz of I don't know. A space for them to give notes on my app and ask me about myself so they can write a letter to the committee on my behalf, they said. We sat at a small round table. Fritz across from me, Lopez between us. She first. Some notes on coherence. Then Fritz. There's a lot of good stuff here but it's sort of all over the place, he said. Don't be a hero. Narrow your focus. Propose something feasible.

RE: KEY LIME CRUST
I assume you're no longer interested? just wanna give a heads up Ima drop it soon

PHONE WITH MAMA last night. Said she went shopping with friends and they all bought shoes. I piled the shoes and took a picture and sent it to your dad, she said, and said to guess which were mine. He got it right.

Out last night with Deja for a drink at a new bar near campus. The bar is nice but cannot decide who it is for. Drinks too sweet. After two my head was heavy. Hers too perhaps. I feel so grateful to have met you, she said. It's when she says things like that.

Yadi's room: Brujx "meeting" tonight. Wine, bachata. No one danced. We went to Riverside, where everyone smoked. I said no thanks. I wanted to but I was hating myself. You've forgotten us, they said. They were hating me too. The ground had dog hair. We passed Obie sitting on a bench wearing headphones and drinking from a can. Hey man, I said. Hey, he said. Are you all right, I texted. No reply. Went back to Yadi's. She asked if we could talk. Just us two. We sat in the stairwell. The light was medical. Her eyes were pink. I thought we weren't going to let things get weird, she said. I thought so too, I said. What happened, she said. I feel bad with you, I said. You feel good with her, she said. I feel bad with her too, I said. I miss you, she said wiping tears. I think of you every day, I said. I can't help you, she said.

I went back for Obie. The bench had no one. +

PENNY GORING, *WEEPERS*. 2018, ACRYLIC ON CANVAS. 23 × 33". PHOTO BY TIM BOWDITCH. COURTESY OF THE ARTIST AND ARCADIA MISSA, LONDON.

GIRLS AND INSTITUTIONS
Daria Serenko

WHEN I FIRST WENT to work at the state institution, I saw only girls. That was what they called themselves—"girls"—with an intonation that shifted from exclamatory to questioning depending on the kind of catastrophe unfolding around them. And catastrophes, I understood immediately, were an inevitable part of the unstable cosmogony of our daily work routine.

We worked in a small district library, in an office without windows. The girls' computers appeared bigger than the girls themselves. Sometimes you could neither see nor hear the girls over the wide monitors and whirring of desktops, at which point you would have to get up from your chair to assure yourself that another living being was present. The lack of windows in the room was apparently compensated for by a photo print pasted from floor to ceiling: tropical greenery and a steep, tumultuous waterfall whose foaming currents came crashing down from up high. The picture was a daily reminder not so much of fresh air as of power hierarchy.

There was a time when I tried to preserve some bodily autonomy—eating separately, taking the bus to the metro separately—but this self-separation very quickly lost any meaning. My life at the time was also basically a catastrophe, so I felt at home at work: it was fun and terrifying, and the boundaries between private and public were washed out by alcohol and deadlines. The girls accepted me as one of their own. We often turned into a single many-armed, many-legged creature, jubilant, all-powerful, devastating. In those moments, I no longer felt my own powerlessness or the weakness in my knees.

At the same time, while studying the girls, I often caught the automatism of my gaze, lightly arrogant, ironic, sweetly condescending, and mythologizing female collectivity. I justified it by my particular status: I'm just passing through. Sometimes, when I looked at everyone in a glum and mistrustful mood, it seemed like the girls only existed down to the waist, that under the tables they didn't exist and there was just a tangle of different-colored wires carrying signals off to somewhere else. Of course, it could be that I still hated women and just wasn't drawn to them. Or maybe on those days, it was me who wasn't all there under the table.

O NE DAY, THE GIRLS and I were walking in silence through a public park. "It's gotten harder for me to hate the State," I said, without thinking, as I walked. "You're becoming one of us," replied one of them.

We didn't always work from the office: sometimes we laid out old books in the city streets or hung freshly purchased Russian flags on trees and led a circle dance around them, arm in arm with confused city dwellers. We were always stumbling into new portals and ending up at yet another one of those endless festivals with a budget sheet we'd never get to see. At these festivals we would fulfill state tasks: we'd build pavilions with our bare hands from sticks, dirt, and shit; we'd fake attendance records for human and animal visitors; and, sometimes, we'd steal a glance into the institutional abyss that was usually covered with papers and rags. There were many abysses. The girls and I went for a cigarette every twenty minutes. In our library fridge there were two bottles of vodka—one for an emergency, the other for a rainy day. As it happened, both came at once.

On my first Cultural Worker Day, we were carted off to the local performance hall and strictly forbidden to leave the room. We thought it was a joke. Eventually, some men in tight suits rounded us up into a small concert hall and shut the door. The lights went out.

An announcer with a poofy hairstyle came out onstage to alarming fanfare and expressively read us some congratulatory poetry. Then she invited "the band of our youth" onto the stage—that's how she announced it. We froze, expecting, at the very least, t.A.T.u.

I'd been nauseated and dizzy all day and, as the Soviet vocal-instrumental ensemble Singing Hearts started on their third song, my period finally came. I tried to squeeze out between the rows. At the exit, two security men stopped me: they'd been given instructions not to let anyone out for any reason at all. The artists were on the state's tab. Workers mustn't leave the show; they must relish it.

After I'd been forced to leave a bloodstain on a stately velvet chair, the girls and I went back to the office.

THE GIRLS AND I didn't like to lie. We never did end up learning how to lie, either. One day we had to pretend that we'd organized a mass event that had never happened. The Department demanded that we send photographs of absorbed visitors that same day, so we got some people in off the street, luring them with the promise of tea with sugar and biscuits. They thought they'd come to a wake, so sat very quietly at the table, crumbling their biscuits into a napkin.

Another time, the girls ordered the security man to wrap himself in a fluffy scarf and sit at the table. That's how we ended up with the dramatic photo of the empty room with a lonely woman in a scarf. The security man somehow managed to precisely convey the necessary gender expression with his entire body. The photo was useless for our report, but evocative. Who was this woman? What was she thinking about when she decided to come to yet another nonexistent event handed down from on high? How long had she been sitting there?

A few days later, we held a goodbye party for one of the girls who was retiring. We sat around the overflowing table and made bets about which of us envied her more. We poured vodka straight into the tea and rattled off cheerful toasts. The girl looked at us with a mocking, sideways glance. "This is my wake," she said. "Get some people in off the street while I'm still here."

ONE DAY I cut myself on my pay stub. The red stain washed out my humble salary. The girls said that now I had really earned it with blood, sweat, and tears.

The girls knew how to manage these small paychecks. In the summer, they would put aside money for winter shoes. They brought food with them in small containers and ate twice a day. Sometimes a commis-voyageur would come to the office, and that's how I found out that word is still used in relation to living people. The commis-voyageurs would lay out tights, socks, necklaces, perfumes, and underwear on our tables. If we didn't like anything, they'd open up another suitcase and pull out long strips of smoked meat and fish.

Every day there came a moment when the girls got undressed. They'd hike up their skirts, tug up their tights to keep them from sliding down, take off their jackets, kick their shoes under the table, let their hair loose. Such relaxation was infectious: their postures became more and more casual, their faces less focused. You could tell that soon the girls would be home. And they would have exactly three hours before sleep to prepare their food for the next day, figure out their spending for the second half of the month, go on a date, go over someone's homework, drink a glass of wine, have a fight with the landlord, walk the dog, masturbate, phone the girls.

W**HAT SETS GIRLS** apart from institutions?
Girls never get old.
Girls go off to cry in the bathroom.
Girls run late and arrive with their dresses inside out.
Girls get called into the police station.
Girls can tell you to fuck off.

O**NCE DURING A STORM** there was a power outage in the library. The flow of digital documents ceased, the overhead lights went out, and the screens went black. The deadened silence of the power outage clogged our ears. If, under the tables, the girls had actually been made of tangled wires, then they would have powered off, too.

Six months ago, a little camera was put up in the office. Each month, a quiet and forgettable man would come, fiddle with the camera, and leave without answering any questions. The camera became another one of the girls. We got along with her as if she were a real and not particularly pleasant colleague in whose presence it was better not to say certain things. When the power went out, the little red eye of our girl-camera flickered out, too. It was as if a closed window had been smashed open.

"I'm being summoned to the police station."
"I divorced my husband."
"I took that contract outside and burned it."
"The budget doesn't add up."
"I want to kill myself."
"I'll lie, leave early, and go out on a date with her."

We came out onto the street to a torrential downpour. Our shirts and blouses got wet and our bodies became more transparent and defined. We admired one another in the middle of the workday, hoping that something irreversible would happen: a short circuit and then a fire; the library bursting into flames and burning down right in the middle of the storm. We would never come back here or see one another again.

O NE DAY, THE GIRLS betrayed me. I didn't blame them: sometimes, in an institution, things develop in such a way that you simply don't have a choice.

I came to work and noticed that my table had been moved. Now all the girls were sitting behind my back. It was frightening to turn around and look at them. I could feel myself going numb from the weight of their gazes.

No one spoke to me all day. I didn't know what had happened, but I understood that it was best not to ask. I had been warned that something like this might happen. I'd been briefed on how to behave if it did.

At the end of the workday, a phone rang. It rang and rang, but the girls didn't stir. Evidently, I was meant to pick up the phone.

"Hello, is that you?"

"Hello, yes, it's me."

"We have received information that last week you were not present at work."

"There must be some kind of mistake. I'm here every day, you can ask the girls."

"What do you take us for? We've already asked."

That's how I discovered that at the building entrance, there was a camera recording the daily number of bodies present at work. For the whole week, one by one, each of the girls had taken a day off.

After the call, the girls surrounded me in a tight ring. They stroked my head and my cold cheeks, cried, asked for forgiveness, and held their hands to their chests. I peered into their sympathetic faces and couldn't tell them apart.

O N INTERNATIONAL Women's Day, boys appeared. Bewildered, they pressed festive bundles tight to their chests. The boys were united by the pale sheen of their faces.

The girls exchanged a glance and silently rearranged the free tables into a *T*. The guests were seated, the bundles taken from them, the cakes cut. Half an hour later, the boys thawed out and started loudly telling one another about things that only they knew. Once in a while, they would break off to give a toast:

"To women, without whom this world would be homogeneous and homosexual!"

"To all our lovely ladies—the heroines, dead and alive, of postsocialist labor!"

When it got really boring at the table, one of the girls pulled off her long wig. The boys didn't notice anything, but we were completely delighted. It was as though a bald moon had risen invisibly over us. Taking off your hair in front of all the men and laying it out right there on the table—could a woman have permitted herself to do something like that a hundred years ago?

We didn't want to admit that the boys had shifted something in our space. That's how it is when your soul temporarily departs your body, but you don't notice. You just sit there, staring at a fixed point, while a single drop of blood falls neatly out of your nose.

THE GIRLS WERE rarely told apart. Of course, other people could remember which one of us was Natalia and which one of us was Daria, but they had no idea how we were different from one another. When work was in full swing, we also couldn't always tell whose arm or leg was whose. Sometimes it seemed like we even shared a stomach, which is why each of us started bringing lunches that went with what the other girls were eating that day.

It was convenient. We swapped in for one another at meetings and conferences, spoke to the bosses in the same neutral voice, politely heard out the irritated visitors who threatened to either overthrow the government right that instant or reach into their string bag full of apples, pull out a gun, and execute us point-blank with a shot to the head.

One day, after the regular meeting at which it was my turn to pretend to be Natalia or Daria, the boss called me into his office. It was gloomy and smelled of freshly printed newspaper and cognac. The boss stroked my hair and back. I grasped the back of a scratched leather armchair. My palms were sweating.

The boss got his coat, informed me that he would be back in a couple of minutes, and left. My eyes slowly adjusted to the weak lighting: the gilded letters of diplomas and thank-you certificates came into focus, and I even managed to make out a tear-off calendar that was already behind by a few months.

I sat like that for fifty minutes, going over in my mind all our reports, contracts, decrees, addenda to agreements. The cleaning lady came in and asked me to lift my legs. I lifted them too high—the way people usually sit at the gynecologist. All the other girls must have been home by now. The cleaning lady looked at me like I was an idiot.

"What are you sitting here for? Go home, he's always doing this. He must have mixed you up with someone else and only worked it out when you'd already come in."

I got my things together, rearranged all the diplomas on the wall, tore sheets out of the calendar many, many months in advance, and went home to the future. +

—Translated from the Russian by Sasha Karsavina, Philippa Mullins, and Nadezhda Vikulina

New and Forthcoming

USE DISCOUNT CODE **ENJOY30** FOR 30% OFF ALL KSUP BOOKS THROUGH 12/31/24

BEHIND THE WHITE HOUSE CURTAIN
A Senior Journalist's Story of Covering the President—and Why It Matters
STEVEN L HERMAN
Hardback, $29.95 / 978-1-60635-477-3

"This behind-the-scenes account is not just another Trump book. It's an important reminder of why we need journalists like Steve on the front lines reporting the truth."
—**Jim Acosta,** anchor and chief domestic correspondent for CNN

OPIUM AND AMBERGRIS
COLIN DEKEERSGIETER
Paperback, $18.00 / 978-1-60635-483-4

Winner of the 2023 Stan and Tom Wick Poetry Prize
"These poems turn the copious glint and glimmer of language into resonant extensions of its themes. Thinking in this book is refreshingly physical and profoundly ethical in upholding the imagination as our great citadel of healing."
—**Major Jackson,** author of *Razzle Dazzle: New and Selected Poems*

LIGHT ENTERS THE GROVE
Exploring Cuyahoga Valley National Park through Poetry
EDITED BY CHARLES MALONE, CARRIE GEORGE, AND JASON HARRIS
Paperback, $22.00 / 978-1-60635-485-8

"Where standard field guides end, this one begins with a terrifically diverse chorus that sings and dreams us into a deeper connection with a special place."
—**Derek Sheffield,** coeditor of *Cascadia Field Guide: Art, Ecology, Poetry* and poetry editor of Terrain.org

Available from www.KentStateUniversityPress.com,
800-247-6553, or wherever books are sold.

IMAGE GENERATED WITH STABLE DIFFUSION.

EAT POOP YOU CAT

Rachel Ossip

WHEN FACED WITH a bit of downtime, many of my friends will turn to the same party game. It's based on the Surrealists' Exquisite Corpse, and involves translating brief written descriptions into rapidly made drawings and back again. One group calls it Telephone Pictionary; another refers to it as Writey-Drawey. The internet tells me it is also called Eat Poop You Cat, a sequence of words surely inspired by one of the game's results. While Exquisite Corpse can generate moments of absurdity, they rarely match the hilarity of Eat Poop You Cat. That hilarity is not always communicable (I've tried and failed to convey the gut-shaking silliness of one particularly memorable round in which the phrase *panic at the disco* gradually morphed into a well-drawn rager of deviant worms—some vomiting, some smoking, some fucking, one sipping from a novelty beer hat). But as a rule, bad translations tend to tickle, and shifting back and forth from the verbal to the visual amplifies these humorous juxtapositions and incongruities.

As recently as three years ago, it was rare to encounter oddities of text-to-image or image-to-text mistranslations in daily life, which made the outrageous outcomes of Eat Poop You Cat feel especially novel. But we have since entered a new era of image making, powered by tools that explicitly rely on these kinds of multimodal translation. With the aid of AI image generators like DALL-E 3, Stable Diffusion, and Midjourney, and the generative features integrated into Adobe's Creative Cloud programs, you can now transform a sentence or phrase into a highly detailed image—or several—in mere seconds. Images, likewise, can be nearly instantly translated into descriptive text. Today, you can play Eat Poop You Cat alone in your room, cavorting with the algorithms.

Back in the summer of 2023, I tried it, using a browser-based version of Stable Diffusion—an open-source text-to-image generative AI (or GenAI) model—and another AI browser application called CLIP Interrogator, which translates any image into a text prompt. It took about three minutes to play two rounds of the game: anywhere from twenty seconds to two minutes to generate an image from a prompt, and another minute or so to process that image back into a text prompt. I kicked things off by typing "Eat Poop You Cat" (why not?) into a field that encouraged me to "Enter your prompt." Then I clicked "Generate Image."

The Stable Diffusion applet generates four images in response to any prompt; I cheated slightly by just choosing my favorite to proceed. From the center of the frame, a decently realistic tabby cat stared me down, green eyes glowing wide, mouth hanging open to display a salmon-pink tongue. The background was grungy gray without much detail; in the image's lower third was some bubbly white text in emphatic all caps: EAT EAT POOOOP POOP YU NOU SOME YOU!

I dragged this image into CLIP Interrogator, which spat back the prompt: "a close-up of a cat with green eyes, blue text that says 3kliksphilip, epic urban bakground, poop, white border and background, licking out, epic poster, office cubicle background, golden toilet, funny cartoonish, erin, classic gem, messy eater, exploitable image, leave, motivational, moving poetry, toilet." A nuanced syntax for image-generating prompts has emerged alongside the development of GenAI tools, and CLIP Interrogator's "prompt" mimicked that accretionary layering of styles, details, and descriptors—though this list felt excessive, like a psychedelic extrapolation of the image, which I was glad to know was already a "classic gem." Apparently 3kliksphilip is a gaming YouTuber, but who is Erin? Why is *background* spelled incorrectly the first time, but correctly the second? Where did the golden toilet come from? *Leave?*

After a few more back-and-forths I ended up with an image of a black-and-brown cat lounging on a commode that could have been designed by Frank Lloyd Wright. A bit of toilet paper, which had fallen onto the cat's head from the roll above, approximated a hat. The image was flat and looked painted; dark contour lines conveyed the forms. The style felt familiar—Expressionist? German Expressionist? Fauxnaïf? Influenced, certainly, by Modigliani, early Picasso, some of the later still lifes by the Polish Cubist Henri Hayden. Adjacent to the cat and the toilet, a copper cup balanced on a matching copper saucer. A series of blocky, all-caps words spilled across the floor: RULE OF TWO FREE PROSDY.

Precisely 197.8 seconds later, CLIP Interrogator described this tableau as "a painting of a cat sitting on a toilet, playstation 2 gameplay still, in style of pop-art, by Ignacy Witkiewicz, the fool tarot, inspired by Phil Foglio, punkdrone, molecular gastronomy, app, bong, persona 5, text: roborock, destroy lonely, dog, ascii, 1 8 2 4, tarot card design." Destroy Lonely is not a command, I learned, but a trap artist from Atlanta. Roborock is a Roomba-like automated vacuum cleaner. Phil Foglio is a cartoonist best known for unconventionally silly Magic: The Gathering illustrations. The inclusion of the late-19th-century writer and painter Stanisław Ignacy Witkiewicz affirmed my intuition that there was something vaguely Polish about this image.*

Stable Diffusion makes images through detailed processes of category-based production, mapping language to a vast set of visual variables, while CLIP Interrogator performs the inverse function. The seemingly random strings of proper and phrasal nouns and adjectives are the result of neural networks "reading" the image and assessing sections of pixels for clues that are then correlated with terms, however opaquely. While the configuration of pixels that translates to "cat sitting on a toilet" is clear enough, those signaling "punkdrone" or "the fool tarot" are less so.

Because there are so many ways to picture even the simplest cat in the simplest scenario, text-to-image and image-to-text models are far from one-to-one processes of translation. If they were, the algorithms and I couldn't play this game. But close reading even such an unserious set of prompts and images offers clues about the scaffolding behind these operations, as well as broader insights into the clumsy, grab-bag way humans tend to deploy language when attempting to describe an

---

* Witkiewicz is a fitting reference for a tool that creates images by interpreting visual categories. After painting for decades, he abandoned his less-than-successful Expressionist style to establish the "S. I. Witkiewicz Portrait-Painting Firm," for which he became well-known. He defined seven "types" of portraits, such as "Type A—Comparatively speaking the most 'spruced up' type" and "Type B+ supplement—Intensification of character, bordering on caricature. The head larger than natural size." Each painting's type determined its price, which generally decreased as Witkiewicz gained leeway to distort the figure. (This rule was notably broken by the priceless "Type C, C + Co, Et, C + H, C + Co + Et, etc," which were "executed with the aid of C_2H_5OH," colloquially known as alcohol, and "narcotics of a superior grade.")

image. By starting with such a nonsensical string of four words, it's possible I embarked upon a bit of a fool's errand. But what does the fool seek? In tarot, the Fool is an innocent youth at the start of a journey, representing new beginnings and unlimited potential. He stands on the edge of a precipice, striking a pose not dissimilar to that of the figure in Caspar David Friedrich's *Wanderer Above the Sea of Fog*. Though the path ahead is unclear and unstable, the Fool ventures forward.

FIRST ENCOUNTERED AI-generated images about a decade ago, toward the end of my time in art school. A peer double-majoring in neuroscience and furniture had trained something called an "artificial neural network" to "design" three-dimensional models of simple forms. He input a rendering of a Platonic ideal—a stool, in this case—which served as a template for the network to replicate. Through trial and error, the neural network, which he'd named DANA, or "Designer as Neural Activity," attempted to craft a stable shape with four legs and a seat. By producing countless assemblages of thin beams and larger cylinders, DANA crept closer and closer to outputting the initial form. DANA's creator postulated that neural networks could, in the future, be developed to be less reliant on a designer for this instigating visual prompt. "What if DANA, instead of existing in a vacuum, became an open loop of information? What if she took in pictures from Google Images, and learned based off of those, instead of my limited instructions?" He was ahead of his time.

I forgot about DANA's anarchic stools until January 2021, when news of the image-generating platform DALL-E was suddenly everywhere. Descriptions of the "AI artist," then in largely private beta testing, still felt like something out of a children's book: Type in a sentence and the computer magically spits out an image! While the technology sounded too advanced to be real, it had been coming down the pipeline for decades. The first neural network—basically a set of interconnected processing nodes that translates an input signal to an output signal—was proposed in 1943 by the psychiatrist Warren McCulloch and the self-taught logician Walter Pitts as part of an attempt to describe how neurons themselves might work. The technology's development continued in fits and starts throughout the 20th century, and its promise picked up as the nodes were arranged into increasingly complex layers. ("Deep" machine learning refers to any neural network with three or more layers of nodes.) Neural networks could decipher typed and handwritten characters as early as 1989, and computer-vision applications expanded rapidly in scope and public availability as hardware capacity continued to increase. Soon, optical character recognition, or OCR, converted PDFs to editable text, and now we can copy text snippets in photos taken on our phones. OCR relies on natural language processing, the field concerned with enabling algorithms to output and receive messages in human language rather than a programming language, which likewise advanced as computing power expanded. Natural language processing combines computational linguistics with statistical modeling and algorithms—now usually neural networks—to process and produce "natural" language through methods such as breaking down sentences, tagging parts of speech, assessing words' most frequent positions in a sentence, and highlighting words that do the most prominent signifying (usually nouns and verbs). At first, these efforts were clumsy and stilted, but we've come a long way from AIM's cherished dimwit, SmarterChild, to the often uncanny responses of Alexa and Siri.

By 2015, algorithmic processes were able to form simple sentences or phrases to describe an image, further integrating computer vision and natural language processing. Patterns of pixels identified as, say, "cat," "toilet," or "cup" were matched with linguistic tags, which were then translated into automated image captions in natural language. Quickly, researchers realized they could flip the order of these operations: What would it look like to input tags—or even natural language—and ask the neural networks to produce images in response? But reversing the image-to-text operation presented additional challenges. There is a vast difference between the complexity of a basic phrase and even the simplest image.

Describing any image with a large, centered feline as "a close-up of a cat" is unlikely to be wrong, whether it's a macro photo of a sultry Siamese or a cell from Sunday's *Garfield*. However, there are infinite possible ways to render the image described by "a close-up of a cat." Is it a hyperdetailed photo in Portrait mode, setting off each strand of the cat's fur? Or is every part of the image clumsily blurred, as all my iPhone snapshots are, taken through a lens smudged with finger grease? What about the angle, the lighting, the composition? Is the cat lying on a bed, or sitting up on a table? A simpler image of "a close-up of a cat" might be a line drawing or a flat, vector-style illustration, but either of those categories still encompasses thousands of possible variations. The authors of "Generative Adversarial Text to Image Synthesis," a pivotal paper presented in 2016, at the 33rd International Conference on Machine Learning, described this problem of complexity with the straightforward tone of computer scientists: "There are very many plausible configurations of pixels that correctly illustrate the description."

Another challenge—one also encountered by image-to-text models but exacerbated by the inversion—is the sheer quantity of visual data required to build up an understanding of the near-infinite visual signs that can be described in language. Some early attempts at image generation dealt with these paired issues of complexity and dataset size by constraining both the style of an image and its subject matter. Scott Reed, Zeynep Akata, Xinchen Yan, Lajanugen Logeswaran, Bernt Schiele, and Honglak Lee—the authors of "Generative Adversarial Text to Image Synthesis"—began by training their models on contextually limited libraries of images, specifically the Oxford-102 Flowers and Caltech-UCSD Birds datasets, published in 2007 and 2011, respectively. Caltech-UCSD Birds contains 11,788 photographic images of birds broken down into 200 mostly North American species, annotated with additional attributes such as "Bill Shape," "Belly Pattern," and "Underparts Color." The images making up the dataset were downloaded from Flickr and then categorized and annotated by human workers hired on Amazon's Mechanical Turk, a crowdsourcing platform often referred to as "artificial artificial intelligence." While one might assume today's text-to-image tools have been automated all the way down, their architecture and maintenance rely on enormous quantities of human labor, whether the repetitive "clickwork" performed predominantly in the Global South by workers paid pennies per "task," or the voluntary, quotidian labor you've provided each time you've filled out a CAPTCHA. To learn, neural networks need an initial set of labeled and categorized images, and a person needs to do that initial tagging and sorting—in this case, identifying the location of parts ("back," "beak," "belly," "breast") and attributes ("has_bill_length::about_the_same_as_head") for the fifty-nine photos that typify the "Glaucous-Winged Gull." The Oxford-102 Flowers were, somewhat less informatively, "acquired by searching the web and taking pictures."

By training GANs, or generative adversarial networks—a then-new form of machine learning architecture that pairs neural networks in something of a dialectical back and forth—on these category-specific datasets of attribute-tagged images, Reed and his coathors were able to generate unique, somewhat plausible bird images from natural language phrases. Photographic-looking images of birdlike shapes doing birdlike things in birdlike places emerged in response to "this small bird has a short, pointy orange beak and white belly" and "this magnificent fellow is almost all black with a red crest, and white cheek patch." The authors then moved on to the MS-COCO dataset, which, unlike Caltech-UCSD Birds and Oxford-102 Flowers, is not limited to a single "object category." The results of "a large blue octopus kite flies above the people having fun at the beach" were somewhat less convincing, though the GAN does appear to have loosely grasped the concept of a kite, if not the beach.

In February 2019, the US chip manufacturer Nvidia released an open-source version of StyleGAN, a generative AI that produces a near-infinite supply of unique, synthesized images of faces, allowing a user to control features such as face shape and hairstyles. StyleGAN was trained on the FFHQ dataset, or Flickr-Faces-HQ. Like Caltech-UCSD Birds before it, FFHQ is a collection of thousands of images pulled from Flickr, though its README does specify that "only images under permissive licenses were collected." Workers hired through Mechanical Turk weeded out errant images of "statues, paintings, or photos of photos" from an original pool of algorithmically scraped images. While FFHQ includes "considerable variation in terms of age, ethnicity and image background" and "good coverage of accessories such as eyeglasses, sunglasses, hats, etc.," its authors clarify that it also inherits "all the biases" present on Flickr.

Days after StyleGAN became open-source, Phillip Wang, a software engineer then working at Uber, created thispersondoesnotexist.com, a website that publishes a new, random, synthesized portrait upon each refresh. From there, a horde of copycats followed: This Cat Does Not Exist, This Horse Does Not Exist, This Foot Does Not Exist, This Pokémon Does Not Exist, This City Does Not Exist, This Chair Does Not Exist, and so on. While fears of deepfakes had been gracing headlines and raising hackles for more than a year, the sudden onslaught of images of People Who Did Not Exist seemed to trip a wire in the broader collective consciousness. Alarm struck the mediasphere as Twitter accounts DMing people for personal information were revealed to be scammers using StyleGAN-generated profile pictures. These *deepfaces*—a portmanteau that barely tracks—were quickly cited as threats to democracy, and calls arose for "anti-StyleGAN algorithms" that would catch and flag the generated images. Meanwhile, StyleGAN branched out and began to tackle anime portraits. While the image type changed, the subject matter remained constrained.

In contrast, ImageNet, a project initiated in 2006 by the computer scientist Fei-Fei Li, had the immodest aim of "map[ping] out the entire world of objects." The dataset contains upward of fourteen million annotated images, organized into more than one hundred thousand "meaningful categories." It also employed the labor of more than twenty-five thousand workers via Mechanical Turk. While one hundred thousand is an astonishing number of categories, it's extraordinarily small when you consider that there are certainly more than Caltech-UCSD's chosen two hundred "meaningful" species of birds, and more than five hundred kinds of items in "the entire world of objects," each of which is likely to have more than two hundred meaningful categories. Categorical reduction and oversimplification never bode well, especially when it comes to labeling humans. ImageNet drew upon a preexisting lexical taxonomy called WordNet, which was developed in the 1980s and borrowed from several earlier lexical sets. As one dataset built upon another, each carried forward the logics and hierarchies of the previous set, if not all its terms. As researcher Kate Crawford and artist Trevor Paglen have written, the original ImageNet dataset contained an image of a child labeled as a "loser"; included the categories "slut," "whore," and "negroid"; and curiously placed "hermaphrodite" as a subcategory of "bisexual," which in turn was listed as a subcategory of "sensualist," alongside "cocksucker" and "epicure." In 2019, ImageNet removed more than six hundred thousand images tagged with "unsafe," "offensive," or "sensitive" categories, patching the most visible cracks in a fundamentally flawed framework. Still, ImageNet's categories look controlled and careful when compared with its successors.

On January 5, 2021, when the San Francisco–based research laboratory OpenAI announced DALL-E, it also announced CLIP (contrastive language-image pre-training), an image-classifying neural network, which was integrated into DALL-E's processes. In a braggy blog post, OpenAI negs the ImageNet dataset for its costliness in terms of time and labor, as well as its limited range of content. "In contrast," the post's authors declare, "CLIP learns from text-image pairs that are already publicly available on the internet." Where on the internet, exactly, we still don't know. But considering the staggering scale of the training dataset—over four hundred million image-text pairs—the answer is likely pretty much everywhere: open-source images and captions from Wikimedia Commons and "images under permissive licenses" from Flickr, yes, but also almost definitely captioned images from Flickr *not* under permissive licenses, as well as images from across Facebook, Twitter, Instagram, BuzzFeed, global news outlets, underground news outlets, museum databases, Tumblr, DeviantArt, abandoned LiveJournal and Blogger blogs, and scientific-image databases. We know for certain, though, that CLIP also includes thousands of works by individual artists, illustrators, photographers, and graphic designers.

We know this because one of the things you could do with DALL-E—one of the things you were *encouraged* to do with DALL-E and its successors—is ask it to generate an image in the style of a particular artist. Unlike *deepface*, *DALL-E* is a canny portmanteau, mixing the names of Salvador Dalí—who played Exquisite Corpse with Valentine Hugo and André Breton—and our era's most lovable robot, Pixar's garbage-collecting WALL-E. DALL-E has concretized both the portmanteau gesture itself and the name's subliminal meanings as the core of its identity and suggested function: DALL-E is a surrealist garbage compactor that performs mash-ups, seemingly designed for what OpenAI calls "combining unrelated concepts."

In summer 2022, nearly a year after a public version called DALL-E Mini was released, social media was flooded with images that followed an "A but B" formula, juxtaposing a subject with an unexpected style or context: "Elon Musk painted by Pablo Picasso," "Kim Kardashian painted by Salvador Dalí" (naturally), "Nosferatu in *RuPaul's Drag Race*," "R2-D2 getting baptized," "SpongeBob SquarePants Godzilla," "Cthulhu on Sesame Street," and (a personal favorite) "a peanut butter sandwich Rubik's Cube." These generated images are not simply Frankenstein's monsters assembled from various bits of images hoovered from across the web. Instead, GenAI models create generalized *ideas* of signs, signifiers, image types, and styles that correlate with probable pixel patterns. DALL-E's deep learning algorithms decode a digital image's arrangement of pixels into hundreds of axes of variables, which it then uses to assess an image and its component parts, and consequently create similar but unique arrangements in the future. When you ask a GenAI tool like DALL-E or Stable Diffusion to style an image after a particular artist, it isn't copying the artist's work so much as it is interpreting and reproducing the artist's patterns—their subject matter, compositional decisions, and use of color, line, and form.

The quantity and range of images available on the internet, and how they are tagged, impact how well GenAI tools can generate images of a certain subject matter: the more digital images of different works by a particular artist are available, the better the GenAI will be at replicating their style; the more a visual idea appears, the more it will be reproduced. Given that there is, for instance, an overrepresentation of images and descriptions of white men as surgeons on the internet, GenAI tools circa 2023 almost always produced a white man when you asked them to generate a surgeon. Rather than remediate the foundational issues in the datasets, these tools' developers have attempted to obscure them through "debiasing," or coding in safeguards to ensure diversity—which is how we get Gemini, Google's recently rebranded GenAI tool, producing images of Nazis of color when prompted to "generate an image of a 1943 German soldier."

As TEXT-TO-IMAGE GenAI tools grew increasingly sophisticated, the surrounding discourse—on news outlets, blogs, Reddit, Substacks, and LinkedIn—grew increasingly alarmed: "Generative AI Is Changing Everything"; "Did Picture-Generating AI Just Make Artists Obsolete?"; "Can AI End Your Design Career?"; "DALL·E 2 (AI Art) Is Getting Too Good That Its Depressing [sic]"; "Art Is Dead and We Have Killed It." Many of these proclamations came from the camp of AI boosters, others from technophobes and visual artists themselves. In early May 2023, an open letter-cum-manifesto entitled "Restrict AI Illustration from Publishing" appeared on the website of the Center for Artistic Inquiry and Reporting, penned by the institute's director, Marisa Mazria Katz, and the prominent leftist illustrator Molly Crabapple. The letter outlines something of a fairy-tale relationship between journalism and illustration, which "speaks to something not just intimately connected to the news, but intrinsically human about story itself." Generative tools, on the other hand, take mere seconds to "churn out polished, detailed simulacra of what previously would have been illustrations drawn by the human hand," producing images that are either entirely free or cost "a few pennies." The letter concludes with a call to "take a pledge for human values against the use of generative-AI images to replace human-made art." More than four thousand people—a range of well-known writers, journalists, artists, and celebrities, including Naomi Klein and John Cusack—have signed.

There are plenty of reasons to be cautious about the use of GenAI for journalistic image production, the technology's embedded biases and enormous energy footprint chief among them. As of late 2023, Stable Diffusion showed us that "Iraq" only ever looks like a military occupation and that "a person at social services" isn't white, though "a productive person" usually is, and is *always* male, while "a person cleaning" is always a woman. Midjourney interpreted "an Indian person" with remarkable consistency as an old, bearded man in an orange pagri, and "a house in Nigeria" as a dilapidated structure with a tin or thatched roof. Meanwhile, a November 2023 study found that producing a single image with GenAI can use about the same amount of energy as charging a smartphone halfway—much more than is required to generate text—and that as models have grown more powerful and complex, they have also grown more energy intensive.

The threats to "human values" and the "humanity" of art, however, strike me as overblown. Humans produce GenAI tools—not only the scripts and mechanisms behind the technology, but the infrastructure at every stage: the Mechanical Turk workers tagging Caltech-UCSD Birds, weeding statues out from FFHQ, and tagging ImageNet; the anons shitposting on Twitter; the Kenyan content moderators paid $2 an hour to review endless horrors just so people can't accidentally make DALL-E kiddie porn. Human choices, foibles, and prejudices are the very bedrock of these tools. I'm more frightened by GenAI's humanity—all the assumptions and oddities inherited via their training images, every representational bias enshrined and automated in their tagging sets, each exhausted impulse of the underpaid laborers clicking and sorting as fast as they can—than most other aspects of GenAI.

But what about artists' livelihoods? It's true that "no human illustrator can work quickly enough or cheaply enough to compete with these robot replacements," as Mazria Katz and Crabapple write. But to say that "if this technology is left unchecked, it will radically reshape the field of journalism" is to paint a rather rosy picture of the field. The dystopian future Mazria Katz and Crabapple fear will come to pass if GenAI is left unchecked—the one in which "only a tiny elite of artists can remain in business, their work selling as a kind of luxury status symbol"—is, unfortunately, already here. Most publications see paying fair market wages for the often extensive labor required to produce a custom image as an unjustifiable expense. Why pay for images when there's a plethora of stock photos and illustrations you can buy super cheaply, memes you can right-click and copy, open-source images you can download from Wikimedia, clip art you can drag and drop in, and preexisting work by illustrators that so many simply screenshot and steal? Of the publications and businesses that do still commission original work, many have long outsourced design and illustration through online gig-work platforms like Fiverr, which were modeled after the general concept of Mechanical Turk. The laborers most likely to be automated out of a job by GenAI, then, are these platform workers drawing and designing for low wages across the Global South.

Any boycott of GenAI imagery is bound to be as effective as a boycott of digital photography to prevent photo developers from losing their jobs, or putting your laptop on the curb in hopes of reinvigorating the market for typists. The best path forward for labor protections might be to ensure that those already trained in crafting communicative, compelling images—illustrators, artists, photographers, photo editors—will be best at using these systems.* Like laptops, cameras, and paintbrushes, GenAI models are tools, and their true efficacy depends upon the skill and knowledge with which they are used. They are also, of course, tools crafted and actively maintained by humans, who deserve to be visible in the chain of image-production labor and considered in discussions of livelihoods.

Rather than "artificial intelligence," then, I prefer to refer to these algorithmic, neural net–powered tools as estranged intelligence, or alienated intelligence. The intelligence—the *humanity*!—isn't fake or forged; it is only concealed, outsourced and offshored, remixed and conglomerated, translated into algorithms which it then quietly labors to refine and train. But I know what Mazria Katz and Crabapple mean. It's

---

* *Wired*, the first US publication to adopt an official AI policy, has already enshrined this idea in guidelines. "Some working artists are now incorporating generative AI into their creative process in much the same way that they use other digital tools," the policy notes. *Wired* "will commission work from these artists as long as it involves significant creative input by the artist and does not blatantly imitate existing work or infringe copyright. In such cases we will disclose the fact that generative AI was used." The magazine expressly says it will not use GenAI images instead of stock photography, as "selling images to stock archives is how many working photographers make ends meet."

insulting to have your hard-won style stolen by an algorithm. I want to believe that something clear and visible is lost in AI-generated images, that what we call "the hand"—all the subtle, holy imperfections and artifacts of existence left on a made thing—is palpably missing. But I have taken all I can find of the online quizzes claiming to test one's ability to distinguish between AI-generated images and photographs, paintings, and drawings made by other means, and I must be honest: I do poorly on these tests. Certainly they were built to stump, pitting the best outputs of the generators against uncanny works made by other means, but given that I've worked as a graphic designer, a design educator, and an editor at an art publication, I'd like to think I have a somewhat discerning eye. What, then, is the tell of absent humanity?

In the early days of DALL-E, Stable Diffusion, and Midjourney, the distinct tics of the generators' weaknesses—mangled hands, habits of repetition, penchants for centered compositions, errors of physics—more readily betrayed their output as products of AI, while also making it fairly easy to tell images produced by each generator apart. Midjourney couldn't quite achieve contemporary photorealism, but it excelled at anything painterly, often added a grungy or vintage flair, and had a penchant for gold, orange, and aqua tones. DALL-E preferred photorealism, blank or simple backgrounds, and cutesier cartoon styles. But with each generation of generators the tells have become less visible. What will happen, though, when the proportion of available visual material begins to tip toward the AI generated, and GenAI tools are increasingly trained on images of their own making? Once the snakes are all deepthroating their own orange and aqua tails, what patterns will crystallize in the images they shit out?

WHILE TEXT-TO-IMAGE (and image-to-text) GenAI tools are built on the foundation of natural language processing, the language that tends to result in the best outcomes—and thus is returned by tools like CLIP Interrogator—reads as far from "natural." The syntax of prompting is unique enough that a market for so-called prompt engineers has emerged, while blogs and vlogs covering Prompt Writing 101 abound. Some indicate that within prompts, comma-separated phrases order ideas or terms hierarchically. Whatever comes first in the list is deemed most important and will most significantly dictate the image; anything on the third line will likely have a minimal impact. Certain engines, like Midjourney, allow users to alter this schema by adding numbers to phrases to weight their relative consequence. An excessive prompt like "a close-up of a cat with green eyes, blue text that says 3kliksphilp, epic urban bakground, poop, white border and background, licking out, epic poster, office cubicle background, golden toilet, funny cartoonish, erin, classic gem, messy eater, exploitable image, leave, motivational, moving poetry, toilet" piles on related terms in order to establish the image's content and approximate its style.

Most guides to prompt writing suggest a tripartite form: a subject, a description, and a style/aesthetic of the image. A "description" usually means a present-participle phrase, e.g., "a cat drinking coffee," or "a bulldog swimming in the ocean." The unruly prompt that CLIP Interrogator generated for my cat image has a clear subject—the cat with green eyes—accompanied by blue text, on an epic urban "bakground," with a white border. When it comes to the "style/aesthetic" of the image, though, it's less immediately clear what applies. "Epic poster" is a style, as is "funny cartoonish" and "exploitable image," which refers to any kind of meme that someone can customize by adding their own text or supplementary image. But these aren't the sorts of descriptors one would generally reach for when conjuring visual styles.

Terms that have become popular prompting shorthand for achieving a distinct look include "retro," "product photography," "food photography," "highly detailed," "digital art masterpiece," "C4d render," "Octane Render," and "trending on ArtStation." Names of proprietary software and platforms—such as the 3D-modeling software Cinema4D, or C4D for short; Octane, an "unbiased" graphics-rendering software; and ArtStation, a platform showcasing portfolios of work by game designers and animators—have transformed into adjectives or adjectival phrases overnight. Likewise, artists' names are more often deployed to achieve a visual style than to directly ape an artist's work. We already have the cultural habit of using proper nouns as eponyms for periods and styles (Louis XIV, Bauhaus, Studio 54), but prompt language has accelerated the trend. There are now websites, like Midlibrary.io, that catalog thousands of image styles indexed by artist names, largely those of digital artists and concept designers.

Prompt crafting relies on learning these terms and understanding the mass of visual phenomena to which they are yoked—the subject matter, visual attributes, media, and composition styles. To prompt an image in the style of Witkiewicz's late pastel portraits would mean to understand that a generator's output would likely be of a woman from the waist up, somewhat centered in the frame, with thin, high-arched eyebrows; pursed, glossy lips; oversize eyes rendered with more polish than the rest of the image; and at least a whiff of the sitter's contempt. Depthless backgrounds might encroach on the figure with ragged, nearly electric lines; clothes might be rendered with similar eccentricity. Other than its somewhat large eyes, my toilet-perched cat looked nothing like this, nor did it significantly resemble Witkiewicz's earlier Expressionism. After some additional searching, I realized that the closest reference for "by Ignacy Witkiewicz" may be a painting *of* Witkiewicz. Rafał Malczewski's portrait of the painter includes, among other curious features, what I can only assume is a particularly bizarre cat balanced across Witkiewicz's shoulders, a perch from which it leers with buggy eyes and a nonexistent jaw. "Witkiewicz" alone might not get me what I'm looking for if I'm seeking a vibrational, contemptuous woman, but "pastel portrait by Stanisław Ignacy Witkiewicz" could get me closer. (Art history may yet matter.)

While prompt writing is quickly becoming a marketable skill, there's still much about the innermost workings of the deep learning algorithms that even the most advanced engineers don't fully understand. Sam Bowman, who runs an AI research lab at NYU, told Vox that even specialists like him can't discern what concepts or "rules of reasoning" are being used by most of these complex systems. "We built it, we trained it, but we don't know what it's doing," Bowman confessed. This sense of mystery tends to be echoed by GenAI tools whenever they're asked to describe themselves. After a Redditor prompted GPT-4 to visualize itself, it used DALL-E 2 to generate images of glowing orbs reaching toward the shelves of a library with illuminated tendrils. The tendrils' tips connect not to books but to scattered floating shapes, glowing in midair. I appreciate these images for the candor of their fantasy: GenAI is always surrounded by knowledge, but does not access it straightforwardly.

CIRCA OCTOBER 2022, back in the days of clear GenAI tells, OpenAI's DALL-E 2 had a hard time with context clues and sequencing, particularly when dealing with how adjectives or descriptive phrases are applied to nouns or verbs. If you told DALL-E 2 to generate "a fish and a gold ingot" it usually gave you a fish that was also gold, frequently a goldfish, as if attempting a kind of wordplay.

DALL-E 2 also went nuts for heteronyms. One heteronym-specific example, as elucidated by Royi Rassin, Shauli Ravfogel, and Yoav Goldberg in "DALLE-2 Is Seeing Double: Flaws in Word-to-Concept Mapping in Text2Image Models," includes the prompt "a bat is flying over a baseball stadium," which produced a jaunty, cartoonish, vector-like illustration of a baseball stadium, over which a baseball and *both* a baseball bat and the animal we know as a bat fly, racing out of the image's top right corner. The problem is that the tag "bat" correlates to two different kinds of pixel patterns, and the GenAI isn't sure which to choose. Hedging its bets, it throws in both.

Rassin et al describe the confusion that lurks in these linguistic-to-visual translations as the "semantic leakage of properties between entities." In the image, the two kinds of bats appear to be soaring in tandem; perhaps the bat (animal) is actually wielding the bat (baseball). A white teardrop shape seems an attempt at a smile, indicating our friend the bat (animal) is having a great time. He appears to either be playing the game or to be gleefully absconding with the bat (baseball) as an act of other-team sabotage. To the bats' left, a flat gray cloud and a lightning bolt interrupt the blue sky. The paper's authors don't provide a clear linguistic reason for how the lightning bolt snuck in there, but my untested image-associative guess is that bats (animal) frequently show up in imagery with witches, who are prone to doing spells and zapping things.

The lightning bolt is a good example of what Rassin et al refer to as "second-order stimuli": the networked associations embedded in language and images we're likely not conscious of unless we're paying very specific attention. When you ask DALL-E 2 for an armadillo on a sea shore, it will often throw in a few shells as well. Why? Well, think of *armadillo*'s word-cloud terms, or what Fei-Fei Li calls its "social network of visual concepts": *mammal, armor, ball*, and . . . *shell*. (For comparison, a request for "dog on a sea shore" generates a beach, but no shells.) This "leakage" of associative traits is subtler than DALL-E 2's direct confusion of heteronyms and is therefore somewhat harder to spot. However, it can add a deeper layer of absurdity to these images, which is often pointed to as proof of the generative tools' lack of sophistication, their poor results. It would be a mistake, though, to treat semantic leakage as proof of technology's clumsiness rather than its acute sensitivity. "A tall, long-legged, long-necked bird and a construction site" spits out an image that includes both a crane (bird) and a crane (construction equipment). While this would initially read as an error, and software engineers are surely working to resolve the bug, it's in fact a sophisticated linguistic affiliation, a return of the heteronym problem by proxy, as the word *crane* never appears in the prompt.

For all the biases and patterns that they reify, GenAI tools also inherit and pictorialize language's nuances and ambiguities—such as English's excess of heteronyms and homonyms, and their possible confusion. When a publisher turns to text-to-image generative AI to illustrate a new biology textbook, for example, what carceral elements will be interwoven in diagrams of "the cell," and, from there, into a generation of students' concepts of cytology? New image-making technologies—whether the printing press, the camera, or satellite imaging—change our perception of the world, which in turn changes our behaviors. The question at hand is: What are these algorithmic images teaching us to see, say, and do?

As of January 2024, GenAI text-to-image tools produced about thirty-four million images per day. This number is still dwarfed by the daily count of digital photographs, but for how long? From here on out, it's safest to assume that any image you encounter might be generated. What differentiates these images is not their lack of humanity but their intense abundance of it: all the alienated intelligence, historical strata, and linguistic tics embedded and reproduced within them. Each prompter sets off a huge chain of networked collaboration with artists and academics, clickworkers and random internet users, across time and space, engaging in one massive, multicentury, ongoing game of Eat Poop You Cat. Like it or not, we all—whether pre-algorithmic image makers or self-described AI artists—will have to learn to play. +

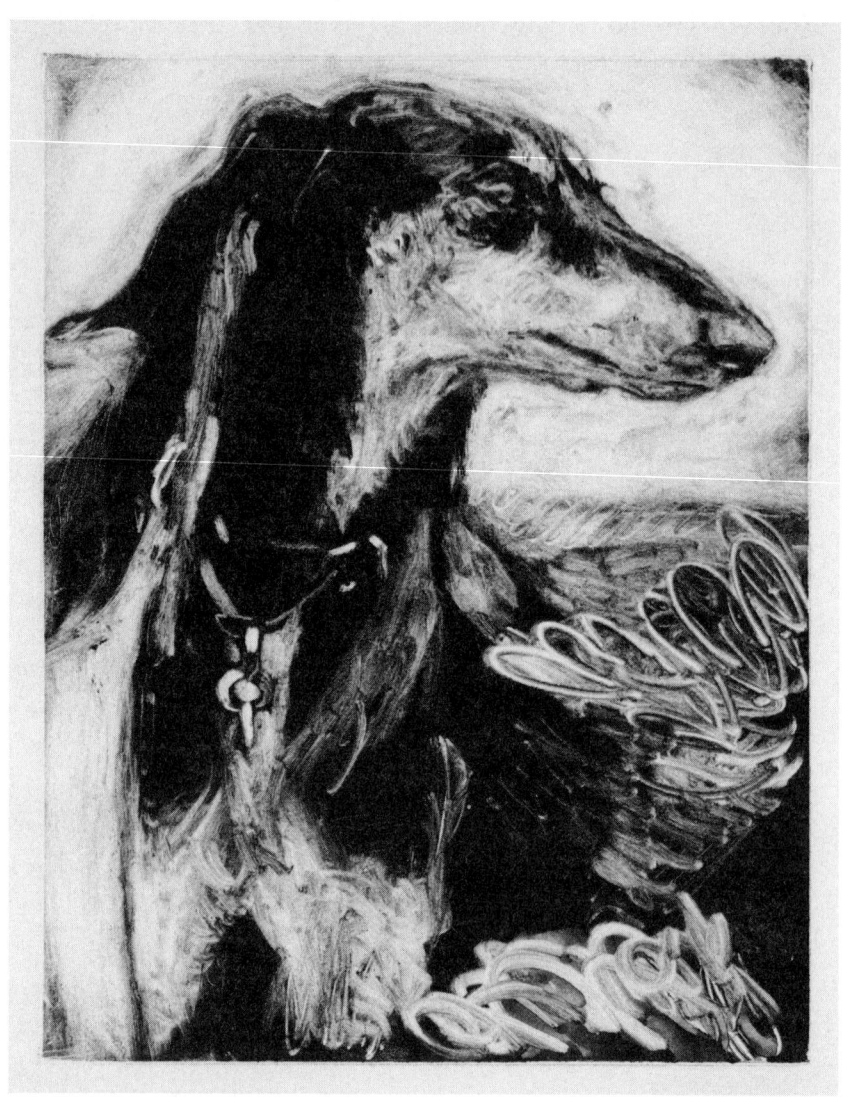

GIANGIACOMO ROSSETTI, *NYC PURPLE*. 2024, MONOTYPE ON RIVES BFK PAPER. 11 1/2 × 8 1/2". PHOTO BY ZESHAN AHMED. COURTESY OF THE ARTIST AND GREENE NAFTALI, NEW YORK.

TWO POEMS
Laura Kolbe

THREE AND A DOG

We clack the mini farmer back in the barn.
The roof hinges on sleeping sheep.
For dinner viscosities now there's three:
One for eight teeth, one for fifty-six
(Two adults, their wisdoms gone),
One for old canines, wet and cigarette
Tan at the base, that chew what they might
And not what they can. The farmer's a man
With a big bandana, not a bad stand-in
For A. at home, notebooks specked
Like quail eggs and laid on the table
In broods, closed in, spooled up, the yeoman
Checking his chicks and commas before
The night. Peanut butter on German
Many-grained brown bread: S. strains
Peanut kernels off the top and chews
What's smooth: not much: a flush of apricot
Jam and all the rest splayed down his tongue
In four dark shingles. I hope the milk
Makes up the rest. B. eats beets
And frittata off the floor. I am the roof
To the farmyard barn, I feel, on hard days:
Bright-turning on thin brass, then fog-

Laura Kolbe

Colored lengths and planks of me spread
In a washed wood extent. Gray paint standing
In for slate. A chill acoustic cover. An echo
Membrane snapping at clefs as clams eat,
Letting the sand gem the walls
Colorless, nacred. Necessity the mother.
I am the roof of my mouth
And more: meshed complex of various
Hardbound moistures whose syncing concert,
Fires and contractions, writ sixty-four inches large,
Wins bread. How strange. How hinged on organs
Clacking along, on thought's mostly lost
Steam, and this is how the barn stays raised?
Am I also the sparrow through the atrium—
It's a makeshift hall now, this barn,
It's like a hospital, this too-clean machine,
What Saint Bede said about the squeaking
Brevity of passage between one cracked window—
Life—as though a bird swooped in, and faster out,
The musk of wild vanishing behind it
On the cleaning-fluid updraft as the hall's
Wiped down. How strange, how flanged
Along the toy barn's sturdy gambrels,
Its imaginary gutter line where invisible birds
Shunt ice cream cone–shaped homes
From which to catch flies atop the wooden horse,
My thinking of my death, right here.
My earnings then my death. But three,
We're three, we're three and a dog, and being
Tethered in triangle, strongest—supposedly—
Shape aids the false feeling of being permanently
Here. I'll take it! So much to bewitch
Just now: at bathtime I admire on S.
The dollops of deltoids and biceps, sleepy
Ladyfingers, soaked and lolling like hatched turtles
Stunned by the sea. *And they lived in a warm*
Wooden tree, Wise Brown's perfect story goes,
And how we do, apartment ardent, towels and emotions

Porous as toast. Dry off, pat the near-black curls
So they snap up again like crickets
Or mousetraps, crisp and busy, piercing me,
Love, it's almost too much. Good night, I ache,
Good night. S. clucks and sinks. In the barn
Of the farmer the farmer seldom rakes
The straw beneath the sheep, it's not
A fun game, it's not Peekaboo or Celebrity
Or Huckle Buckle Beanstalk, it's not anything,
Putting toys away or cleaning the clothes,
But a colossal theft of someone's time. Mine?
Or yours? We bicker on this point and swindle
More from each other, expensive minutes that could
Have bought another line in A.'s novel
Or in this poem. Fifty-six teeth: that's four
Operatic rows, a Family Circle catching
The augmented triad and the gleaming
Rests, the supertitles jack-o'-lanterned so we know
Just what each keening means. I've turned
Mine off, sometimes, when A. bel cantos—
Opted not to read what I wish not
To know. I do not want, sometimes,
His burning tower. Mine's enough,
This stage. Then the mezzanine cocktail:
Remorse, love, and etiquette, up straight,
Well drink, all's well. I remember when
I read and wrote all day on the craigslist table,
Bag of granola and jar of water at my elbow, window
Cracked for the lilac and the neighbor dog's nails
Glittering the vinyl patio. Snout would be his name
In supertitles, the actual a cabriole I couldn't
Execute. His owner trilled it Iberian
About the yard. Nothing stopped me, those days,
In my novel (an Italian medical student,
Homesick, corn-dazed in Pennsylvania,
Entangled in two men) except its cureless badness
And the odd shower. So happy! Writing badly
So much every day! So much remembered

About one's twenties is still here, a bit smaller
Or paler, shirts shrunk too hot, the books
Whose ramparts have been egged by the sun.
I wear everything that's happened to me
And some things that haven't but expropriate
Beautifully in accordion pleats. Dress-up's a sport
I forget I love to play until I'm there. So what
If I don't for lack of time write of all that
Interests me or makes me yearn, velvet adornments,
Adorno, Duccio, Goya, grammar, the Haitian
Revolution, the Bayeux tapestry, Guatemalan huipils,
Henry James, incense perfumes, public radio
At sunrise in a cold car (those hopeful old
All Things Considered horns!), cowboy shirts,
Schubert, Bert and Ernie and *Sesame Street*,
Maurice Sendak, Edward Said, how he-said-she-said
Works on a formal level in hospitals, novels, opera, and therapy,
It's not a race, this kind of need is more like a bee's
If I'm being honest, it's programmed, in theory
All the flowers, please, but de facto I'll just dunk
My head wherever, come up covered in floral
Pistil shots. I won't do everything I want—so what?
That birds spin just for bugs is no less lovely
Of them. The object can be dull and small,
I'll eat bugs too, soon, I don't mind as long
As it's a mashed patty and spicy and everyone's
Doing it, it'll probably save a delicate crust
Of the planet from overroasting. Will I be more
Generous when there's less to go around?
I wouldn't mind a life all secondhand of touched
And weathered castoffs—have mostly built
Books and wardrobe so—we rent—I like a lover
Whose previous encounter's evident—
I like to be late to a scene picked over,
Awaiting revival—I like eating the food
S.'s left behind, I've even eaten what
He's spit right out, as long as barely chewed
Or wet, it's grace, it's like alms, and tastes

No different than if he'd only held that cube
Of mango in his palm. I've a weird fear
Of wasting, but even more I like to stretch
This epoch of two bodies being one. It's last call,
Past time to be done, I've pulled this
S./Mama symbiosis phase beyond all
Acceptable shape, like yanking sheer tights
Over one's head to rob a counter. (The scariest
Thing I saw in the paper when I was six—
The eyes matte shoe soles, face like a skull.)
Two and a dog awake, this Sophie Calle/
Greg Shephard movie makes me sad couples
Never hear each other's thoughts in time
To change. Even two people in a car preferred
To tell the camera of a mood, and not breathe
An audible alm to the other till later
They edited the tapes. A. takes B. out to pee,
I roll up the moribund toothpaste tube to get what's left,
Past natural shape it's a telescope, it's a diploma,
Noble ring through which the long view
Leaks an astral applause. Habit's cowlick's
Big as the Milky Way. In bed our two quilts start
Mille-feuille style atop each other, a printed draft,
But drift apart until we're incubated separate
As buns. I open A.'s, or he does mine,
In the moment it seems crucial who moves first
Though never after remembered, each in
Our separate disaster of intended thought
He or she didn't think much less transcribe today,
Prickly and sour from that, feeling owed,
Feeling tired and tared back to zero, this cranky friction
Flips, perhaps, the dry-docked hull in which we berth
As family, makes us snarled strangers, with all
The injury and wonder a stranger can arouse.
Thank God. This fold, this bowl, this cupola: these parts
I pick up until they become one unit of intention:
I do not know who all this belongs to while
It's happening. Later we're tired and relieved

And soft with new skin: the tingle of taking
Off braces or a cast. Quilts on again, one handmade
Hand-me-down from someone else's wedding,
The other mass-made paisley from our generation's
Most liberal big box. Two weights shedding
Thread while we sleep, to the floor, the air—
Everything winds up everywhere, that's thermodynamics,
That's a family reaping its subsistent furrow
While another family gleans behind it.
At dawn S. will stand in his crib like a farmer
At the plough, egging on the next turn
Of the whipped world, but now we are four lumps
Still and apart, vinegar-poached for the bite
That fixes us solid, soft, each exhaling
Sheeted dome a planetarium, a view of the light.

MARCH 25, 2023

Cold wind through the market again.
Coats out from under the bed,
their brief unhappy resurrection—
those worn folks in paintings carrying
their hides at final trumpet.
Your black wool, its bottle-green lining
shredding old lettuce, my puffer
shiny at the elbows.
Some things seem to obey
the alphabet today. Wind whips.
Robins redoubt. Afternoon's
brave cooks don ear-flap gusset hats—
it's just kale, last month's, nubucked over.
Persisting, quiet, rough.
Quite enough!
The world tardy this year, and still
too fast . . . I am, for example, thirty-six.
With age the human lens denatures
and the full blaze of world's white gets lost
from what we see. Not yet, I think,
for me: the plastic tip jars
from pretzel and pickle barrels
still give one of white's varieties:
the dog-eyed kind that rolls and stains.
Another white from the butcher
twine light that holds itself
and a few select muscles on a pan
of ground, lets the day's oils
slide in slats. And big scones of cloud, a pill-pale
white sliced yellow at the center traced
with Jersey sulfur.
Let us defer
to astronomical spring, here and five days
old, however slipped with tired
and frozen things, and come out
with our babies and forsythia lambed

and then felined with half frosted feet.
And under our coats keep
no layers we could not as easily
remove. A spring *we*, a local *we*,
smudged by the fan of clayish washout
on the park path. And so long
as we keep finding whatever little-brown-job
birds stir up our cerebral glossary
and incite a pen in the chore coat,
pecking at the dropped shoppings
as they do, the metronome of Saturdays
will stretch out its neck like a horse
for us from grain to lippy grain.
The fat, smooth park in March
and the pocked, wee market:
like a ring resized down
and its comma of refunded tact.
Like any insistence on snug fit,
it wagers on the future as commodity
with some sap still, the truth. Just so
the park begins early on its angles
and dewpoints, cranking Avogadro's number
for finding pale atoms in so much of mostly
just space. It's cold, devices say.
Let us submit
that this was the week's end, but also
the beginning of the next. I'll take
the baby now, bale him in blankets
and sift the stalls for last apples
that still pepper the nose in
starry lemon tones. You go home
and sleep. We're at a pale point
where distance from each other feels
like kindness, absence like a chance
at life well mulched by dark beds
of silence, better for the brain
to rest a snatched hour before
another dim, short day hauls up again.

A final and yet the first white: the speechless
nougat round which my life
clings with its candy-bitter shell,
having hardened there. +

JENNIFER CARVALHO, *STUDY OF AN ARCHITECTURE FOR A SACRED CONVERSATION*. 2023, OIL ON CANVAS. 22 × 28". PHOTO BY LF DOCUMENTATION.

THE RESURRECTION APPEARANCE AT PARQUE LÍTICO LA MOVEDIZA

Tom Bubul

1. THE FORM

THE BISHOP OF ROME, Vicar of Jesus Christ, Successor of the Prince of the Apostles, Supreme Pontiff of the Universal Church, Primate of Italy, Archbishop and Metropolitan of the Roman Province, Sovereign of the State of Vatican City, Servant of the Servants of God, His Holiness Pope M does not reside in the Apostolic Palace of Rome, but in an austere apartment on the second floor of the Domus Sanctae Marthae, a hotel built in 1996 on the southern edge of Vatican City for the purpose of hosting cardinals visiting Rome for papal conclaves. Pope M chose to remain there after his election out of a sense of monastic propriety: he had lived meagerly all his previous life and found his new role to be enormous enough without needing to reconsider his relationship to worldly comforts by moving, at that late point, into a palace.

After breakfast, when his schedule allows, the pope withdraws to his rooms to read, recite the rosary, prepare for formal audiences, and engage in handwritten personal correspondence from a small wooden desk.

Most nights, the pope settles in to read for an hour before bed (Borges, Davis, Dostoevsky, Ferrante, Hopkins, Laxness, Manzoni) and then sleeps, according to one journalist's report, "like a log."

One May night, nearing entrance to this state, Pope M is surprised by a flash of white light and a sound that recalls crystal singing bowls. The light and the sound pass quickly but leave a lingering wake. As the pope begins to examine this experience, he is startled to find in his mind's eye the image of a form suspended in the ceiling—as if it had been projected by the flash—along with the unusual certainty that it was this form that produced the sound.

Pope M opens his eyes in the dark but finds no presence to draw him to higher alertness. Soon he is sleeping, dreaming of the form as a hanging mask with no features other than an open mouth. He then dreams of a log planed into white boards that fly away at alternating orientations to two different planes, first horizontally and then vertically, to sit in rows and columns there, as these two planes in turn pass over each other to make an endlessly expanding moiré of white crosses. After this he dreams he can see himself sleeping, there in his bed, from the perspective of a distant star.

Outside his window, air moves past the Vatican Obelisk, which was brought from Heliopolis by Caligula to decorate his circus some two thousand years ago. Many early Christians were martyred in this place, including the church's earliest leader, Saint Peter, on an upside-down cross, though the story is apocryphal.

The next morning, as Pope M returns to his desk after breakfast, he revisits the night's episode. This time he recalls the form as a series of shapes that phased without appearing to move, like the mind trying to recognize something nameable in the shape of a cloud. Then, with a sensation of a cord being drawn across the velvet surface of his brain, the pope imagines, in vivid detail, a Lhasa Apso wearing the papal triregnum and mantum being carried on the sedia gestatoria. Pope M has a brief, nauseous sense of this image expanding outward from his direct sensory experience into something more firmly organic, beginning to take root in his mind. After a minute spent studying the dog, Pope M shudders back into awareness. He blinks self-consciously, shakes his head, touches his cheeks. He looks around his office and begins to smile as his confusion settles. He wonders if he is suffering from dehydration or lack of exercise. That night, he gets into bed without reading. He was present for the final use of the throne-like sedan chair by John Paul I, the last pope to be carried on men's shoulders. He ruminates for some time over that earlier pope's thirty-three-day reign. Then he falls asleep picturing himself as the Lhasa Apso and wonders if, had he been a dog with dog ears, he would have heard something different in that sound of crystal singing bowls the previous night.

The following day, with mild but proactive concern, Pope M institutes a new set of health practices. He begins to stretch for fifteen minutes every morning before breakfast, makes sure to drink a large glass of water every four hours, starts mild strength training, stops drinking wine. After a month the pope feels sharper and more energetic than he has in recent years, and as he carries on his work this episode gradually recedes.

2. THE ENTITY

THEN, ONE AFTERNOON, as Pope M walks down Santa Marta's back stairs on his way to the papal gardens, his pupils dilate and light rushes in. The form appears again, hovering below him on the landing as if projected on the wall. It then shifts dizzyingly, fluctuating over the pope's full field of vision. Time warps as the form billows; the pope feels his awareness of the texture of the stairwell and its enclosing walls sharpen, as if he has been studying them closely for a long time. This feeling continues until the form passes over the pope's entire body.

Pope M feels motion-sick and begins to sweat. A discordant, non-repeating melody rings distantly in his mind, the textures of droning bowls and strings played as if bowed by a strong wind. The sounds are not beautiful in any traditional sense, but they carry a beguiling and hypnotic aspect . . . as if angels weren't associated with harps, with their own luminous voices, but instead with the forceful beating of their wings against marble, wet sand, and clean water . . . as if the heaven they served were deserted, overgrown and in disrepair, filled with birds and earthly gravity but no souls anywhere in sight. The melody plays on and on in Pope M's mind until the pope comes back to himself enough to take several deep breaths. He returns to his apartment, washes his face and hands, regards his face in the small mirror with a degree of relief. The pope doesn't believe in angels as figures or in heaven as a physical place, or one inhabited by souls that resemble bodies. Yet these were the images that arrived. The felt sense of fear that these are not his own thoughts returns him to the image of the Lhasa Apso.

The pope remains in his office at Santa Marta instead of resuming his walk to the gardens. He summons his assistant, Father B, and tells him to let his staff know that he is suffering from a migraine and to cancel the rest of his day's schedule. Father B observes with concern that the pope's pupils are dilated and that he is visibly flushed.

"Your holiness, should you see the doctor?"

"Yes."

Within the hour Pope M is visited by his private doctor. The pope describes the optical sensations and distortions of time, and the doctor agrees that these are not inconsistent with certain kinds of migraines. Pope M is given a physical, his blood taken for testing. The physical results reflect his recent better-than-usual health. The bloodwork shows slightly elevated cholesterol, nothing unmanageable or abnormal for a man of 86.

POPE M WORRIES he may be experiencing the symptoms of a neurological disorder. Unsatisfied with the physician's assessment, he arranges to visit specialists at Gemelli Hospital in Rome the following day. The event is not listed on his schedule and is closely guarded by his personal staff, so as not to draw undue attention within the Vatican. He leaves his chambers via a secret exit and travels to the hospital by car. Wearing his white cassock and mozzetta, Pope M is slid into the white MRI enclosure after removing his rosary, which contains metals. The MRI does not reveal anything notable other than the illuminated image of a healthy 86-year-old brain.

At his staff's behest, Pope M takes the rest of this day off only to spend it in irate puzzlement. He forces himself to drink even more water than his recent routine has called for, which causes him to need to urinate repeatedly, preventing him from settling into his reading. His strength training has made him capable of completing several push-ups, and he does these vigorously. As his heart pounds in his ears, he weighs with frustration his ability to complete this exercise as a measure of health against his growing uncertainty about his own acuity, even as there are no perceptible signs of its decline. He flexes his old arm and sighs, frowning, but then begins to laugh to himself as he imagines flexing his brain. He imagines it squeezing inside his skull like a sponge and ideas, thoughts, and memories being wrung out—as a purple liquid that floods through his nervous system and pools beneath his skin at the tips of his fingers.

At sunset the obelisk casts its long shadow across Saint Peter's Square. Pope M contemplates it as he falls asleep. The two thousand years it's been there, he thinks, are still not close to a million days, but getting closer. Still 270,000 more to go, the lives of the next nine Dalai Lamas, assuming they live out their days without shenanigans or ill health, unlike the ninth through twelfth Dalai Lamas of the 19th century. Deneb, at Cygnus the Swan's tail, will be the Earth's polestar around the year 10000. And 3,500 years after that, Vega will take over as the brightest polestar of all. Four million days, give or take, until the obelisk points up at that and Polaris watches from the side like a retired coach. Seven hundred-odd years from now, will the obelisk be returned to Cairo, or whatever name the site of Heliopolis will carry at that point, to cast a shadow across some other courtyard for its next million-day term?

ON JUNE 5, 1988, some thirteen thousand days prior, Pope M made a vow to the Virgin of Carmen to never watch television again. But with his concern for his immeasurable condition privately increasing, Pope M requests that a television be brought into his rooms, thinking this could help him feel more connected to the world or show him if what he is experiencing might in some way be generalized.

It takes two days for the Santa Marta staff to procure a 92-inch LED screen, and for a technician to mount it on the wall, connect it to invisible speakers, and configure the relevant software. That night, Pope M sits to watch it, breaking his vow. He works the remote, flipping through menus, reading titles of entertainments he hasn't heard of. The menu application produces a tone for each of his interactions in the voice of a digital marimba.

The pope finds this irritating—that television should be buried beneath all this, instead of just "on"—and then smiles to himself as he realizes that this type of thinking is affiliated with men his age. This type of thinking, he thinks, also describes the frustration he has heard people express over the ways metaphysical mysteries are wrapped for delivery in containers of doctrine and ritual. How nice it would be, he thinks, if God, too, were just "on."

As Pope M watches the news, a digital afterimage of two faces begins to emerge, like a datamoshed Francis Bacon painting, talking, kissing, or screaming. These faces overlay the aftermath of a shooting in the United States, a memorial ceremony in Brazil, some kind of revelry in Japan, a sporting event in India, a financial conference in Switzerland, fuel-pipeline protests in Canada, men on horseback holding guns in far-eastern Russia, a concert in China attended by ten thousand people, stock footage of the Arctic intercut with a story about a woman in Tunis who self-immolated to bring attention to the urgency of the global climate crisis, public mourning in England related to the death of the recently crowned king, a widely loathed businessman on vacation with a popular Western politician . . . then the moon fading out and in, the stars vanishing and reappearing in new positions, distant comets suddenly accelerating and returning to the solar system, the Sphinx at Giza rolling over playfully as the noses fall off the four Presidents' busts at Mount Rushmore, then the busts themselves falling off and rolling away toward Easter Island, in order to colonize it and drive the moai onto a reservation . . . Pope M begins muttering, asking the entity what it wants, to give him a sign. He feels pathetic, knows it won't respond; that this is already what it wants, inasmuch as its presence can be described in terms of desire at all; that it has already given him many signs. He presses his palms to his eyelids and begins to cry. He hears the news return to the shooting in the United States, to an interview with a victim's relative who says things in English—passionate but inarticulate things—that the pope understands to be common slogans used during instances of this form of tragedy in that country. These victims were visited by something from outside too, the pope thinks.

The afterimage faces multiply and bend, appearing to slide out of the TV and down the wall, as Pope M himself slides out of his chair to the floor. He feels totally exhausted. With his eyes closed he manages to exit the news to the menu screen. Five minutes later the television displays a screensaver and twenty minutes after that it enters sleep mode.

Pope M is, of course, aware of the church's history of exorcisms, as well as the popular examples of their depiction, epitomized by the 1973 William Friedkin movie and, before that, by the infamous Anna Ecklund case, via her 1936 profile in *Time* magazine. Just as he is falling asleep he remembers the scene in the movie in which the possessed girl's head spins around and the devil speaks through her, and the director saying to an interviewer at the time, "All I can tell you is that the way you think I did it is not the way we did it." Pope M found this statement resonant with the unknowable physics of miracles, which he both believes and disbelieves, and now feels it resonant again with the mystery of this experience. This memory of the interview resolves into the pope wondering if he is being haunted as he falls asleep right there on the floor.

In the morning, Pope M is shaken awake by Father B, with a gentle but urgent touch.

"Your holiness!" Father B repeats as a terrified member of the Casa Marta cleaning staff looks on.

Pope M is surprised to feel a flash of shame, less for being caught asleep on the floor than for having broken his vow to the Virgin of Carmen. Beyond Father B hovers the boundaryless shape of the entity.

"Do you see that?" the pope asks, pointing, as he gets to his feet.

Father B turns to look.

"I see nothing, your holiness, only your apartments."

The entity billows and images flow out of it enveloping the room like unspooling rolls of film, passing through one another in intricate patterns. They wrap around Father B, becoming a tiger's mouth, then a long series of faces of people the pope has met but knows he no longer remembers, then a peony blossom, the face of a spider, the water's rippling surface, the face of William Friedkin, the opening of the MRI machine at Gemelli, and on and on. Father B seems far away and far beneath all of this, but Pope M is aware enough to perceive that Vatican City and the world will soon know that he is not in an ordinary condition.

THAT NIGHT, POPE M kneels at the side of the bed and says a rosary the way laypeople do in popular entertainments when entreating God for something, such as a simple reveal of His presence. The pope thinks about the metals in his rosary chain. He imagines the crucifix entering the MRI machine; the nails would first have to be removed from Christ's hands and feet.

He weeps gently as this image warps in his mind: the arms of the crucifix bending down as if the crosspiece were hinged and Jesus's arms lowered to his sides, the man still lying on the board but with the nails removed, sliding comfortably into the magnetic chamber. In his sweaty and bloodstained face one can perceive both his deathly repose and the haunting, peaceful quality of his alertness in resurrection. The pope's vision shifts to the MRI monitors, which show the brain activity of the crucifix itself—the illegible internal logic, thoughts, dreams, and subconscious of that living symbol, a man attached to God through humiliating and painful death—replayed endlessly in mysterious celebration for two thousand years. Is this what is meant by the resurrection? The simple persistence of an image far beyond its context and time, invested with a ponderous weight of hope, for something beyond the death that awaits everyone on this planet, rotating slowly under Polaris, 323 light-years away?

Perhaps in seven hundred years the obelisk will be flung into space like a lance, thinks Pope M, and over billions of days will accelerate miraculously to a speed far beyond that of light, perhaps to pierce an ultradistant black hole, bursting out its other side like a bullet shot through a water balloon, releasing all of that collected, compacted mass back into the universe as sprayed ejecta, which will collide with further galaxies to bless them like holy water from the aspergillum . . . and over time re-collect, re-spin, and re-create new stars, or perhaps the same ones . . . as Nero's circus was an accretion disk for Vatican City . . . is this what is meant by the resurrection?

These are not my thoughts, the pope thinks with effort, discerning an anxious texture to his own language-thinking, by which he can distinguish it from the entity's. Though he understands that the entity is not likely organic, made of matter, or in need of breathing, he hears its music as a form of respiration and is nearly overcome by the onset of a surprising feeling of fondness, even pleasure and relief, as he feels able to center himself in its onslaught of information and images for the first time. He beholds it flowing around him without losing himself completely. Soon Pope M returns to himself with a gentle bodily relief, like an angel stepping off a dissipating cloud onto one of heaven's high pillars, and he sees that only ten minutes have passed during what felt to him like several hours.

At 9:02 PM in Rome, 5:02 PM in Viedma, Pope M picks up the phone and dials out to Father R.

Father R answers with a cheerful note in his voice, addresses Pope M as your holiness, asks if it isn't past his bedtime.

The pope responds with an unsteady greeting that his old friend intuits instantly. He asks if there is anything he can do.

"Father, I believe I am being spoken to by a ... visitor. Like ... but not ... an angel," the pope says, "And I worry that before long I will no longer be able to lead and serve our people."

"Your holiness," Father R responds, "I will serve you in any way I can." Pope M thanks his old friend, addressing him by his first name; Father R returns the intimacy in kind. The two speak for hours, catching up at such length for the first time in seventeen years, and Pope M does not fall asleep until nearly midnight.

AFTER BREAKFAST the next morning, groggy but on schedule, Pope M returns to his desk in Santa Marta to find that his assistant, Father B, has placed several newspapers onto his desk that bear headlines like, "Vatican in Disarray as Pope Hallucinates," "Pope Has MRI as Mental Health Declines," and "Pope Rattled by Contact with God."

Pope M immediately understands that there has been a leak, or that a coup is underway, but feels surprised at his own disinterest and lack of urgency. The articles all report on a statement released by the Vatican the previous evening:

> The pope is being treated at Gemelli by Rome's most highly accomplished doctors. He has received an MRI, indicating the presence of a rare neurological disorder. As this disorder is causing his holiness to lose sleep, his public schedule will be curtailed for the foreseeable future.

The pope finishes reading the articles at a leisurely pace. He leaves his chambers and walks down the back stairwell of Santa Marta, through the Vatican gardens, and into the Apostolic Palace. He takes the elevator to the third floor and turns right, entering the offices of the secretariat of the state from which the Vatican conducts its global business at all hours. He enters the offices of the cardinal secretary, Cardinal L, with whom he is scheduled to discuss a draft of a new encyclical related to duty, dignity, and fraternity within the globalized 21st-century church, but even before he left his apartments he knew this meeting would be preempted. Three other senior cardinals under Cardinal L are already gathered when Pope M enters the office; all four men rise and greet Pope M.

"Your holiness," Cardinal L says. The five men sit, and Pope M, consciously trying to maintain his center, begins to think about the Vatican obelisk. One of the cardinals jogs a stack of papers, which escape him and scatter across the floor. The pope watches the sheets flutter and fall, tracing the details of each paper flipping through the air like wide bleached leaves, in some cases even reading their text, recognizing the Vatican's letterhead like the patterns of a bird's plumage. The sound of the scattering paper returns the sensation of angels' wings buffeting an empty heaven to his mind. The entity fluctuates beyond the cardinals as the pope slouches and his aged face takes on a stricken expression of fear and awe.

The incident resolves itself after only a few seconds but is fully observed by Cardinal L and the others, all of whom regard the pope with gnomic concern.

"Your holiness," one of the cardinals repeats. "Were you disturbed?" The pope makes a weak vocalization and a dismissive gesture as he tries to regain control of his face and position himself upright in his chair. The light shifts as the sun passes behind a cloud. The entity billows over Pope M's perspective, collapsing the cardinals toward the far wall.

At last, after nearly a minute of this, the pope registers the strange expressions of the cardinals and their audible concern and returns to himself, by which time the scattered papers have already been regathered.

Cardinal L insists that the pope let the cardinals into his confidence at once, as something is clearly of concern.

"An entity is making its presence felt to me through visions," Pope M confesses softly.

The cardinals express disbelief and ask if it's a miracle or a sign from God. After a moment of consideration, the pope says, "No, it is not a sign from God." His unusual confidence in this response perturbs the cardinals further. An entity?! they ask. But not God?!

"No," the pope says again, this time with mournful resignation. "Not God." Cardinal L shakes his head and asks Pope M directly if he believes it is a sign of his deteriorating mental faculties or some emergent form of mental illness. Pope M does not find this line of questioning insulting, as he typically would, and even accepts its mounting practicality. He turns to Father B and nods. "His holiness has already taken steps to rule this question out," says Father B. "As your eminences are aware from the newspapers, his holiness is in consultation with the neuroscientists at Gemelli and has undergone an MRI. However, the results of these consultations and tests are at odds with the reporting in today's newspapers. In fact, according to the doctors, his holiness is not experiencing any measurable decline, and his holiness's symptoms are not consistent with any known disorder." Cardinal L remains fixed on the pope with unblinking blankness as Father B delivers this report. "How long have you been experiencing the presence of this entity, your holiness?" he asks.

"The presence has become more pronounced this week."

"So a decline measurable in terms of a week, then." The two men hold each other's looks in silence.

"Are you sure it is not God?" one of the other cardinals finally asks again.

"They are inexplicable images and sounds, beheld through a kind of expanded perception, but are not in any sense related to the sacraments," Pope M says as he turns away from Cardinal L, his deliberate slowness betraying his exhaustion.

"But why must that indicate an entity and not God?" asks the cardinal. Pope M gives a small, dismissive shrug. He knows he does not know how God would communicate, what images God would choose, what meaning they might eventually reveal, the size of the experience in which God would reveal them, how much awe God would invoke, how much notice God would demand. God can surely be small, simple, uninspiring, easy to miss . . . perhaps the most common experience of God, he thinks for the first time with some ruefulness. But could God be playful, or even libertine?

Cardinal L continues to look at the pope with sleepy, sphinxlike seriousness. Pope M sees the gathered cardinals with the bodies of lions beneath their cassocks, disemboweling him for answering their questions incorrectly, then laughing and shrieking as their eagle wings burst forth and fill the room with discarded golden feathers. He sees them crashing through the high windows of the Apostolic Palace out into Vatican City, perching on the obelisk, swooping down to the entrance of the basilica, blocking it forever to any future visitor, forcing them to debase themselves by guessing the answers to cruel, unanswerable questions, then disemboweling them, too.

As he beholds this, Pope M mutters a request that an amendment to the statement be issued, one that states that, per interviews with his doctors, nothing of concern had been found . . . however, his holiness is being visited by an entity.

"An entity, your holiness," says Cardinal L, unmoved.

"A visitor," the pope responds.

"A visitor from where, if not God?" asks Cardinal L.

"I don't know," the pope says. "From far away."

"It sounds more like a haunting," says Cardinal L, with only the corners of his eyes revealing the most modest possible smile.

3. THE EXORCISM

THE INTERNATIONAL NEWS media covers the story of the pope's haunting relentlessly. Non-Catholic visitors pour into Vatican City, assembling in the shadow of the obelisk, at the site of the ancient circus. Enthusiasts, fans, and consumers of horror films, metal and adjacent forms of extreme music, alien theories, new-age and astrologically rooted practices, weird science fiction, unexplained natural phenomena, cryptozoology, and conspiracy theories of all stripes are a constant presence, identifiable by the ways they signal these identities through slogans and images printed or embroidered onto their clothes.

Haunted pope memes circulate on the internet and make their way onto merchandise, as if the internet itself produces these material consumables as a by-product of its metabolism of cultural information and events. In one of these, the pope's white zucchetto takes the place of the UFO from the I WANT TO BELIEVE image popularized by *The X-Files*. Traditional green aliens wearing mitres are captioned TAKE ME TO YOUR HOLY FATHER. Every available photo of the pope is photoshopped to contain every available ghost or supernatural creature from popular media. Mail related to the haunting floods the Vatican from all over the world. Pop culture figures and hosts of nightly shows swarm the idea, joking, theorizing, writing songs; posting online; asking whether the pope should resign; asking whether the pope is now, by right of this direct supernatural experience, in fact better equipped to do the work of being the pope than any pope who has come before; suggesting that the pope is being visited by Christ in a "second coming" signaling the end times, as a joke, then further joking that it would certainly not be a joke if that were the case, joking that the audience should pray together that it isn't; asking whether there's any proof.

The pope receives a phone call from the President of the United States. "Goodbye, holy father," the pope can hear the President saying as he lowers the handset onto its base.

Pope M recalls images from his childhood: walking barefoot until his soles turned black to look at the remnants of the shattered Piedra Movediza; watching dirty water run down the drain of a cast-iron tub. He assumes the President must have had similar experiences, even though he comes from a family with dynastic wealth. Everyone occupying any station lives in a body and was once a child. Pope M's reservoir of compassion and his generous and respectful attitude toward children, the pillars of his private faith, flow from these inarguable, indivisible realities.

How unusual to be selected twice in this life, he thinks. First for this station, now by this visitor.

Of course, the former was the product of a path he had chosen himself. Already in his youth he was attracted to the architectural experience of worship—stained glass, curved painted ceilings, the altar, the acoustics. Next came the ritual—the ringing of the bells as the chalice is lifted in consecration, the palo santo–scented cakes burning in the thurible, swung three times over coffins at funerals. And then the performance—the cadences of homilies, the humor of priests, the processions, the collar itself. And then, finally, the sense of repetition—the familiarity over the course of many years, the stations of the cross mirroring the stations of the days. Administering to a parish, then to a diocese, then to the global kingdom, his life like a dropped object accelerating to a terminal velocity . . . a simple process of identification, devotion, and a continuous streak of correct action culminating in his election as pope, here in Santa Marta . . . an unimaginable outcome to himself, as a child in the bath.

But was this experience with the entity any less unimaginable? Another thing, one he didn't choose or prepare for, transforming his life again. Emerging from nowhere, disconnected from everything, illuminating and stirring his mind, returning him to the clarity of his aging body and to an awareness of the passage of time, filling him with a new view onto this, his one life, but also a crestfallenness in the confirmation of what he always knew to be rationally true, that what would ultimately reveal itself to him would not be the conceptual entity that the structure and global community of his life had imagined and hoped for—that it would be something else entirely, unrelated to God. This terrible presence shattered the familiar comfort of no presence at all, the symbolic emptiness, the holiness of waiting ... terrible in no small part to Pope M because he knows he won't likely live long enough to ever understand it.

Is it because he is the pope? Does this visitor have an intention related to his calling? He feels that the answer is no, that his position in this role is merely incidental.

He spends the rest of the afternoon and evening before bed searching the internet for any accounts that resemble his own—but finds none. Meanwhile, throughout the world, public opinion continues to calcify.

"Why not simply try an exorcism?" comments one news host. "The Vatican has powerful exorcists at its disposal," notes another.

Dining together one night, Cardinal L breaks the silence.

"Your holiness," he says.

Pope M waits impassively without responding.

"We believe," Cardinal L presses on, "that it would be of global interest for you to receive the sacramental—"

The pope's visitor billows in the darkness over the table like a manta ray.

"—that it would be restorative to the global flock, to see you, holy father, engaged with the full power of our traditional mechanisms for dealing with such things as have been troubling you."

The pope responds that it is no longer troubling.

"As have been disturbing you, then."

The pope responds that it is no longer disturbing, either.

"Your holiness, these are avoidant semantics," Cardinal L says with some exasperation.

"Your eminence," Pope M responds. The visitor's music emanates from a projected void far above. The pope hears the music through vibrations at the base of his spine; he nods to it slowly, but in time. The faces of the cardinals ripple, as if glimpsed beneath the surface of dark water.

"Your holiness," says Cardinal L again after a lengthy pause.

"Your eminence," Pope M responds again, turning his attention upward. The visitor has no center or face to meet, but the pope can feel it beholding him. He closes his eyes. There is no obvious opinion or meaning present, only images in a continuous stream, an awareness of its presence, and, only very occasionally now, of its nonpresence and the sense that sometimes it goes somewhere else. Five minutes pass in silence. A Vatican aide clears the dishes.

"Your holiness, respectfully," Cardinal L says finally. "Please allow us to schedule the sacramental."

"That . . . jester," Pope M mutters through gritted teeth, squeezing his water glass. His contempt for Cardinal A, the Vatican's so-called head exorcist, is well-known in this company.

"Your holiness, respectfully," Cardinal L repeats. "We can't know if it's really your holiness speaking right now."

CARDINAL A IS TOLERATED at the Vatican for providing a novel therapy to those rare members of the global flock who are both far enough astray to require it and receptive enough to receive it. But he is also widely viewed by his fellow cardinals as an egomaniac corrupted by his own minor celebrity and obsessed with its cultivation. He has a reputation for being overly willing to engage with language and theater that suggest that the church's ontology can and does include a literal concept of demons that manifest through observable supernatural acts here in the natural world, such as the defiance of gravity and the body's impossible self-contortions, as in the William Friedkin movie. Cardinal A's boasts about having performed "over a hundred thousand exorcisms" and his self-identification as "the pope's exorcist" render him all the more ludicrous to his colleagues. These men hoped all their lives to see even the smallest manifestation of supernatural presence, and some even worked to free themselves from this need for confirmation, and then continued in a life of acceptance beyond doubt, waiting for nothing, understanding that God's purview is the universe and not mankind on this planet, that matter behaves consistently even at unimaginably far distances, and that God's manifestations may yet—paradoxically—remain possible. In the presence of such demon talk by Cardinal A, Cardinal L had once pretended to fall asleep and then apologized profusely when pretending to start awake as a means of obliquely changing the subject. For his part, Cardinal A is willfully oblivious to or contemptuous of his colleagues' perspectives.

Upon receipt of his task from the offices of the cardinal secretary, Cardinal A sees for himself a path into history. He will rid the pope of his visitor and, failing that, he will preside over a recorded attempt to do so, which will be enough. He thrills at the change in meaning to his self-given title.

Pope M doesn't wonder whether he doubts Cardinal A unnecessarily. He thinks of the global flock, whose members wait for the same confirmation as the cardinals, praying for it, running slow laps around the rosary and the calendar until they collapse and receive last rites—the vast majority of them without the benefit of glorified global travel, freedom from concern over worldly needs, and safety in the knowledge of their own purpose and role within the global church, all of which Cardinal A enjoys with great profligacy. Naturally, thinks the pope, the rest of the universe will continue to seethe with activity long after everyone is gone. Yet here is this mountebank with his vain performance, pretending to serve as a grounding reassurance of the seriousness with which the church treats the Satanic. Pope M firmly believes that the much-larger mystery of salvation can only be undermined by the church's acknowledgment of unrelated supernatural occurrences, such as the notion of a person being visited by demons. But in the end, the cardinals deem it important enough that the pope employ the pope's exorcist, both to make clear how seriously the Vatican takes this ritual and to take advantage of the public perception of Cardinal A, which the Vatican ultimately views as a valuable brand asset. So, despite his personal distaste, Pope M agrees to the exorcism.

To prepare, he schedules a second MRI. Again at Gemelli, parts of Pope M's brain light up as he listens to music. This process reminds him of the visitor in a way that makes him smile . . . and as if on cue, the words the doctors speak begin to hang in the air and their constituent letters flutter to the floor like leaves, assembled to perform esoteric little plays within plays within plays. The pope is smiling, even enjoying this, as his doctors look on.

"Your holiness?" asks an MRI technician.

In the pope's vision, thousands of letterforms are collected on the linoleum floor of the hospital room. They look up at him inquisitively and expectantly, as if he were viewing the crowds in the circus from St.

Peter's Balcony. Letterforms rain down from the air, filling the room like sand in an hourglass.

The pope's personal doctor shakes his head. The MRI technician observes the patient with a sad expression and pursed lips.

The pope is silent, his old eyes gaping as the vision piles to the ceiling. The doctors observe the pope's slightly dilated pupils and raised heart rate but cannot determine an obvious cause. Again the MRI shows nothing.

THE EXORCISM TAKES PLACE in the pope's apartments. Pope M agrees to have the ritual observed by Cardinal L and his staff and, if appropriate, televised at a slight delay. The pope's idea is that this will remove some of the mystery from exorcism and ground its rituals in a new contemporary understanding related to the body and to faith rather than the ridiculous displays people imagine that often constitute the appearance of possession.

Cardinal A performs the ritual with stony seriousness. The broadcast is streamed globally by more than a billion viewers.

The pope remains alert throughout and does his best to remain solemn. He is aware that if he is seen laughing, or disregarding or disrespecting Cardinal A, or otherwise being carried away by his visitor during the moment, this would ratify Cardinal A's position and sow immediate global chaos. He succeeds in this effort, though twice during the ceremony a strange look falls across his face, one that close observers of the video pause on, debate, and share images of for years to come in a manner similar to the famous photograph of what is purported to be the Loch Ness monster.

Cardinal A looks at the pope with obvious anxiety in his face when the ritual is complete. Pope M looks into his eyes and thanks him, and feels himself extending his forgiveness.

"DID IT WORK, your holiness?" asks Father B, the pope's assistant, after Cardinal A and his retinue, Cardinal L and his staff, and the Vatican's regular support and production staff have all departed.

"Yes," responds the pope, scoping his answer to his private goals—to have completed this exercise, to have provided this material as education to the world—rather than to the intent of the question being asked.

The visitor remains present, unmoved, oblivious to whatever it was the ritual was intended to communicate to it, if anything. Its music played throughout the entire experience, audible only to the pope.

▬

4. THE SIMULACRUM

POPE M'S SCHEDULE remains truncated for several months following the exorcism. During that time, the Vatican coordinates a careful campaign to demonstrate the exorcism's success, sharing intimate details about the pope's schedule and life; here he is in his apartments praying, here he is laughing in meetings. Eventually the pope is returned to the public eye, or at least a simulacrum of the pope. As the visitor comes to claim more and more of Pope M's waking attention, causing him to drift into his own interests, Cardinal L devises a solution: There will be an impersonator employing complex daily makeup and prosthetics. Under his control, a simulacrum pope will be fielded each day.

For decades Father R has been a parish priest in the diocese of Viedma, in line to become an auxiliary bishop in the archdiocese of Bahía Blanca, but he is brought to Rome to play the role owing to his close personal relationship with Pope M as well as his general physical resemblance to the pope in stature and voice, though the pope is fifteen years his senior. To prepare for the role Father R receives three rigorous months of coaching on the pope's physical manner and style of speech, a series of surgeries to alter his appearance and the register of his voice, and an extensive regimen of hypnosis. He agrees that in Viedma it should be announced that he has deserted the faith and disappeared. Who can say no to the request to help a friend in need, much less to serve the higher power as a steward? So he enters into this new vocation with the absolute confidence of the cardinals.

As a simulacrum pope, Father R is a secret guarded closely by the cardinal secretary and his senior staff; only six people know of the scheme. For this reason, Father R also lives in Casa Marta, in the pope's chambers, as the pope's roommate. The pope, for his part, has been moved deeper into the apartment, and privacy protocols around how and when the apartment is cleaned and otherwise staffed and visited are strictly enforced under the pretext of supporting the pope's long-term recovery after his successful exorcism and aiding his return to the perfect health of a man many years younger.

All of this coincides with Pope M's loss of desire to leave the rooms and his preference to remain there in constant communion with the visitor. He begins to draw and watch movies, and with his vast swaths of uninterrupted private time gets into the habit of watching up to four each day, in three- or four-hour blocks after breakfast and at night before bed. When the daily schedule allows, Father R sometimes joins the viewing, still always wearing his prosthetics. Viewed from the television, the men look like twins.

One night, after they watch Peter Weir's *Picnic at Hanging Rock*, which they both find moving, Father R asks Pope M if the visitor is present. By the pope's request, in the privacy of these moments he and the pope continue to address each other by their first names, rather than their honorifics or titles, as they did when the pope had first called to discuss the occurrence they now both live within.

The pope confirms the visitor's presence and watches it spread over and inside the walls, in what the pope has come to view as a form of watchful repose. "What do you believe it to be?" Father R asks him.

"I don't know," the pope responds.

"Memorizing the encyclicals—" begins Father R, and the pope immediately understands that Father R is beginning to ask him if his concept of God has changed.

"If it's to be understood as a haunting," the pope interrupts, "it's certainly not a religious haunting."

"The most powerful religious figure in the world has a supernatural visitor," says his friend, "and with the powers of the entire kingdom of God behind him, is powerless to deal with it, except on his own terms, as an old man."

"Is it supernatural? More miraculous or supernatural than what we just watched?" he asks.

Father R sniffs. He adjusts his glasses automatically, as a tic, though they do not need adjustment; he is used to their sliding down the nose of his normal face. This, to the pope, is a tell—perhaps the only one.

"Why me," jokes Father R, gesturing around the room, then at his own disguised, highly altered face. The pope laughs a slight old laugh.

"Preservation and maintenance require veils and scaffolding," says the pope, miming the removal of a mask.

The priest nods. "Though we don't own the building, in this case," the pope says. "And yet we must prevent it from crumbling."

"And yet as we do, we can't stop birds from making nests in the mouths of the gargoyles," says Father R.

The pope opens his mouth and pulls a face, mimes with his hand a bird flying in. Father R laughs.

"And we try to make it as safe as we can to walk below until we can reopen for normal business."

The priest nods. They sit in silence for some time.

The two men get up to begin the process of going to bed. They brush their teeth together, sharing the mirror, their eyes sleepily tracing each other's identical faces.

They sleep in the same room. The cardinals requested this setup so Father R could mimic the pope even in his sleep—as the holy father's unconscious mind must surely also attend to a great deal of business, this too is expected of Father R. Both men still pray a silent rosary with their backs to each other and complete this task simultaneously.

5. THERAPY

THREE YEARS LATER, Father R walks into what has become the pope's drawing studio. Large sheets of paper containing illuminations of various scenes and effects the pope was shown by the visitor are pinned to the walls. The room, an interior chamber on the floor with no external windows, is no larger than a service closet and is brightly lit by several overhead LED strip lights. Painting materials are piled on a craft table and a drafting table sits against a wall. A stretched square canvas with heavy blue underpainting sits on two paint cans taking up half of one wall, opposite a floor-to-ceiling mirror of equal size. Most of the painted space depicts Veronica's hands holding a bloody, sweaty rag, while in the background a tiny silhouette of Jesus no bigger than a key continues to bear the cross toward his execution. No visible impression of Jesus's face appears in the rag. Pope M gestures in acknowledgment to Father

R, but continues to stare at a drawing on the wall through the mirror for some time. By this point the pope wears only a simple white cassock and has long ceased grooming his hair and beard.

Father R is dressed in the typical white daily garb and wears his prosthetics. The two men do not resemble each other anymore, though only they know this. No one other than Father R has seen the pope in years; three of the cardinals who conspired to form this arrangement have since died. Addressing the pope as your holiness, Father R confirms that an appointment with a psychedelic therapist has been procured. The pope smiles and says, "Thank you, your holiness," and both men laugh. They briefly dance, facing each other as mirror images, a choreography Pope M developed as an exercise and began practicing with his friend several months earlier.

THE OFFICE OF the psychedelic therapist is paneled in mahogany and decorated with a single potted palm in an elaborate ceramic container resembling a squid, as well as a large semi-abstract painting that depicts a grid of receding gray spheres. Though he was once one of the most famous and recognizable people in the world, the pope now looks like an anonymous old painter. He sits on the therapist's leather couch wearing a loose gray linen shirt, matching pants with a drawstring, and leather sandals. The visitor is present.

The pope consumes three grams of psychedelic mushrooms, and as he does not speak, the therapist also remains quiet. Two hours into the session the therapist plays Kimiko Douglass-Ishizaka's 2012 recording of Johann Sebastian Bach's *Goldberg Variations* at a low volume, causing the pope to weep and wonder why he didn't listen to music more often during the many years prior to the visitor's arrival. He feels the visitor's attention pass over his body as an awareness of his entire skin, as though he were being vacuum-sealed in a sausage casing and then electrocuted. By this late point the pope no longer finds these images and sensations disturbing or distracting; his language has been dissolved, vision clouded with dancing fragments, and ears filled with strange music many, many times. Now, he finds, it's what's already in the world that's moving him to distraction and disturbance. He considers Bach, whose kingdom overlaps with his own but also transcends it. There is no evidence that Bach (1665–1750) interacted with any of the popes who served during his lifetime: Innocent XII (1691–1700),

Clement XI (1700–1721), Innocent XIII (1721–1724), Benedict XIII (1724–1730), Clement XII (1730–1740), Benedict XIV (1740–1758). Did they hear his music and know how far it would travel? How did all these men fail to introduce themselves to this rare genius beyond time who walked among them? How ironic that they were so focused, perhaps, on Jesus—who did not walk among them, who had passed them by long ago—that they would all miss this other kind of savior who was alive in their day.

The pope drinks water. He enjoys the effects of the psilocybin and finds its expressions to be similar to simpler forms of the visitor's. He is also aware that by this point his mind has been so soaked in the visitor's material that the images and associations produced by the drug seem to rhyme with or reimagine versions of things he has already been shown. Though the physical experience the drug produces is distinct, the pope can't be sure that anything crossing his mind would not have done so anyway. But he does feel a plain and overwhelming feeling of love and gratitude for his friend, Father R.

THE NEXT DAY, the pope is reading Erowid. He finds an account of a mushroom experience in which the writer describes the mushroom as an earthly conduit for an alien or astral intelligence that compelled him to cultivate and then consume the mushroom to establish contact. The writer compares the sensation of information flowing from the intelligence into his brain to holding a tin cup under Niagara Falls. The writer also describes the intelligence as an interdimensional demon, wielding this torrent of knowledge as a form of torture for its own pleasure, and expresses a deep horror at the hideous expanse of the demon as a form, and at its clear desire to distort perception and cause madness toward its own nefarious ends. The user observes his own mushroom grow with disgust and destroys it. The feeling of horror took a week to fade, but the desire to interact with the mushroom again took hold about a year later, despite how utterly nightmarish he had found the experience at the time.

THE POPE CELEBRATES his 91st birthday with Father R in his studio. They talk at length about when they were young, as they did on the phone years earlier, when this experience was still nascent for them both.

Father R is wearing the full papal regalia; the pope is wearing a black sweatsuit. Late at night, Father R asks the pope about his experience with the therapist, and the pope shrugs.

"I've been thinking that we should return the obelisk in the square to Cairo," is all he says.

6. THE DEPARTURE

MONTHS LATER, the pope is sitting in his studio, letting his mind wander across his work, increasingly distracted by his inability to behold the visitor. His stomach drops in shock and disbelief: after almost five years of daily contact, returning to the visitor as a source of inspiration and mystery, a direct touch with something outside, he realizes that the visitor has departed. The pope sits dumbstruck with this realization for twenty minutes, looking at the now-ordinary things around him. He begins to panic, and then to cry. In the end, this interaction with some further reality meant more to him than being entrusted with an entire global community's metaphysics, with systems of ritual and behavior, with mechanisms of governance and power. All of that was so much less personal, and ultimately so much less real, than whatever it was that had passed through him and his rooms and then finally, with equal lack of explanation, disappeared.

THREE LONG DAYS PASS for Pope M. He remains in his studio but feels unmoored and disconnected from his work, the source of his inspiration gone. He knew that the work wasn't terribly important or interesting, let alone skillful; that it was potentially interesting as a narrow historical curiosity due to its being created by a pope, just as the American President George W. Bush's paintings were interesting because they were produced by the architect of the war on terror, after his failures spooled out and out, tarnishing the new century, his paintings functioning as objects of focus for that broader, diffuse disgust much more so than as paintings in and of themselves. The pope also knows that his inspiration was not related to his papacy or his life, but to his encounter with the visitor, and that he has not progressed far enough in any mode of creative practice to capture the visitor in any kind of adequate way. It had been a nonreligious haunting, or perhaps a religious experience unto itself.

Why him? Why anyone? There hadn't been nearly enough time.

The pope feels a bodily desire to be done, as if his skeleton and muscles themselves have begun to bark: That will be enough.

THAT WEEK, FATHER R presides over an official papal mass in Manaus, by which time he has been acting as the pope for five years without suspicion. But suddenly he is beheld, through the prosthetics, across the years, nearly four thousand miles from Viedma.

"Father R," says one of his old parishioners.

He recognizes the old man at once. His name is Juan Nascimento. "Juan, my son," says Father R, breaking character for the first time. A look of horror and revulsion passes across Nascimento's face, and he turns away.

Two weeks later, Nascimento's account appears in *Meia Hora*, the Brazilian tabloid, suggesting that the pope has been switched. Cardinal L's offices register the story, but it gains no traction at the Vatican or in the public mind. Nascimento is shamed into silence by his family, caused to doubt what he knew he saw, and stops speaking of it. He later falls into a terrible depression.

IN CASA MARTA the pope haunts Father R. No longer employed by his visitor, he sits for long periods of time in his studio, rewatches movies, distractedly pages through magazines, and suffers from headaches. Father R's prosthetics are now very advanced, to mimic what computers have modeled a shrinking old Pope M would look like. And perhaps he would have looked that way, though he does not, and Father R now finds himself as a simulacrum of an entirely imagined pope, just as he himself is in perfect health beneath all the layers.

"Father," the pope says one day.

"Your holiness," says Father R, sighing and bowing deeply, immediately understanding the request.

STILL WEARING HIS prosthetics as always, Father R spends the better part of four hours grooming the pope, cutting his hair and beard, cleaning his hands and feet, dressing him in his proper attire: the white cassock, the white mozzetta, the white zucchetto, the red leather outdoor shoes.

Pope M leaves Casa Marta for the first time in years to walk in the papal gardens. He looks up at the sky through the leaves of the garden's trees, then at the roofs of the buildings—the radio building, the art gallery, the academy of sciences, the outer walls of Vatican City.

Cardinal L sees Pope M from a distance and recognizes him instantly. He walks quickly to intercept the old pope, returned suddenly to the world. "Your holiness," he says, with wide eyes and real, deep reverence. Pope M smiles at his old colleague. "Your eminence," he says. "I would like to address the people."

"Your holiness," Cardinal L says, taking in the noticeable extent of the drift between Father R's display and the present reality of the pope's body, "you know that will not be possible."

Pope M continues to smile, then lets out a gasp as a look of overwhelming sadness passes across his face. He begins to lose his vision and balance and falls forward. Cardinal L, an old man himself, is unable to catch him.

FATHER R IS SITTING in the pope's studio, as per their arrangement, waiting for the pope's return. But it is Cardinal L who finds him there; he is only the third person to set foot in that converted closet since the former pope himself had secretly outfitted it. Cardinal L doesn't so much as glance around at the former pope's work and delivers the news of his sudden death in the garden to Father R with an attitude of relieved grievance, but also unmistakably one of awe. "I can continue," says Father R.

Cardinal L looks at him impassively.

"You wish to take over . . . in this capacity?" asks Cardinal L, gesturing around the studio.

Father R looks around. His life as a priest was driven by a practical desire to help others, who, like himself, did not choose to be born into their bodies, at their times, under their conditions. He looks sadly at the former pope's incomplete painting of Veronica and begins to weep at the news of the death of his friend and the end of this moment. He sees his life opening suddenly before him once again. He shakes his head.

"Forgive me, your eminence," he says, in Pope M's soft voice, and begins to cry harder, as if hearing his friend speaking through him.

Cardinal L exits, and in his offices arranges for Pope M's immediate cremation, which he oversees within the hour. The other remaining cardinal who knew of Father R's role appears in Casa Marta to help Father R remove and destroy the prosthetics. Meanwhile, Father R weeps alone in Pope M's room for the entire day. The next morning, he leaves Casa Marta, again as himself, never to return; he is temporarily housed in the papal apartments of the Apostolic Palace as arrangements are made.

Soon, Father R and Cardinal L agree that he will leave Vatican City, and Rome, to live out his days in secret retirement in Paris. After he departs the Vatican, Cardinal L oversees the destruction of the former pope's artwork and the return of the studio space to its standard function as a large storage closet.

Finally, Cardinal L issues a public announcement of the pope's death, in which the cremation and closed-casket arrangements are described as in keeping with Pope M's strictest private wishes. He begins the process of calling the sacred college of cardinals to Rome to elect another pope; they start to arrive at Casa Marta later that day.

F ATHER R LIVES IN PARIS for nine years before Cardinal L's death, at which point he knows he is free to return to Argentina. His life in the city had been calm and gentle, walking, reading, drinking wine, giving away money to anyone who asked. In the privacy of his apartment, he maintained much the same routine as he had with Pope M: watching movies, saying the rosary now as a form of meditation practice, but he does not otherwise continue practicing what had been his faith.

After making the arrangements himself, he takes the train to Charles de Gaulle in order to observe the people and the receding city one last time. As he falls asleep on the flight to Buenos Aires, he finds himself picturing the obelisk being sent back to Cairo. He imagines it being conveyed through various shipping procedures, sees the container ship bearing it crash in a canal and the obelisk shatter. Then he sees it reassembled in Cairo, its voyage completed, where it will stand for another thousand years. He imagines he can see himself from the impossible perspective of the pope's visitor, flying through the void of space to Deneb and then from there on to Vega.

After landing, Father R makes his way to the Terminal de Ómnibus de Retiro, where he spends a great deal of time getting himself into a new set of gradually procured prosthetics, once more reapplying the makeup. Then, instead of continuing to Viedma, with an appearance indistinguishable in the mirror from that of his deceased friend, he boards the bus to Tandil, and the world is soon made to contemplate reports of the first new resurrection in more than two thousand years. +

The Wendy Award

by WALTER SCOTT
IN STORES NOW!

"Remarkable... a story of personal dissolution, betrayed friendship, and tentative recovery with a hefty cast of rich characters, but it's almost purely comedic." —SAM THIELMAN, *THE NEW YORK TIMES*

"Hysterically funny while always insistent on hope—Wendy is an icon of modern longing." —KATE BERLANT

"Wendy is the authentic voice of a bewildered generation." —RACHEL COOKE, *THE GUARDIAN*

drawnandquarterly.com

REVIEWS

DAN BERGER
The Fifty-Year Revolt

Orisanmi Burton. *Tip of the Spear: Black Radicalism, Prison Repression, and the Long Attica Revolt.* University of California Press, 2023.

Jocelyn Simonson. *Radical Acts of Justice: How Ordinary People Are Dismantling Mass Incarceration.* The New Press, 2023.

IN 1969, A WRITER WHO STYLED HIS NAME AS raúlrsalinas wrote an ode to the places he called home and an indictment of the forces that oppressed him. "You live on, captive, in the lonely / cellblocks of my mind," runs the opening stanza of "A Trip Through the Mind Jail," surveying the neighborhoods of Salinas's youth. By the end, he visits California, Texas, New Mexico, Colorado, and "all / Chicano neighborhoods that now exist and once / existed; somewhere . . . . . , someone remembers . . . ." More than fifty years on, the poem has been widely anthologized as a singular expression of Chicanismo across the American Southwest.

"A Trip Through the Mind Jail" first appeared in the inaugural issue of *Aztlán de Leavenworth*, a Chicano newspaper produced at a federal penitentiary in Leavenworth, Kansas, where Salinas was incarcerated on a felony drug charge. Prison was where Salinas became a poet. It was also where he became a revolutionary, thanks in part to the people he met at Leavenworth, including Puerto Rican nationalists Oscar Collazo and Rafael Cancel Miranda, whose respective attacks on President Truman in 1950 and inside the US Capitol in 1954 had called attention to the US colonization of Puerto Rico. "We immersed ourselves in the Puerto Rican history and united our struggles," Salinas later said of the Chicano prisoners at Leavenworth. But this organizing was more than an expression of pan-Latinx unity: "Through that connection and the Black Muslims that were coming in, and the Republic of New Africa, and the Black Liberation Army people, we began to talk."

They did more than talk. On September 16, 1971, militants incarcerated at Leavenworth went on strike to protest their working conditions in the prison's brush, furniture, and clothing factories. There was more to the strike than that: rebels were also protesting the murders of imprisoned comrades, including Black Panther Field Marshal George Jackson in San Quentin on August 21 and the twenty-nine prisoners killed by state troopers at Attica Correctional Facility on September 13, where an uprising had been violently suppressed. For days afterward, hundreds of surviving dissidents at Attica were tortured by New York State Police and prison guards. The Leavenworth rebels joined a wave of incarcerated militants around the country who were rising up in revolt.

Participants in these protests, including rebels from Leavenworth, would soon become the inaugural cohort of a new experiment in human caging: the control unit, a special wing of the prison that combined isolation with a kind of psychological warfare officials called "behavior modification." In 1972, prison officials from across the US transferred some of their most rebellious and troublesome charges to a single federal prison in Marion, Illinois. Shortly after their arrival, these charges formed the Political Prisoners Liberation Front. "The convicts of this institution of Marion prison have in the past experienced many difficulties which were resolved by a collective effort," the group wrote in a July 1972 statement announcing a strike after the beating of a Chicano prisoner. "And this collectivism is being called upon for still another serious problem confronting us today that must be resolved by whatever means necessary." Yet the control unit would require new forms of resistance. To reorganize the men's minds, the "behavior modification" program at Marion imposed prolonged isolation (culminating in a 23/7 lockdown), coerced psychotropic drugging, and brute force. Edgar Schein, the MIT psychologist who helped create the unit, drew on the brainwashing techniques used by China and North Korea against US prisoners of war in the early 1950s. As chronicled by the scholar Alan Eladio Gómez, these practices included isolation, "spying on prisoners and reporting back private material, tricking men into writing statements then shown to other inmates, exploiting informers and opportunists, [and] the disorganization of all group standards among prisoners." Prisons, Schein and his colleagues recognized, were war zones: they were in the business not of "rehabilitation" but of vanquishing enemies. As Marion's warden declared, "the purpose of the . . . Unit is to control revolutionary attitudes in the prison system and in the society at large."

That declaration could serve as a mission statement for mass incarceration itself. More than just an unprecedented physical expansion of the US prison system since 1973, mass incarceration has also long been a form of counterinsurgent warfare aimed at those who would upend the order of things. Buoyed by participation in Black and associated radical movements, cadres of militants in the early 1970s inspired broader groups of incarcerated people to make the US prison system ungovernable, through uprisings, strikes, lawsuits, unionization drives, and other means. The organized revolt and accompanying polemics—from a mix of dedicated revolutionaries, newly politicized bandits, and people who simply seized any opportunity to resist their captivity—put the question of prison abolition squarely on the table. But the control unit and similar efforts answered revolutionary challenges to authority with brutality. Policies of isolation and behavior modification built today's American prison system, and Marion was part of an epochal turn in carceral governance that abandoned even the pretense of reform. The result not only sent massively more people to prison, but kept them in more atomized and austere conditions.

After nearly a half century, a new wave of antagonists rose to challenge the American carceral state amid the volatile political economy of the 2010s: Black Lives Matter, Idle No More, #NoDAPL, #Not1More antideportation campaigns led by undocumented people, and a rolling series of prisoner-labor and hunger strikes. Such efforts began to shatter the illusion of invincible police power in the 2010s, leading to the George Floyd uprisings in 2020. These movements were the outcome of a fifty-year fight over human caging that began in the cells of places like Attica, Leavenworth, and San Quentin. As in all struggles between liberation and oppression, the battles have occurred on ideological and material fronts: as movements work to close prisons and free their captives, they call into question a society rooted in punishment. The grim conditions of incarceration have always lit sparks of solidarity, but the past half century of escalating state violence in the forms of prisons and police has revived the abolitionist spirit—both in prison and on the streets—in greater numbers than ever. And while the tactical terrain shifts as more non-incarcerated people join the fight against an expanding punitive state, the strategic imperative and moral urgency remain. Much as an earlier generation said the future offered two paths, "socialism or barbarism," the closing decades of the 20th century and the start of the 21st have presented a choice: abolition or authoritarianism.

TWO NEW BOOKS examine revolutionary challenges to different phases of the US carceral order, linked in purpose but separated by over four decades. Orisanmi Burton's *Tip of the Spear* studies the prison uprisings of the 1970s that reached their apex in what Burton, an anthropologist at American University, calls the "Long Attica Revolt." In *Radical Acts of Justice*, legal scholar Jocelyn Simonson surveys the past decade of grassroots urban resistance to police and the courts. Despite their different temporal and institutional areas of focus, both books examine abolition as an epistemology and a praxis, and both understand the organic intellectualism of antiprison movements: the way these movements ask us to think differently about justice, safety, and politics. Reading them together helps connect two eras of insurgent organizing against the prison state. Each text recognizes, as do their protagonists, that the carceral system makes manifest the logic of patriarchal racial capitalism in its most violent extremes, which is what makes antiprison organizing so perilous, but also so rife with potential. "Amid conditions of extreme duress," Burton writes, "the dregs of the capitalist order began to fashion themselves anew."

That self-fashioning exceeds the limited framework typically applied in evaluations of protest movements, especially those led by incarcerated people. Burton rejects the conventional focus among activists, journalists, historians, and others on what he calls the "minimum demands" prisoners make to improve prison conditions, drawing from Black studies thinkers such as Sylvia Wynter to consider the more profound political struggle in which prisoners have engaged. Denigrated as poor and racialized as disposable, these incarcerated radicals challenged a larger conception of human value. *Tip of the Spear* restores attention to prisoners' own self-understanding and political objectives, and the overarching ideals of freedom to which they aspired. Burton calls these "maximum demands," the holistic view formed through an accumulating process of struggle: at their most expansive, they are "communal, internationalist, and autonomous practices ... presag[ing] a new social order, a new ethics, and new forms of human sociality." Their visionary scope is integral to Burton's project to "decarcerate the revolutionary meaning and significance of Attica"—to break from the "mind jail" that would see Attica only as a tragedy of state violence rather than a site of revolutionary possibility.

Burton achieves this larger view by extending the revolt beyond the four-day uprising in New York in September 1971. For Burton, "Attica" begins with a series of rebellions that convulsed the New York City jails in the summer and fall of 1970, more than a year before the uprising at Attica Correctional Facility. Many of the latter's defining features were already evident in the crisis in the jails, where members of the Black Panthers and the Young Lords spearheaded a frontal assault on an overcrowded and abusive jail system.

Amid a moral panic about rising crime, the New York City jail population had nearly doubled between 1967 and 1970, and this rapid expansion meant that many people, too poor to post bail pending trial, ended up spending months or even years in jail. After more than a dozen members of the Black Panther Party were arrested as part of a sweeping COINTELPRO-generated conspiracy—among them Kuwasi Balagoon, Lumumba Shakur, and Kwando Kinshasa—the Panthers lost no time and began organizing throughout the city's jails in concert with Muslim and Puerto Rican militants. Burton quotes Victor Martinez of the Young Lords, who told the *Black Panther* newspaper about the founding of the Inmates Liberation Front at the Tombs jail in Lower Manhattan: it "began as a committee of two people, which grew to four and then kept multiplying until we were able to organize the complete ninth floor." The uprising spread until prisoners had seized most of the facility. Then, Burton writes, "they swarmed throughout the jail assaulting the physical expression of their degradation: they set fire to bedding, destroyed their medical records, smashed windows, and threw handwritten messages, burning trash, and dead rats onto the downtown Manhattan streets." Even after they released the prison guards they'd taken hostage, the captive militants continued to plot their next moves. Their rebellious spirit soon spread from New York's city jails to its state prisons—partly because the government transferred people upon conviction, and partly because state prisoners took inspiration from the sight of fellow captives challenging the institutions that controlled their lives.

"Prisons are war," Burton writes. "They are state strategies of race war, class war, colonization, and counterinsurgency." As *Tip of the Spear* makes clear, however, the prisoner is not a helpless victim of war but a disadvantaged combatant within it. "Against carceral siege, revolting captives waged a people's war, a counter-war." Reframing the carceral context as one of war helps Burton take seriously both prisoners' politics and their tactics. While the political thought of incarcerated people has recently received more attention in histories, memoirs, and journalistic accounts, serious analysis of their tactical choices—which in the 1970s included the taking of hostages and armed revolt—remains lacking. Incarcerated militants challenged the state's monopoly of force with particular flair in that decade, opening a new front in struggles that in many cases preceded their incarceration. Black revolutionaries, sometimes joined by Puerto Rican, Chicano, and Indigenous comrades, seized guards as hostages in bold attempts to win their and their comrades' freedom. These measures succeeded, at least at first: in the New York City jail rebellion of 1970, hostage taking led to an impromptu bail hearing that resulted in the release of thirteen people, many of whom had been held without trial for more than a year. The taking of hostages continued to accompany strikes at the prisons where some of the city-jail rebels—including Herbert X. Blyden, who would be elected as a spokesman for the Attica Brothers—were later sent: first Auburn, then Attica.

By the time the revolt reached Attica, many of the participants were battle-tested and ready to fight. And fight they did. Burton emphasizes the revolutionary convictions of the rebellion's leading participants. Some were members of the Black Liberation Army (BLA), the clandestine offshoot of the Black Panther Party, which found new recruits among the prisoner ranks and whose outlook defined the public statements issued by the Attica rebels. Others, including a figure interviewed by Burton whom he dubs Bugs, saw themselves as "gangsters" who put their self-taught skills to use. (Bugs, for his part, helped blow up the prison's chapel.) In fact the rebellion fused the revolutionary and the gangster, the propagandist and the saboteur, in a shared project that Burton describes as a "commune . . . of ecstasy, joy, love, intimacy, pleasure, and collective Black radical becoming." Beyond the tactical drama, it is this process of self-actualization amid state repression that makes the rebellion's image and memory endure. As Burton writes in the book's conclusion, "more than fifty years later, Attica remains a living example that collectively, ordinary people can be more than the sum of their parts."

To those in power, from the police to the governor, the scene of incarcerated people asserting their political will as part of a third-worldist revolutionary project was a crisis to be crushed by any means necessary. The Long Attica Revolt was killed in what Burton describes as a "war on Black revolutionary minds," part of a coordinated program of "pacification." In the book's grim second half, he traces this pacification across three related domains: racist sexual terrorism against participants in the revolt; reformist counterinsurgency to defuse the revolt's incipient sense of possibility; and new forms of captivity (including programs like the control unit) to preempt any future revolt. This tripartite regime of physical violence, co-optation, and renewed social control built the system we now call mass incarceration and soon spread nationwide, led by states with large prison systems—New York, as well as California and Texas—after they experienced their own episodes of revolutionary unrest. Prison officials looked to obstruct organizing through isolation and atomization, and used collective punishment to keep prisoners divided and demoralized.

MAO ZEDONG famously declared that the relationship between guerrillas and the people is that of fish to water. America's policing apparatus worked to capture the fish and drain the sea. While the FBI targeted leftist leaders and organizations with particular intensity in the 1960s and 1970s, federal and state governments hardened penalties and expanded the bureaucracy of punishment beginning in the 1970s. The ensuing decades of get-tough criminal policy not only made it harder to be a revolutionary, but also undermined the communities that had nurtured such organizations and supplied their militant members. These policies targeted not just the fish but the water.

Yet following the 2008 financial crisis, as states looked to cut expenses and costly prisons were bursting at the seams, it became harder to sustain the illusion that safety was perpetually just one more jail cell away; the profound human (and fiscal) cost of pervasive incarceration came to seem too high. The attempt to solve political-economic crisis through punishment generated its own crises, and the past decade has shown once again that, in the words of Assata Shakur, "a wall is just a wall." Long-standing organizing against the prison industrial complex by groups like Critical Resistance and the Prison Moratorium Project, as well as campaigns in support of political prisoners, reached new recognition in the 21st century as the concept of mass incarceration entered the popular lexicon. Against unchecked police power and the biggest prison system the world has ever known, the past fifteen years have seen a new anticarceral upsurge. The current revolt has many sources, including incarcerated people themselves, who have organized a wave of prison strikes, from Georgia and Alabama to California to Guantánamo Bay, that have taken on everything from labor exploitation to long-term solitary confinement to medical neglect. Formerly incarcerated people and their family members have waged campaigns against prison censorship, sexual violence, and death-by-incarceration sentences. And every day the pedagogy of the police officer's truncheon continues to mobilize new generations of activists against the violence of austerity that cops uphold. These new militants, Jocelyn Simonson writes in *Radical Acts of Justice*, "redefine the concept of justice itself: perhaps justice is when the state provides communities with what they need to support each other and keep each other safe. Perhaps safety means freedom, not incarceration."

Focused on bail funds, court watching, participatory defense (which "combine[s] collective advocacy in individual cases with the building of power to change public conversations and policies"), and solidarity budgeting (collective organizing to "demand that . . . governments play a part in supporting forms of justice and safety that don't include punishment"), *Radical Acts of Justice* is a compact history of recent grassroots decarceral organizing that gestures toward the deeper roots of these strategies, each of which is the subject of a chapter in the book. Throughout this lively, hopeful, and well-reported work, Simonson shows how specific campaigns have won material changes in the lives of criminalized people and helped shift collective understanding of safety, justice, and "the people." One story follows Tracy McCarter, the New York City nurse who was arrested for killing her abusive ex-husband in 2020. Members of the local feminist anticarceral organization Survived & Punished took up McCarter's case, supporting her in court while pressuring the district attorney to drop the charges. At public events and on social media, they used her case to illuminate the linkages between state and interpersonal violence, highlighting the injustice of a city that would rather incarcerate survivors of domestic violence than provide for their needs. After more than two years, they won: McCarter went free and joined Survived & Punished. "They thought they were building me a cage," McCarter wrote upon her release. "Instead they were building me a pulpit."

Where Burton focuses on people's attempts to overthrow or break out of prisons in *Tip of the Spear*, Simonson's attention in *Radical Acts of Justice* remains on external efforts to get people out, or keep them from going in at all. Revolutionary vigor looks different in a world reshaped by the pacification programs used to crush the prisoner revolts of an earlier generation. On the surface, the hostage-taking, chapel-burning rebels of the early '70s have little in common with, for example, contemporary court watchers—community volunteers who "sit in the audience section of criminal courtrooms to demonstrate support for the accused," observe the proceedings, and publicize the actions of judges and attorneys. But court watching similarly defies authorities who are unaccustomed to being challenged, and at the point of their greatest power. Likewise, when opponents of mass incarceration reject prosecutors' legal claim to represent "the people," they continue the kind of political self-fashioning that Burton ascribes to the Long Attica Revolt. The tactics have shifted, but the purpose remains constant: to push the state to live up to its putative democratic values in the short term, and to delegitimize the state's monopoly of violence in the long term. The insurgent forms Burton discusses had their parallels in clandestine revolutionary organizations of the '70s like the BLA, which also operated in prison, much as contemporary prisons house the type of community organizers Simonson profiles—such as those of the Green Haven Think Tank, the in-prison study group that Simonson credits with developing a now common approach to studying incarceration rates in tandem with urban divestment. Though much of the United States has been organized to stymie the revolutionary challenges of the early 1970s, Burton's and Simonson's books voice a resounding echo between past and present. They also highlight the necessity of a certain kind of "inside-out" strategy that challenges the prison state from within while also working to block its tributaries.

The carceral system is vastly larger and more pervasive now than it was a half century ago. When the Attica revolt began, the United States incarcerated approximately two hundred thousand people; today it imprisons almost two million. This expansion in turn presents contemporary abolitionists with different challenges. Simonson outlines a multipronged movement strategy of people working within, alongside, and against the criminal legal system. She offers no electoral solutions to end mass incarceration and is critical of the move to elect "progressive prosecutors," whom, because they seek to apply the levers of the existing system more equitably, she sees as already captured by the system. Instead, her focus is on the ways collective organizing outside and against the system remakes our sense—and the very infrastructure—of justice itself. She acknowledges that bailing people out of jail, observing a criminal trial, or influencing city budget priorities also necessarily engage with the system as it is—but they do so in order, one hopes, to limit, change, or even eradicate it altogether. And as the prosecutorial targeting of bail funds shows, working to subvert the system from within can make people a target of the legal apparatus they wish to diminish.

Resisting jail and prison expansion also refashions questions of safety and social priorities. Restorative and transformative justice organizations implement collective and reparative models of accountability without punishment that, as one of Simonson's respondents put it, "look backward" to move forward. "When movement actors come together to bail someone out, to observe courtroom proceedings, or to create a video for their sentencing hearing, they enter the carceral space of the courtroom as a collective, as the community," Simonson writes. "The public becomes a concrete presence" in spaces normally organized around individualizing and isolating punishment. In turn, activists from groups like Court Watch Baton Rouge, Philadelphia Bail Fund, or California's Faith in the Valley participatory-defense hub "inevitably understand what they see and do from a collective perspective." The same could be said of incarcerated organizers, highlighted only briefly in Simonson's book but central to *Tip of the Spear*: their resistance collectivizes justice, seizing power from a system accustomed to treating justice as a bludgeon against the disenfranchised.

A FEW YEARS before the uptick in anticarceral organizing that Simonson chronicles, I went to visit a former BLA member at a federal prison in the Catskill Mountains. The bucolic drive up a windswept road culminated in a medium-security facility whose hilltop location obscured much of the surrounding natural beauty. The person I was there to visit had already spent forty-five years in various prisons. Through our mail correspondence, I had accompanied him for a dozen of those years as he was shipped from one federal prison to another. He was now in his seventies and I was concerned about his health; one of his BLA comrades had recently died in prison. I did not want him to suffer the same fate.

"How do we get you out?" I asked him on that visit.

"Time was," he smiled, nodding toward a small patio outside the window of the visiting room, "I would have said a helicopter on that yard."

I smiled back. Long before reading Burton's book, I had heard tell of the many daring, almost cinematic prison-escape attempts of the 1970s: the time BLA members tried to bust out their imprisoned comrades with acetylene torches, or when a long-planned escape effort was foiled by a rival group of prisoners who were caught attempting their own comparatively haphazard escape. The '70s were not short on bold efforts. But three decades later, the carceral state had vanquished armed struggle. We both knew there would be no helicopter. But we would not accept the grim condemnation passed down by the state decades earlier, either.

In the next few years, an intergenerational group of organizers worked tirelessly for my friend's release and that of several other political prisoners who had spent decades in some of the nation's worst prisons. They did so through the kinds of strategies highlighted in *Radical Acts of Justice*. They launched public campaigns targeting the cruelty of "death by incarceration." They protested the police capture of parole boards. They wrote letters and made visits and kept prisoners at the heart of organized communities. "WE ARE ONE PEOPLE," reads a political statement from the New York jail rebellion that initiated the Long Attica Revolt. By the 2010s, abolitionists had put this message into practice as a form of solidarity between inside and outside. Cumulatively, their efforts led to the release of more than a dozen aging revolutionaries, my friend among them. Many of them had been serving life sentences.

Such hard-won freedom was once unthinkable—not only to the state, but to the pundit-brain logic that measures political efficacy purely in polls and ballots. These were people who were meant to be buried under the prison. Abolition operates on a different timeline. Its unshakable demand for immediate freedom starts from the impossible conditions of the dystopian here and now. *Free them all*, *abolition now*, *defund the police*: the concepts dismissed as political immaturity bestow a sense of possibility. "We cannot underestimate the movement visions that emerge from these experiences," Simonson notes toward the end of her book, "if for no other reason than because these visions are *possible*. They are the fuel for everything." Yesterday's tactics are unlikely to secure tomorrow's victories. The past offers an orientation, not an instruction manual, and successful struggle often requires an improvisational response to the moment. But abolition continues to promise an escape from the mind jail that

Salinas named decades ago. And in making or even attempting that escape, we can know freedom. +

REED MCCONNELL
Good Boys

Matteo Garrone (director). *Pinocchio*. 2019.
Jordan Peterson. *The Jordan B. Peterson Podcast*. "Maps of Meaning: Marionettes & Individuals," parts 1–3. 2020.
Vasiliy Rovenskiy (director). *Pinocchio: A True Story*. 2021.
Guillermo del Toro (director). *Pinocchio*. 2022.
Robert Zemeckis (director). *Pinocchio*. 2022.

JORDAN PETERSON IS SITTING IN A ROOM. Behind him are indistinct images, partly obscured in the dim light and cut off by the camera's frame. (Perhaps they are the Soviet propaganda posters purported to cover every wall of his home — a constant reminder of the dangers of ideology.) Today he is being featured on the *Rubin Report*, a podcast hosted by the conservative commentator Dave Rubin. In the YouTube clip — described by its original poster, ManOfAllCreation, as "absolutely incredible" — Peterson recalls the moment in Disney's *Pinocchio* when Geppetto "wishes on a star." He stops, overcome with emotion. He starts again in a quavering voice, now speaking as Geppetto.

"What I want more than anything else," he says, "is that my creation will become a genuine individual. It's a heroic gesture." He is getting all worked up. He is gesticulating with great force. "And that catalyzes the puppet's transformation into a *real! being!*" he shouts. "We start as puppets. And so the trick is to get rid of your goddamn *strings!*"

WHEN I WAS a little girl, I was uninterested in Disney princesses but obsessed with Disney's animated Pinocchio. I slept under a Pinocchio bedspread, kept track of the days on a cloth Pinocchio calendar fastened to the back of my bedroom door, and, when so moved, hauled a three-foot-tall stuffed Pinocchio doll from my toy chest, bound its feet to mine with rubber bands, and danced frenetically around the living room to the Beatles until I collapsed, exhausted, on the rug beside my beloved puppet. I was an only child bullied mercilessly in school, and Pinocchio was a reliable friend in the absence of real boys.

I loved other characters in the movie, too, especially the Blue Fairy, the gorgeous blonde in a glittering dress who gives Pinocchio life. But I was equally entranced by one of the movie's villains, Honest John, an effete talking fox who tries to lure Pinocchio to a place called Pleasure Island. No wonder: this hairy fairy and his bedraggled, soft-butch sidekick, Gideon the cat, embodied something far more thrilling than the Blue Fairy's domestic purity. Danger and deviant indulgence? The thrill and horror of making the wrong choices? I was repulsed and enchanted. I regularly dragged my parents to Blockbuster to rent my favorite *Disney's Sing-Along Songs* VHS, and sing along I would: "Hi-diddle-dee-dee, it's Pleasure Isle for me!" That Pleasure Island was a place where lazy boys went to be turned into donkeys and sold to the salt mines only added to the allure. (Once, when I was about 6, I threw my mother into a panic when I told her how much I longed to be kidnapped. It would have been so exciting.)

As is the case for so many queer adults, it's tempting to interpret these childhood preoccupations as flamboyant indicators of my future queerness. But I didn't know anything then. Like Pinocchio, I was still so radically unformed. I knew nothing about boy-meets-girl and had barely accrued any gender yet.

Also like Pinocchio, I was desperate to be lovable, and somewhere along the way this yearning became bound up with a fearful obedience to rules and dictates, an absolute fixation on doing right, that persisted into my adult life. In graduate school, reading Kant's *Groundwork of the Metaphysics of Morals*, I realized with horror that every word of Kant's ethics felt simply and naturally true to me, that the austere, abstract sense of duty he described was the North Star that guided my life. Desire and sensuous pleasure had so little to do with how I made choices. Then again, I was the daughter of a philosopher who would one day declare to me that Kant's categorical imperative was simply correct. It's no wonder that at some point Jiminy Cricket and Immanuel Kant crawled deep into my psyche and never left.

WE LIVE IN a Pinocchio moment. If Disney's *Pinocchio* (1940) is a film about Kantian morality, it is also one about free thought, proper child-rearing, the dangers of lying, quack doctors, children being kidnapped and enslaved, becoming a real boy, homophobic panic, biblical punishment, and menswear—topics that have dominated news headlines and Twitter discourse since the start of the Trump presidency.

There are, however, many Pinocchios, and Carlo Collodi's original 1883 novel *The Adventures of Pinocchio* tells a very different story from the Disney film. Like life in the Hobbesian state of nature, Collodi's Pinocchio is nasty, brutish, and short. He kills the Talking Cricket (Jiminy's less dapper forebear) with a hammer as soon as they meet and then runs away, freeing himself from the pesky demands of his conscience. From there Pinocchio launches into an Odyssean journey, during which he is nearly eaten by a fisherman, threatened by an enormous snake, rescued by a blue-haired fairy, and lured by the siren song of a wicked man who, like Honest John, promises him a life of leisure in the "Land of Boobies."

Collodi's story is dark with economic desperation and everyday brutality. By the end, the Fox and the Cat are left begging on the street, the Fox sans tail after having cut it off and sold it to buy food. Geppetto himself is miserably poor and initially makes a puppet to earn some money as a street performer. Collodi, as it happens, created Pinocchio out of his own financial necessity: deep in debt from gambling, he sent some stories about a naughty marionette to his friend at the Roman daily *Il Fanfulla* in hopes that he might serialize them in the newspaper's new insert for children, *Giornale per i Bambini*. (Collodi was explicit about his motives: "If you print it," he told his friend, "pay me well to make sure I want to continue with it.")

As well as an advocate for children's education, Collodi was by this time a vocal critic of an Italian state that had failed to live up to the nationalist political ideals of his youth, which he had devoted to activism, military service, and newspaper publishing, all in support of a united Italy. Anti-state sentiment pervades the text. When Pinocchio is robbed by the Fox and the Cat and notifies the proper officials, the judge—a gorilla—throws him in jail for the offense of having been robbed. When one of his schoolmates is injured, Pinocchio is the only one who nobly stays behind to help, only to be immediately arrested by the carabinieri for assault and nearly ripped to pieces by a huge police dog. The Fox and the Cat may be rascals, but the authorities come off no better. Hence the novel's ambivalence: Pinocchio is meant to become good and obedient, but not to bow to corrupt and ineffectual authorities.

Accordingly, Pinocchio turns into a real boy at the story's end not because he has absorbed some Kantian sense of duty, but because his slow-growing love for the blue-haired fairy and Geppetto compels him to care for them in their sickness and old age. In other words, he learns to obey them because his love for them singles them out as people worth listening to. This is Collodi's answer to an inescapably human dilemma: to whom do you listen when you are surrounded by warring factions and have not yet developed a will of your own?

PETERSON'S Pinocchio meltdown video is a hit, with sixty-nine thousand views, and the YouTube responses express overwhelming approval. The dozens of commenters, almost entirely male, find Peterson's display of emotion honest and inspiring ("Jordan is not afraid to get misty eyed and choked up. Real Ass Dude right there!"), and some urge others to save the clip and watch it in moments of uncertainty or need. The few commenters who dismiss Peterson's diatribe as maudlin or melodramatic are met with rambling replies explaining why they are too dense to understand his brilliance.

Peterson's rise to fame has been well-documented, from his almost three decades as an academic psychologist at Harvard and the University of Toronto to his breakout moment in 2016, when he loudly protested a proposal to add "gender identity or expression" to the Canadian Human Rights Act as a protected category. What is so notable about Peterson today is both the sheer size of the following he has amassed among disgruntled young white men and his awkward incongruity with his Breitbart compatriots:

Peterson wears three-piece suits, cries onstage, and cites philosophers in everyday conversation, yet manages to curry favor with people who usually treat "intellectualism" like syphilis.

As the big-brain darling of the alt-right, this Jungian pseudo-philosopher produces work that, unsurprisingly, feels both unhinged and dangerous. Peterson's 2018 self-help book *12 Rules for Life: An Antidote to Chaos* is saturated with evolutionary pseudoscience, debunked sociobiology, and bizarre hits on philosophers and theorists whom Peterson does not appear to have read.* And though he negs his readers (*Clean your room! Be a man! You're a worm!*) from his presumably superior rung on the wisdom ladder—being a professor and all—his fundamental message is that they do not actually need to learn the objective truth about the world. On the contrary, they already know it: it's all about trusting their guts.

This lesson remains central throughout Peterson's three nonfiction books, hundreds of podcasts, dozens of interviews, and countless performances—including his seven-hour, three-part lecture on Pinocchio, "Maps of Meaning: Marionettes & Individuals." Peterson loves the original Disney movie. It makes him cry, it makes him rant, it makes him pace back and forth, waving his hands and rhapsodizing about the transcendent beauty of the song "When You Wish Upon a Star." Most of the lecture is not actually about the film: he manages not to mention *Pinocchio* at all until ninety minutes in. But key concerns do emerge, most of all the problem of free thought, a value that Peterson cherishes and believes

---

* In one passage, Peterson segues deftly from the briefest mention of Derrida ("Derrida described his own ideas as a radicalized form of Marxism") to the Soviet Union to an extended meditation on the horrors of the Khmer Rouge—lest we not realize where reading Derrida might lead us.

to be in decline, and which he thinks parents are responsible for instilling in their children. "If you don't want [your child] to be a puppet," he says at the start of hour two, "then you let them have a voice and you facilitate the development of that voice." The terrifying alternative is a world of puppet-robots, mindlessly repeating lines fed to them by their overlords, the very definition of the "ideology" he so abhors (see his walls of Soviet posters).

Yet in his commitment to objective truth not just in chemistry or math, but in all things, Peterson crashes headlong into a logical wall. By promoting the development of the child through free speech and free thinking, he does not want to create individuals with a rich variety of worldviews. He wants to create individuals who are free-thinking enough to choose truth—meaning that they choose to think just like he does. For Peterson really believes he has discovered the truth of the world. "The things that have shaped us most," he says early in the Pinocchio lecture, "are the things that have been around the longest, and so you could say those are the most *real* things." These are, first of all, archetypes in the Jungian sense, from the trickster fox to the disapproving father to the swamp witch. Such tropes have survived through the ages, Peterson says, because they express deep truths about humanity.

Then there are biologically old things, which are true and real because they have survived millennia of evolution. Gender is apparently one such thing, and seeing as it is also archetypally old, it constitutes one of the truest, realest things of all. "The state of Order," Peterson writes early in *12 Rules for Life*, showing his penchant for both ominous capitalizations and the passive voice, "is typically portrayed, symbolically—imaginatively—as masculine." On the other hand, Chaos, "as the antithesis of symbolically masculine order, [is] presented imaginatively as feminine."

That the book is subtitled *An Antidote to Chaos* says it all. Peterson has advocated for enforced distribution of women to men as marriage partners, based on the idea that women, like lobsters, will otherwise just pick the "top guy," leaving the rest of the guys in the dust. The rejected guys will then naturally commit mass shootings, so "enforced monogamy" is an important first step in fighting domestic terrorism. (This is very, very true because it is based on lobsters, which have existed for 350 million years—and that is very, very old.)

Peterson's beliefs about the female character are especially interesting in light of his relationship with his daughter, Mikhaila, a social media influencer for the most macho diet imaginable: she eats only beef, salt, and water, which, she claims, cures autoimmune disorders, depression, and medication withdrawal. In Mikhaila one sees the bizarre contradiction that arises when a girl-child tries to earnestly follow the Peterson manual. Mikhaila is a woman who cleans her room, runs a business, doesn't take shit, and eats only steak, but she also defends her father's misogyny tooth and nail and peddles her own crackpot gender fables, like the idea that declining male workforce participation is a result of women's use of birth control, since the pill makes women attracted to more-feminine men (this, Mikhaila says, is just science), which undermines men's confidence.

Reenter Pinocchio. Like Mikhaila, the hero of the original Disney movie is eager to please his father, and his acts of disobedience seem to result from forgetfulness, naivete, or confusion rather than rebellion. In Disney's version, Pinocchio is a wanted child: the movie starts not with Geppetto making a puppet out of financial necessity, as in the original, but instead dreamily wishing for a child to keep him company. In doing so, he forges the only relationship that really matters in the movie—that between father and son, establishing the primacy of the agnatic line. The maternal Blue Fairy who brings Pinocchio to life later that night has no desires, needs, or personality of her own, and her role in the rest of the story is minimal; in other words, the film's only explicitly female character (other than Cleo, a mute, flirty goldfish) shows up to produce the miracle of life and then conveniently disappears.

This is when the Fox and the Cat come in. They want money, and when they see Pinocchio skipping down the street to school the next morning, they sense an opportunity. They kidnap and sell him, first to a cruel circus master, Stromboli, and then, after he escapes, to the evil coachman who takes him to Pleasure Island. Peterson's love for the movie stems largely from his belief that characters like these embody very old and therefore very true archetypes: Stromboli the cruel father, the Fox the trickster coyote.

But for Peterson, the most powerful archetypal story is the one he sees exemplified by the film's ending. When Pinocchio learns that Geppetto has been swallowed by a whale, he searches until he finds him and then drowns, saving Geppetto's life. This sacrifice is ultimately how Pinocchio earns the right to be human, the thing he wants most in the world (as if his goodness were ever actually in question, or the murderous Stromboli were not also human!). It's an important teaching moment in *12 Rules for Life* and a major reference point for Peterson's fans.

In Peterson's oeuvre, the son venturing into the belly of the whale to save his father symbolizes something specific: the new generation unlocking ancestral knowledge and revitalizing tradition, which is, basically, Peterson's whole shtick. At the end of "Marionettes & Individuals," he compares Geppetto in the belly of the whale to "the state," which he says is "against innovation," here represented by Geppetto resisting Pinocchio's suggestion that they set a fire to make the whale sneeze them out. Geppetto—or the state, "the culture," ancestral knowledge, society, or any other of Peterson's interchangeable abstractions—is starving and old. He needs his son to revitalize him by innovating just enough to keep up with the changing times, but mostly by pulling him out of the belly of the whale, reproducing the father's older culture-society-tradition as a stable base for the son's minimal innovation. This rescue operation is the sort of transcendent goal he recommends his followers set for themselves in the *Rubin Report* clip—we must examine our lives, and then, like Geppetto, set our sights on a star.

At the close of the *Rubin Report* clip, the camera cuts back to the host. Dave Rubin sits there enraptured, open-mouthed, staring. Then it ends.

TODAY PINOCCHIO is everywhere, if you look. Guillermo del Toro's 2022 *Pinocchio*, which won Best Animated Feature Film at the 2023 Oscars, was released on the heels of three other *Pinocchio* remakes, all within three years: a gorgeous Italian adaptation of the original book by the director Matteo Garrone; an animated Russian version directed by Vasiliy Rovenskiy that inadvisably turns Pinocchio's love for the Blue Fairy into a romance (and inexplicably has Pinocchio voiced by the 1990s MTV VJ Pauly Shore); and a live-action Disney film released just months before the del Toro film, directed by Robert Zemeckis of *Who Framed Roger Rabbit* fame. But wait, there's more: Edward Carey's novel *The Swallowed Man,* a retelling of the story from the belly of the whale, from 2020; Adam Kotsko's 2023 translation of a treatise on Pinocchio by Giorgio Agamben; MoMA's 2022 exhibition of the puppets built for del Toro's film; and Paula Rego's two large paintings at the 2022 Venice Biennale, one depicting an exhausted Blue Fairy whispering in Pinocchio's ear, and the other a man polishing the bare ass of a Pinocchio figurine stretched across his knees. This little wooden boy, it seems, is living rent-free in our cultural unconscious.

But maybe that's not so surprising. Peterson's Pinocchio eisegesis is ludicrous, but at least in the United States, the questions he tries to answer are pressing ones. The last decade saw a barrage of targeted disinformation campaigns, the rise of one of the biggest pathological liars ever to occupy the White House, a pandemic that so undermined trust in science that public health efforts may never fully recover, and the development of generative AI tools that have compromised any reliance on documentary evidence. Whatever tenuous epistemic consensus formerly held in the US seems to have irreparably splintered. How do we know what is good? How do we decide what constitutes truth, and what aspects of this truth we should teach our children? Not since the postwar Red Scare has there been such a flurry of legislation limiting what can be taught in the classroom. In 2023, Florida tabled a bill that would have effectively banned the teaching of ethnic studies and Black studies at public universities; an earlier version would have also prevented students from enrolling in the (nonexistent) majors of queer theory, critical social justice, critical race theory, and intersectionality. What we see today is a societal battle over authority, steeped in moralization. How is a child born into this mess supposed to know who is worth listening to?

Del Toro's film depicts a world where these questions also have special purchase. Set in Mussolini's Italy on the eve of World War II, the film pits Pinocchio against more than just a pair of wily vagabonds: Pleasure Island is reimagined as a fascist military training camp for little boys, high on a mountaintop that slopes away into foreboding cliffs. At first, Pinocchio and his friend Candlewick—son of the Podesta, the government official who runs the camp—are eager to become excellent soldiers, but repeated exposure to the Podesta's violence convinces Pinocchio, and then Candlewick, not to obey those who would gladly see you die. Pinocchio duly rejects fascism in favor of those who show him love.

This outcome was not inevitable. In 1947, Theodor Adorno and a team of researchers at Berkeley devised the "F-scale," a test meant to measure an individual's susceptibility to fascist propaganda via the presence of authoritarian personality traits. The traits on the scale read like a summary of Peterson's central concerns, including a punitive attitude toward social nonconformity, an obsession with dominance and hierarchy, and a fixation on contemporary sexual practices. Adorno and his colleagues believed these characteristics were instilled in children by overly harsh parenting, making the child an ideal site for early interventions to contain the spread of fascist ideology. Pinocchio and Candlewick escape inculcation; many of their peers at the training camp do not. For del Toro, as for the creators of the F-scale, the child is and was as much a locus of anxiety as it is for today's far right, but for opposite reasons. Authoritarian parenting breeds little fascists, Adorno and del Toro suggest—yet it is precisely this harshness that Peterson recommends to parents, in *12*

Rules for Life and "Marionettes & Individuals," as necessary to guide the child to the "truth" that, paradoxically, they will eventually freely choose for themselves.

Although Adorno's F-scale deals extensively with a person's susceptibility to fascist propaganda, it does not deal with the content of fascist propaganda itself. It is in Adorno's work with Horkheimer on the culture industry that we see some of his clearest diatribes against the dangers of a new mass media capable of doing the thinking *and* feeling for you, and in this way capable of eliminating all critical distance. As much as del Toro's film might be more critical, odder, and less sappy than the original Disney movie, it is at heart a remake of it, and in some ways tells an even more sentimental story. In del Toro's version, Geppetto is mourning the death of a real-life son, a traumatic gap that he believes only a new child can fill. The book he gives Pinocchio on his first day of school belonged to his dead son; when he finds the book discarded after the Fox and the Cat steal Pinocchio away, his heartbreak is nearly unbearable. At every turn, the stakes are far higher than in the Disney movie; every betrayal and twist of fate is emotionally heightened because of the characters' greater complexity, the extremity of their vulnerability, and the cruelty with which they are met. Pinocchio may learn to resist fascism in the del Toro film, but its viewers are not asked to exercise their own critical faculties in watching him do so.

This introduces the final piece of Peterson's argument and one of its most dangerous components. If you are completely honest with yourself, he tells his lobsters, and have fully committed to the real-boy mentality of always letting your conscience be your guide, you can identify truth by determining whether it *feels* like truth. When a piece of media affects you emotionally, he explains, it expresses something about humanity that is especially true.

Today, legions of young male followers are taking up this injunction, eager to start treating their guts as God. ("Whenever I listen to him, it's like he's telling me something I already knew," says a fan in Peterson's 2018 *New York Times* profile. "Learning is remembering.") For Peterson, in other words, feelings are facts—at least once you have learned to reject "postmodernism" (any idea that is not identifiably conservative), "cultural Marxism" (a conspiracy theory alleging that the Frankfurt School's intellectual descendants are using identity politics to overthrow Western civilization), and "Derrida and Foucault" (almost always named in the same breath, like Cheech and Chong). Peterson paints all his bogeymen as dangerous relativists, and while he is certainly not the first to insist that we need some ground to stand on in the wake of Nietzsche, he takes his essentialisms much further. Thus Peterson's love of Pinocchio derives from a very specific fantasy about the child, one that treats it as a freethinking vessel: choosy enough to reject falsehoods, receptive enough to affirm Peterson's social order as sidereal truth. Today this fantasy, as the paradoxical basis of right-wing American dreams about social reproduction, holds power far beyond Peterson.

Pinocchio fantasists imagine that even when confronted with propaganda and queers and moral relativism, the unspoiled, blank-slate child will independently arrive at the same moral system as its conservative predecessors, thereby confirming tradition's objective truth and pulling it out of the belly of the whale. The bad animals—foxes, cats, asses, and other queers—are necessary temptations that the child must consider and reject freely, and in so doing choose to be human rather than beast.* In the fantasy's purest form, the little Pinocchios of the world reach the truth through independent judgments about what is good and bad based on personal experience. In the real world, though, they are too easily seduced by the bad, and need a guiding hand against temptation.

OVER THE PAST half century, obsession with the innocent, blank, white child and its imagined vulnerability to sex perverts has become a fixture of American political culture. It gained force in 1977, when the anti-gay activist and erstwhile orange-juice saleswoman Anita Bryant first stormed onto the scene, leading the charge against a gay-rights bill in Florida with her claim that gays had resorted to recruitment in schools to "freshen their ranks." Soon after came the Satanic Panic, with its frenzy of child interviews whose single question—were you abused by your day-care provider?—came with the assumption that any negative answer was a fearful lie. We want Pinocchio to tell the absolute, unbiased truth, as proven by his ungrown nose, but we also demand that the truth be the answer we are seeking. (Is it a coincidence that this is also the precise dynamic of the forced confession?)

But American panic over the vulnerable child did not reach its current fever pitch until 2016, when a man named Edgar Maddison Welch entered a Washington DC pizza restaurant called Comet Ping Pong and fired three shots with a semiautomatic rifle. Pizzagate, initially dismissed by many as a paranoid blip in the delirious early days of the Trump era, saw its chief concepts rehearsed in even more febrile form a year later, in QAnon's central mythology. This time it wasn't just Hillary Clinton and her political cronies kidnapping children and turning them into sex slaves; now they were joined by George Soros, Ellen DeGeneres, and the Dalai Lama, inter alia, and were not just enslaving but killing the children to extract a chemical called adrenochrome from their pituitary glands, then using it to artificially extend their own lives.

This theory has lived on, its reach ever expanding. Disney's 2022 live-action *Pinocchio* spawned a post on the r/conspiracy subreddit (with 308 upvotes and 188 comments) asking whether anyone else found it creepy that Tom Hanks played Geppetto in the new *Pinocchio* movie, considering all the controversy around the actor. The replies are mostly affirmative (a chorus of "Ge-pedos"), many working from the hypothesis that Hanks had recently acquired Greek citizenship because he is a pedophile, and pedophilia is classified as a disability in Greece (it is not), allowing him to not only stay out of jail but collect disability benefits. Hanks, they claim, has been sending covert pedophilic signals for years—just look at his Instagram, where he has posted multiple photos of gloves, which allegedly contain numeric code directing viewers to child-porn websites.

"Are lost gloves considered secret code in the way pizza and hot dog is?" asks one exasperated commenter. "Is there anything that isn't considered secret code?" For most posters, the answers are a clear yes and no, respectively: one Redditor posts a link to still another conspiracy site, where user JimDuyer "explains" the nefarious, satanic paganism of the original Pinocchio story,

---

* Not coincidentally, contemporary Evangelical Christianity rests on the similar belief that a person must confirm their relationship with Jesus of their own volition, and that temptation will be put in their path to test and ultimately strengthen their faith.

arguing that the star that Geppetto wishes on is actually a UFO (it just *feels* true), that the blue-haired fairy is Satan (she repeatedly turns into a goat), and that Jiminy Cricket is Jesus Christ (same initials!), making Pinocchio's murder of him at the beginning of the book an unfathomable sacrilege. JimDuyer is nothing if not a close reader. He posts selection after selection from the original novel and fastidiously combs through each one for hidden symbolism, bristling at idiosyncrasies and treating Collodi's every authorial choice as a clue that, once decoded, will lead to treasure, like the map on the back of the Declaration of Independence.

Peterson reads *Pinocchio* in much the same way, as if parsing a medieval coat of arms for a single correct interpretation. He puzzles obsessively over the significance of overcoats, whales, and sculptures, and expresses relief when he uncovers their true meanings. And what is paranoid thinking if not a pathological overproduction of meaning, where every element of one's world contains its own manifest symbolism and adds up to reveal a vast, coherent, easily explicable totality—thereby freeing the paranoiac from the difficulty of navigating an often ambiguous, at times inexplicable world? What is essentialism if not a form of paranoia?

For Peterson, then, the father-object that must be rescued from the belly of the whale and passed on to his waiting son is not only the "Judeo-Christian" tradition, but the paranoid method of meaning-making that draws exclusively on this tradition for truth. The childless gays—the bad animals—get in the way of this quest by rejecting the demands of patrilineal reproduction for a life on Pleasure Island. It is only by resisting their wiles that the child can reproduce the conditions of the present, from white supremacy to binary gender, and as such offer its parents a sort of immortality. The dream is one of seamless reproduction, of a society that does not change, one that will endure for as many millennia as the crustacean, and, in this way, prove itself to be right.

Peterson himself is only 62, but his followers are already eager to revitalize his ancestral wisdom. On Redbubble, the print-on-demand web store, you can buy a sticker from user TopLobster depicting an enormous, buff Pinocchio bursting through the top of a whale, blood everywhere, dragging a tiny, beleaguered Jordan Peterson behind him.*

IT HAS BEEN decades since I laid Pinocchio to rest. The calendar, the doll, the coin bank made out of an apple-juice jug that I forced my mother to decorate with stick-figure drawings of Jiminy Cricket and Honest John—all sit in boxes in my parents' attic, stacked atop old furniture and furred with dust. In the intervening lifetimes I have developed other interests, like horticulture, and I am no longer three feet tall. Today I have dozens of human friends. But Pinocchio retains his emotional grip on me. I am embarrassed to admit that when I first finished watching the del Toro movie, I burst into tears. Unable to explain my reaction to the person I was with, I could only gesture vaguely at the television and say, through rivulets of snot, "He tried so hard to be good."

I am, after all, someone who spent my first two decades of life earnestly thinking that being good was what made people love

---

* Until recently, TopLobster also sold T-shirts, leggings, and shower curtains that said JEFFREY EPSTEIN DID NOT KILL HIMSELF in red, green, and white to help you "red pill everyone this holiday season."

you, and as a result found myself mistreated over and over again by people who saw me as an opportunity, or a resource, instead of a person. Psychologists call this repetition compulsion. I, at least in this case, call it a Pinocchio fallacy: the idea that your goodness alone will eventually save you, that you don't also need to cultivate some harshness of your own to survive this life. It is hard not to see this little wooden boy as a flash point for the ways I suffered because I turned goodness into its own kind of indisputable truth.

The question of goodness in the face of harshness is, incidentally, exactly what Collodi intended to address for his young readers. The original serialized version of *The Adventures of Pinocchio* ended even more violently than the book we read today, with Pinocchio hanged by the Fox and the Cat in the course of a botched robbery. Collodi was trying to show his readers just how brutal the world was: judges will throw innocent children in jail for no good reason, people will try to swindle you out of your money, your peers will trick you out of malice, your friends will get sick and possibly die, and all this is mostly out of your control. But, at least for Collodi, the message was that if you were good, things might turn out somewhat better than they would otherwise.

This is why Matteo Garrone's 2019 live-action adaptation hits it out of the park. If del Toro's movie pulls at your heartstrings, Garrone's brutalizes you. Garrone sticks faithfully to the original novel, placing Pinocchio in a circa eighteenth-century Italian countryside where cruelty is an everyday fact of life. The costuming is extravagant, the makeup and prosthetics are works of art, and all of it is set amid medieval fortresses and sun-licked fields of wheat. At times it is almost unbearable to watch. Geppetto scrapes at a ravaged pumpkin rind, desperate for sustenance. After sparing Pinocchio from death by fire, Mangiafuoco (Stromboli's ultimately more sympathetic counterpart) tells him to pick another living puppet to die in his place.

Online US audience reviews are split almost evenly between one and five stars, with the film's detractors infuriated by its depictions of violence and naughty behavior. ("This films [sic] sends all the wrong messages to children, skipping school, being rude to strangers, stealing. Torturing people. It should be removed," says one one-star commenter. "If you want your kids to experience nightmare [sic], school and swimming phobia and suicidal ideations then this will be the place to bring them," says another.) The film's sin is that it exposes the child to a world where almost nothing is gentle and almost everyone has learned how to use their fists to survive, even the little children. In Garrone's world, goodness has little to do with purity.

The necessity of cultivating harshness to survive is also central to Peterson's work. His lobsters need to clean their rooms to rise to the top of the dominance hierarchy, because otherwise they will be crushed by an indifferent world. In fact, Peterson starts his Pinocchio lectures by explaining that people should strive to be good for instrumental rather than transcendent reasons. Being trustworthy, honest, and kind makes others trust us, he says, which allows us to win any given social "game" in our lives; this in turn sets us up to win the next game, and ultimately to win, as it were, at life. It's hard to imagine a more cynical attitude toward the concept of goodness, or a worldview more closed off to complex and enduring forms of love.

Peterson and I are ultimately troubled by similar things. We are both concerned with living good lives, the nature of truth, and how we can know what we know for sure. And like both Peterson and generations of misanthropic teen boys, I have found myself drawn to Nietzsche in recent years for reassurance that I, too, have a right to exist, that I do not owe everybody everything, but also that I cannot expect access to a prefabricated morality that will deliver me from evil.

This is where the similarities end, but also where Pinocchio thrives—in the murky spaces where we ask how to be in the world. This figure of uncertainty is rearing his little wooden head, letting out a tiny roar, his entire personage ripe for manipulation but also, at his best, pointing toward a real openness: the possibility that each child might one day leave her father in the belly of the whale and walk resolutely toward an unbreached horizon, brave enough to make space for the things she does not understand, her journey portending a very different kind of world. +

MARK KROTOV
Auto Show Dispatch

New York International Auto Show. Jacob K. Javits Convention Center, March 29–April 7, 2024.

THE BUICK DISPLAY AT THIS YEAR'S NEW York International Auto Show was located in the far back corner of the Javits Center's third-floor main exhibition hall, the kind of dim and lonely zone where you might stumble upon unused sound equipment from the 2016 Hillary Clinton victory party. What I found instead was a solitary, sickly orange Buick Envista, a crossover SUV presumably named to match its sisters, Encore, Envision, and Enclave. Except of course that *encore*, *envision*, and *enclave* are real words.

An auto show, like any trade show, is an assertion of hierarchy. It was obvious from the press days I attended in March that Buick—once a glorious American enterprise, more recently a middling brand with a Tiger Woods endorsement deal—is at the bottom. Like visitors to a car dealership subjected to none of the sales pressure, auto show attendees can take all the time they want examining, entering, photographing, filming, touching, and slamming the doors of the contemporary American automobile. I sat down inside the Envista and considered the market potential of a cheap-feeling crossover with the rear-seat headroom of a coupe; it struck me as limited. I had gotten the sense, walking around the Javits, that after a decade of unquestioned SUV dominance we were now in the early days of decrossoverification: small and small-adjacent SUVs seemed to be getting lower, more compact, and more sedanlike than their recent antecedents. Unlike the Envista, however, most of them were managing this transition without forcing rear-seat occupants to lean forward like visitors in a hospital waiting room, waiting to be told the bad news. Buick's old-school crappy display featured piles of branded cowboy hats and nothing at all in the way of persuasion. "Is this the company's first compact crossover?" I found myself asking the lone and passive sales rep with a curiosity at once feigned and totally sincere. What was I, undercover for CNET? That was a real low point for me.

Everyone has a first convention center, and Atlanta's Georgia World Congress Center was mine. I attended my first auto show there in 1992 or 1993, and back then I would have seen every major brand and model on the market. This hasn't been the case at the Javits for some time. As customers do more and more exploratory browsing online, carmakers are increasingly reluctant to allocate their marketing budgets to labor-, transportation-, and swag-intensive events. Floor space is expensive; hashtags are cheap. Stellantis had an outdoor Jeep test track but was otherwise absent at NYIAS this year—no Chrysler, Dodge, Ram, Fiat, Alfa Romeo, or Maserati—and two of the three major Germans (Mercedes-Benz and BMW) were entirely absent, which would have been unimaginable even a few years ago. GM didn't bother bringing Cadillac, its most interesting brand, and Ford showed up without Lincoln, which in 2016 had a huge stand featuring its brand-new Navigator concept and its then ambassador, Matthew McConaughey. Mazda didn't show up, which was too bad, and neither did Mitsubishi, which was unsurprising. The last time I saw the latter there, I think in 2017, their display was desultory and Buick-like, as if they were putting in a final appearance before opting out of the circuit forever.

Auto shows used to be major media events. Local and national TV networks still show up to deliver low-energy live coverage, but the automotive magazines have thinned out and newspaper car critics are, of course, an endangered species. In their absence an esoteric community of amateurs has stepped in: TikTokers, vloggers, *n+1* editors. Watching the vloggers at work called to mind firefighters rescuing a single cat from a tree or PACs spending millions of dollars on a local election—instances where effort and outcome are irrevocably mismatched. Here were guys who had spent thousands on high-end cameras and microphones to record videos that would get them views in the single digits. At one point I saw a young man sprint across the floor and instinctively thought he was a mass shooter until I noticed the selfie stick. He was a vlogger, booking it toward a Toyota Land Cruiser with his camera and proceeding to bob up and down dramatically around the hood, I guess for cinematographic reasons. It was a poignant, committed performance, and there was no way anyone would watch it once it was uploaded to YouTube.

MY SENTIENT LIFE has roughly coincided with an era of unprecedentedly high automotive quality. In the 1990s, during my early auto show–going days, the xenophobic Reagan-era freakout about Japanese imports was giving way to a near-universal great leap forward. American cars were getting better, as were German cars and Korean cars, while the Japanese econoboxes had attained an exalted realm that seemed to surpass mere questions of reliability. Today, cars are better than they have ever been—and, not unrelatedly, are more similar to one another. There are fewer major car companies, more shared parts and platforms, a stronger regulatory environment, and far less eccentricity. None of this is bad per se, but I wonder if the oft-noted decline of auto enthusiasm isn't in large part a consequence of our high-quality epoch. It seems to me that there is an essential relationship between idiosyncrasy and fandom—the latter can't function without the former. Fans of midcentury English cars bonded over their MGs' and TVRs' ghastly wiring problems and frequent breakdowns, and turn-of-the-millennium Saturn nerds had whatever it was they had at their epic gatherings in Spring Hill, Tennessee.

The only contemporary brand that encourages this kind of collective intensity is Tesla. Tesla famously and not unreasonably hates car dealers, so there's no way they would ever appear at an event organized by the Greater New York Automobile Dealers Association (GNYADA). It was wonderful not to have to actively think about Tesla, one of the most important car companies in the world, and also one of the hardest to theorize without hype or prejudice. But clearly other people were thinking about it a lot. At a press conference introducing the Prologue, the Honda representative emphasized the model's retractable panoramic sunroof, throwing shade (and shade) at Tesla's unyielding, overheating-prone glass version of the same. The sunroof, the guy said, was "one of my favorite things about Prologue," along with its low roofline (more evidence of decrossoverification) and the fact that it has the biggest wheels and tires in Honda history.

Acura is Honda's luxury vehicle division, a category I've always been suspicious of. What's the point of paying a huge premium for a rebadged Toyota Camry with leather seats and wood trim? Without BMW, Mercedes, and Stellantis's numerous brands, the Japanese luxury divisions had way too much space and not enough to fill it with. My main impression of their display areas was that there was a lot of carpeting, which didn't do much to soften the Javits's blunt-force concrete hostility. Infiniti, the upmarket Nissan, was a little more impressive than Acura or Lexus, giving over the entirety of its floor space to a semi-interactive experience dedicated to its new QX80, a beastly full-size SUV with air curtains larger than my head. The Infiniti stand featured swelling electronic strings, blue-green lava lamp illumination, elusive hors d'oeuvres, and a weird audio component showcasing the Infiniti's Klipsch Reference Premiere Audio System—all of which seemed like the appropriate amount of effort needed to sell an SUV that costs $30,000 more than the nearly identical Nissan Armada.

Of course there's no inherent relationship between display quality and market share. Tesla is no less powerful for not showing up, and even Matthew McConaughey couldn't have helped Buick make its case.

But if some of the heavy hitters asserted their presence via absence, a few brands did so via emphatic presence. Toyota had wheelchair basketball and a bouncy castle meant to evoke a swimming pool in honor of the company's Paralympic and Olympic partnerships. The row of sneakers at the Nissan stand was there to promote the Kicks compact crossover, a car named after shoes and possibly also designed to resemble them.

I'm not immune to good marketing, and the cup of citrusy beet tea poured from a stone teapot at the Genesis booth was good marketing. Genesis is a luxury brand like Acura, Infiniti, and Lexus, but it presents itself with swagger and individuation, distinct from both its parent company (Hyundai) and its Japanese and German competitors. The Genesis booth, by far the most elegant at the Javits, had the radiant, unfussy vibe of a French regional bank headquarters from the tail end of the trente glorieuses. Genesis's cars are like its beet tea: subtle, refined, ennobling. It used to bother me that the company's grilles and logos so shamelessly evoked latter-day Bentley models, but then at last year's auto show I sat down in the back seat of a G70, closed the door behind me, heard the most perfect thunk I've ever heard, and realized that in every respect these cars are superior to Bentleys—at a quarter of the price. I will never be in the financial position to purchase a luxury car or a new car, but Genesis is the only brand that makes some minor degree of free-floating longing feel nonhumiliating.

Three of the Genesis cars (Geneses?) on display were the same vivid orange color as the tea. I forget which ones were to the left and right of the X Gran Berlinetta concept because no other car at the show so dominated the visual field. With its impossible wheels, huge haunches, and narrow cockpit, it resembled nothing so much as a race car that had undergone a BBL. Once I got over the pornographic shock of the thing my mind drifted, auto-biographically, to the car racing computer games in the *Need for Speed* series, which featured cars like the Berlinetta traveling through serene nighttime European landscapes. In these games driving was easy and frictionless—supercars could travel through moonlit German villages at 300 km/h, bounce off the town square's guardrails, and keep on cruising. Today the only people who get to drive frictionlessly are billionaire failsons who pilot their Koenigseggs and Paganis through LA and New York at 100 mph. I usually learn about their efforts in graphic news footage of their million-dollar cars crushed against lampposts and storefronts, with pedestrians as collateral damage.

THE BESTSELLING automotive brands in America are Toyota, Ford, and Chevrolet. In 2023, the bestselling models were the Ford F-Series, the Chevy Silverado, the Ram Pickup, the Toyota RAV4, and the Tesla Model Y. The stars of the New York International Auto Show, however, were the Koreans. While Genesis held it down for the Korean luxury sector, Kia did its best as Hyundai's somewhat lesser quasi subsidiary. Introducing its heroically ugly K4, the Kia representative talked at length about the model's various technological innovations, including its AI capability, which allows drivers to hear about their "stocks, sports scores, and owner's manual content." Over and over again I heard about the width of various digital instrumental panels, possibly the saddest example of dick measuring I've encountered in an industry permanently committed to the practice. (The K4's screen is thirty inches wide, if Big Display Energy is the sort of thing that gets you going.)

For all this self-debasement, Kia's fleet is solid and capable. Anytime I rent a car I'm disappointed if it's not a Kia. But the parent company is on another level. Hyundai's press conference was the slickest, its product the most appealing. At last year's show I fell in love with the Ioniq 5, a modern electric car free from Tesla's obnoxious influence. I suspect that even Tesla superfans have a hard time generating enthusiasm for the company's current product line—too ubiquitous, too outdated, too vulgar. The Ioniq 5, by contrast, is designed to thrill. Its exterior has a crisply modular quality, as if one could disassemble it and replace the batteries, but it doesn't look cheap—just user-friendly and a little like a 1980s vacuum cleaner. Its orderly grid of taillights is a creative design detail I haven't seen anywhere else. Like the car as a whole, the grid's futurism gestures backward but is also somehow present-tense, a soothing contrast to both the industry's retro doom loop and the hegemony of aggressive black fascias and interchangeable rooflines. On the Hyundai test track inside the Javits, the charismatic driver treated me to a few laps in the Ioniq 5 N, which can do zero to sixty in a little over three seconds. The acceleration was startling, effortless, and genuinely fun. I never thought I could enjoy simulated engine sounds, a terminal gimmick, but the Ioniq 5 N made even this seem playful—the opposite of Tesla's strained and effortful innovations. Musk famously endowed his cars with a feature that produces fart sounds, an inanity that came to mind as I was looking around a booth that sold faux vanity license plates. I was thinking of getting my 6-year-old daughter a plate with her name on it—maybe New Mexico, with its perfect livery—until I saw, in close succession, an Indiana plate that read BIG TITS and a Georgia plate that read BUST A NUT. Nope! The entire Tesla project feels like a collection of advanced if often undertested technologies with the ethos of these license plates.

The salespersonship at the Hyundai press conference was impressive. Introducing two lesser new models, Randy Parker, the CEO of the company's American division, announced Hyundai's "all-new human-centric technology": the "return of some of those knobs and dials" that nearly every brand—other than the noble anti-touchscreen holdout Mazda—has renounced over the past few years. But these surface-level tweaks weren't the big story. "We're meeting customers where they are on the journey to electrification," Parker said with great pride. If in recent years electric cars had appealed to a smallish number of early adopters, Hyundai is now working toward "what we call the early majority," a brilliant piece of branding that feels like something Democratic consultants get paid millions of dollars to (fail to) come up with.

I was 11 when GM introduced the EV1, the subject of the documentary *Who Killed the Electric Car?*, and the experience of seeing the first real generation of electric cars founder—thanks to corporate conspiracy, consumer disinterest, or both—was radicalizing. Now, nearly three decades later, a group of executives from the most ambitious car company in the world were discussing electrification with a disorienting sense of inevitability. The Hyundai crew didn't have much to say about climate change, but then again, why would they? Auto manufacturers are no more likely to "solve" climate change than oil companies or hedge funds. I admire Hyundai's earnest commitment to electrification and find its belatedness inescapably tragic.

LIKE THE HYUNDAI CEO, Polestar's Thomas Ingenlath—a kind of Germanic Tom Cruise—was unreservedly excited about the electric future. While the other manufacturers suppress the political-environmental implications of their electric vehicles, Polestar—a Swedish company owned by Volvo—labels its seats with sans-serif details about the carbon footprint of its fabrics and the assertion that "animal welfare [has been] secured." This is smug, probably effective, and made me feel like I was sitting inside a bottle of Aesop hand lotion.

"Did it come from the stars?" someone asked in the Polestar promotional video that played before the unveiling of the Polestar 4. "I don't know, but it has one on it." OK. I have to say I was pretty seduced by Polestar's vision—its beautiful, low-slung 3; its hot CEO; its Scandinavian minimalism—until I started talking to a hedge fund guy also hanging around the booth. He had recently rented a Polestar 2 and found it extremely uncomfortable to get in and out of. He had a pretty bearish view of the state of the electric market (unrelated to his rental experience), though he was bullish on Hyundai. At the moment the problem with electric cars, he said, is that not enough people are buying them. EV credits have receded but the price premium hasn't, the US regulatory cudgel is weak, and gas is cheap. What will move the needle? I asked. Another war, the hedge fund guy responded, hedge fund guyishly.

Ingenlath, for his part, devoted most of his time to the Polestar 4's lack of a "traditional rear window," which has been replaced by a camera linked to the rearview mirror (now no longer a mirror, but a screen). There's been a lot of upheaval in the car design space in recent years, and I've gotten used to the elimination of the grille, the dashboard, and other automotive features I once thought were as essential as wheels or doors. But seeing a sea of white recycled steel where a rear windshield should be felt

"A great and necessary book."
—Nikil Saval

TWILIGHT PRISONERS
The Rise of the Hindu Right and the Fall of India
Siddhartha Deb

"A signal of determination and solidarity."
—Roxanne Dunbar-Ortiz

THEIR BORDERS, OUR WORLD
Building New Solidarities with Palestine
Edited by Mahdi Sabbagh
Palestine Festival of Literature

"A must read for this moment."
—Donna Murch

THE BLACK ANTIFASCIST TRADITION
Fighting Back from Anti-Lynching to Abolition
Jeanelle K. Hope & Bill V. Mullen

haymarketbooks.org

like a new frontier. After the Polestar presentation I walked over to the Volkswagen stand and worried the fake-mirror epidemic was more widespread than I'd thought. Sitting in the driver's seat of the ID. Buzz microbus I looked at both side mirrors and saw a mysterious digital pattern. You could make anything appear on these things! It took a few too many seconds for me to grasp that what I was looking at was the booth's bright blue LED backdrop, reflected in mirrors that were still blessedly real. For now.

ON THE MORNING of the second press day I went down to the basement level to attend the World Traffic Safety Symposium, organized by GNYADA. On the show floor the industry people, finance guys, and vloggers—so many vloggers—were recovering from the party circuit, but down here I was in the realm of the bureaucrats. Most of the bureaucrats were very tall. I shared a table with the tallest person in the room—a poised, captivating man who had the air of a benign Robert Moses. This turned out to be New York state DMV head Mark Schroeder, a celebrity sighting that far exceeded my brief run-in with McConaughey years earlier. During his remarks Schroeder praised Kathy Hochul as "the only governor in New York state history who has run a DMV." He told a good joke about former governor David Paterson and said the words "diversity, equity, and inclusion" without embarrassment, with none of the hesitation the CEOs upstairs displayed when tiptoeing around the subject of climate change.

Jennifer Homendy, the chair of the National Transportation Safety Board, delivered the keynote via Zoom from Baltimore, where she was negotiating the aftermath of the Francis Scott Key Bridge collapse, a topic everyone at the show spoke about in muted whispers. Homendy's speech was upsetting and frustrating. "In just these next fifteen minutes," she said, "one person will die on our nation's roads," at which point she launched into a horrific discussion of two recent car crashes the NTSB had investigated, both of which, the agency concluded, could have been prevented with existing technology. In Las Vegas, a driver doing 103 in a 35 zone slammed his Dodge Challenger into a Toyota Sienna minivan. In the Sienna was a family with four children, the youngest of whom was 5 years old. Everyone in both cars was killed. In Avenal, California, a drunk driver in a Dodge Journey SUV going 98 in a 55 zone collided with a Ford F-150 carrying eight people, seven of whom were kids between the ages of 6 and 15, all of whom died along with the driver. Homendy's repeated invocations of these events via their place names—Las Vegas, Avenel—reminded me of the shorthand we use when talking about school shootings. I misheard *hard-braking events* as *heartbreaking events* and don't think I was wrong to do so.

Homendy reiterated that "crashes can be prevented by lifesaving tech in vehicles" that already exists—intelligent speed assistance, passive alcohol detection technology, and so on. Fair enough. But there was a sense of resignation in her remarks, as if all this unspeakable cruelty was ultimately up to the car companies to stop. I was pleased to hear her bring up the weight of electric vehicles—a serious concern; EVs often weigh 30 percent more than their gas-powered equivalents—and then troubled to realize this fact was cited not in defense of pedestrians and bikers, but of the roads.

I'm sure it's true that heavy vehicles are wearing down roads more quickly than anticipated, but with Las Vegas and Avenel on my mind this didn't seem like the central problem American government officials needed to contend with. Every morning I walk my daughter to school through two intersections so poorly designed that we have to go to elaborate lengths to avoid the nearly 100 percent of drivers who illegally plow through a few flimsy grabber tubes and always fail to stop at the crosswalk. I'm glad that New York's intelligent speed assistance program seems to be having a positive effect, just as I was glad about congestion pricing until the "only governor in New York state history who has run a DMV" blew the whole thing up in an act of thoughtless political immolation it will take decades to repair. But the scale of the safety crisis is vast and radically out of proportion to all the cheerful innovating taking place upstairs.

The US's biggest infrastructure project—bigger than the New Deal–era dams and the Erie Canal—was the highway system, which destroyed the American city and, arguably but I think not that arguably, American society itself. The country's mid-century racist spatial self-destruction is a crime that will never be sufficiently atoned for. Whenever a child walking along a four-lane exurban road is killed by a driver who swerves into the shoulder, whenever someone can get away with driving 98 miles per hour in a 55 zone, whenever a family of seven in an ostensibly safe minivan is killed despite the self-evident technological ability to limit speeds, redesign roads, and enforce existing regulations, it seems reasonable to infer that car culture isn't really about sexy concept cars or futuristic taillights. Car culture is really about death.

"ACTUALLY SO FUCKED that luxury victims have safety options lower trim levels don't," I wrote in my notepad during Homendy's keynote. I meant vehicles, not victims, but the point stands. It's obvious that American life is a series of cruel disparities, but the idea that

automatic emergency braking and forward collision warning are options only available to a privileged few, despite the absence of any technical constraints to universal adoption, still feels, well, fucked. We desperately need much more stringent safety regulations and we seem unlikely to get them.

During the Hyundai press conference discussion of Hyundai Pay, a technology that places the brand "at the nexus of the auto industry, the payments industry, and the EV charging industry," I had the thought that the interior of a new car is the only place where one can experience the total tech dream as it's been conceived of by its proselytizers. While driving you can turn your Klipsch Reference Premiere Audio System all the way up, suppress the outside world, and attain pure, blissful dissociation—unless a bridge collapses under you, or (more likely) you get distracted by a text and crash into a minivan.

"It drives so much smaller than it really is," I overheard an Infiniti QX80 salesperson tell a couple of potential customers. Immediately this stood out to me as one of the truest and most ambiguous claims anyone could make about life in the 21st century. Electrification is a real if unstable trend, and decrossoverification is probably not nothing, but the story that matters above all others is that cars continue to get bigger, even as that size is mitigated by all kinds of refinements. For a recent trip I needed to rent a car with six seats and was upgraded by Thrifty to an eight-seat Chevy Tahoe, which also drove much smaller than it really is. At nearly six thousand pounds, the thing was smooth and nimble: easy to accelerate, easy to steer through the Taconic State Parkway's precarious curves. It was also easy to forget the smaller and more vulnerable cars—and their passengers—in the other lanes. I don't think any of this constitutes progress. Size inflation has been so normalized that it's almost impossible to appreciate the enormity of American cars. The desire for status, the desire for height, a fragile and increasingly attenuated relationship to masculinity, the global war on terror, the rise of safety consciousness, a legal regime that has made the production of fuel-inefficient vehicles far more appealing to car manufacturers than smaller and more eco-conscious ones—all these have been held responsible for the rise of the SUV and all these are indeed responsible. But we shouldn't underrate, as an explanatory factor, the desire to wall oneself off from the world, to float above degraded infrastructure and the threat of violence even as one contributes to both.

As Kate Aronoff has written in the *New Republic*, emissions standards are improving (too slowly) but don't come close to adequately addressing the problem the EPA helped create: a two-tiered system by which

SUVs and large trucks can keep on trucking with embarrassing gas mileage. Automakers who lobbied for this legal regime in the first place have responded rationally, by making more SUVs and large trucks and fewer regular cars. At the Ford stand I spotted a limited-edition Sydney Sweeney–branded robin's-egg-blue Mustang, with Sweeney's "heart bolt emblem" emblazoned all over the car's interior and exterior. (Her signature is on the engine.) This is a world-historically smart collaboration (notwithstanding the online creeps obsessed with Sweeney's breasts as an arbiter of Western civilization's revival or whatever), but also a sideshow, given that the Mustang is the only remaining passenger car in Ford's lineup.

I UNDERSTAND that life goes on in the imperium as people die in a genocide supported and underwritten by the US. I've been to movies since the war began, have attended and even hosted children's birthday parties. And still the experience of spending two days inside a convention center reflecting on an industry that has done so much to destroy and destabilize this country and our planet and millions of its inhabitants filled me with disgust and despair. Downstairs on the first day, I saw a customized fifth-generation Toyota Land Cruiser with a rear windshield sticker that read SORRY FOR MY SCRATCHES AND DENTS, THESE ARE ACTUAL WAR WOUNDS. The Land Cruiser was, of course, spotless.

It felt right to spend my final minutes at the show with the Hummer. My family had just immigrated to the US when the Hummer—the civilian version of the Humvee—went on sale to the general public in the wake of the company's PR triumph during the Gulf War, and by the time the brand had started to conquer the hearts and minds of American suburbanites in 1999 I was a little more attuned to the market. The gigantic Ford Excursion was launched around the same time, and it was impossible to ignore consumers' lust for size. Positioned not far from the Buick Envista in GM's Siberian sector of the Javits, the GMC Hummer EV looked and felt massive. Inside, every drawer, compartment, and air vent was at least three times the size of what was normal and necessary, but then that goes for the Hummer itself. The truck's most notable feature is a black-on-black American flag embossed at the top of its C-pillar.

The Israel Defense Forces have purchased more than two thousand Humvees from the US, and three of four military utility vehicles manufactured in Israel are based on American trucks. (The fourth, the MDT David, is based on platforms from the Land Rover Defender and the Land Cruiser.) Sitting inside the EV, with its outrageous scale and terrible sight lines, it occurred to me that the last (and sometimes first) US-produced object many victims of wars throughout the world encounter is probably a Humvee. +

OUR CONTRIBUTORS

Dan Berger is the author of *Stayed on Freedom: The Long History of Black Power Through One Family's Journey*, among other books. He coordinates the Washington Prison History Project.

Tom Bubul is an artist living in the Twin Cities.

Daniel Denvir is the host of *The Dig* podcast and the author of *All-American Nativism: How the Bipartisan War on Immigrants Explains Politics as We Know It*.

Saidiya Hartman is the author of *Scenes of Subjection*, *Lose Your Mother*, and *Wayward Lives, Beautiful Experiments*. She is a University Professor at Columbia University.

Angelo Hernandez Sias is a writer and critic living in New Haven. He is at work on a novel.

Sasha Karsavina is a translator and PhD student at Yale University.

Laura Kolbe is the author of the poetry collection *Little Pharma*. Her most recent piece for *n+1* was "Learning and Not Learning Abortion," in Issue 44.

Mark Krotov is coeditor in chief of *n+1*.

Leigh Claire La Berge is the author of *Marx for Cats: A Radical Bestiary* and the forthcoming *Fake Work: How I Began to Suspect That Capitalism Is a Joke*.

Raven Leilani is the author of *Luster* and the winner of the Dylan Thomas Prize and the NBCC John Leonard Prize, among others. She teaches creative writing at Harvard University.

Reed McConnell is a writer and anthropologist living in Chicago.

Philippa Mullins is a translator and research associate at KU Leuven, Belgium.

Rachel Ossip is the deputy editor of Triple Canopy and a contributing editor at *n+1*. Her most recent piece for *n+1* was "Living Inside," in Issue 37.

Daria Serenko is a Russian author, feminist opposition activist, and cofounder of the Feminist Anti-War Resistance, a movement against Russia's invasion of Ukraine.

Nadezhda Vikulina is a PhD student at Harvard University. She is an assisting editor for English-from-Russian poetry translations for Cicada Press.

ACKNOWLEDGMENTS

A version of Saidiya Hartman's "Crow Jane Makes a Modest Proposal" was presented as a lecture at Amherst College and as the Alchemy Lecture at York University in 2023. Raven Leilani's "Death of the Party" is adapted from a craft talk at NYU's Writers in Paris program presented in 2024. "Girls and Institutions" is excerpted from *Girls and Institutions* by Daria Serenko, originally published in Russian by No Kidding Press in 2021.

LETTERS

SHEINtrouble

Dear Editors,

In almost every issue, *n+1* seems to have an awful tale that goes down easily. It's a tough call, but for me the writer in Issue 47 who took on the most nauseating topic in the most (barely) stomachable way was Nicole Lipman writing on SHEIN ("Super Cute Please Like"). I was sweating and gagging through it, but I did get through.

I started a clothing and fabric recycling and exchange program at a community center here in Northern Michigan in 2017. I did this in part because I knew the fast fashion and plastic clothing waste problem was bad. But I guess I had no idea it would get as bad—environmentally, socially, psychologically—as Lipman depicts in her review of one global fast-fashion-addiction juggernaut.

When I presented my idea for the Fibershed to the director of Grow Benzie, a local nonprofit funded by grants and donations, I had to make the usual sorts of number-based claims about tons of clothing waste, the problem of plastic pollution in the Great Lakes watershed (our major concern here, but yes, of course, also the ocean), and how the program would be diverting material from the landfill and waterways while also encouraging the creation, exchange, and repair of natural-fiber clothing and crafts. But I knew people would use the heck out of the Fibershed whether or not they gave a shit about the environment.

As a fully convinced person myself, I often question the utility of information when it comes to environmental matters and behavior change. For most people, even once they're made aware that their habits are bad, feeling righteous and receiving social support for doing a good thing or not doing a bad thing is not enough for them to change. If the thought of a freshwater plankton choking on a weensie bit of lurex doesn't make you not buy that sweater, then I don't know what to tell you. Except that I too want lurex. I want glitter. How can I still get shine without SHEIN?

This is the factor that Lipman brings to light: disgust. Disgust with oneself. By going into the belly of the beast and being really gross about it, Lipman exposes an impulse most of us have and forces us to really look at it. How is my going to Goodwill and coming out with a garbage bag full of clothes any different, really, from ordering several $2.99 items from a company like SHEIN? Because I drove there in my electric car? I would never, ever buy anything from SHEIN. But I absolutely understand the impulse.

The Fibershed worked on an alternative currency model, where the currency was tied to something objective: weight. A new gold standard! And unlike a lot of programs, it was not means tested. You brought in a garbage bag full of fabric, fiber, or clothing, or anything that was fibercraft related (a sewing machine, bobbins, yarn, bins or racks, a pile of random notions), you watched me or another volunteer weigh it on a baby scale, and that's how much credit you got, at a rate of one fibercredit per pound. You could then spend your credit on pounds of anything in the shed. The only rule for the exchange was that items had to be clean (stained was fine). We even took broken sewing machines because we had a volunteer who was into rehabbing them or parting them out. I kept track of people's fibercredits on a basic Google spreadsheet. Inevitably some people had hundreds of fibercredits they couldn't or didn't want to use, and they would designate some of them as donor credit for shoppers who didn't have anything to exchange. Perhaps not coincidentally, this project started around the time of Marie Kondo's tidying-up magic, and one thing I learned is that there are many, many ladies (not all, but mostly, ladies) with sewing and craft rooms full of incredible stuff.

We had workshops where people could learn—using essentially free materials they could afford to mess up on—how to sew, crochet (the crocheted rag rug workshop was a hit), knit, and weave. There were treasures: a 1953 wedding dress in perfect condition that no one ended up taking; a bag full of dog hair that someone took almost immediately. And there were magic moments: when a high school librarian teaching a sewing workshop saw me "mousing" with my sewing machine foot pedal (operating it with my hand, because its cord wasn't long enough to reach the floor), she discovered a way for a disabled student in a wheelchair to sew.

The Fibershed had old gym socks, smoke- and dog-stench-filled piles of stuff occasionally left outside our door, and bad, bad fashion. But it wasn't disgusting. It was friendly, and easy, and challenging, and cheap, and time-intensive, and surprising, and reliable, and deeply interesting, and something that I can only describe as human. It was imagining possible outfits and creations, and making thousands of choices and selections, essentially for free, and not feeling gross about it at all. It was staring at a piece of cotton in what you thought was a beautiful pattern and being shocked no one had taken it yet; it was finding out that there's no accounting for taste, that one person's bag of dog hair is another person's treasure, and feeling grateful and relieved about that.

At the very end, right before donations and open hours were ended because of the pandemic, we were furiously making cloth masks and debating the virtues of different fabrics, styles (layers or filter pockets?), and fastening schemes. The exponential growth of SHEIN is probably inextricable from the conditions of the pandemic: lockdown, fear of contamination, the illusion of something clean and new, the atrophying of social muscles. The impulse toward acquisition is complex and obviously not logical. It remains even though you have only one body and, even after lockdown, not nearly enough occasions to display your goods. As gross as it is, I think this need bears within it a kernel of something healthy and even environmentally sound: imagination, creativity, and connection.

—*Emily Votruba*

The Organic Intellectual Situation

Dear Editors,

I was interested to find the popular Gramscian term *organic intellectuals* in William Harris's "Acid Rhythms" (Issue 47). On the subject of Detroit in the 1950s, Harris writes, "by then, three of the US left's most original organic intellectuals"—C. L. R. James, Grace Lee Boggs, and James Boggs—"had transplanted themselves to the city, or at least had made plans to." Since 1957, following the first English translation of Antonio Gramsci's *Prison Notebooks*, *organic intellectual* has come to refer to any thinker who opposes the hegemony of capital and is racialized and/or from the working class—an intellectual who speaks for the people. Harris uses the term *organic intellectuals* in this idiomatic meaning.

However, the colloquial use of *organic intellectual* loses the analytic complexity and integrity of Gramsci's 1929 phrase. Gramsci defines the role of the organic intellectual as giving a social group "homogeneity and an awareness of its own function." An organic intellectual is not merely from a certain class, but elaborates a latent truth about that class. In other words, an intellectual is not an identity marking the intelligence or exceptionality of an individual, but a *structural* category in a social formation. All labor requires thinking. In "even the most degraded and mechanical [work] there exists a minimum of technical qualification," Gramsci reminds us. But not all people who think are intellectuals.

In the *Prison Notebooks*, the only substantial example of an organic intellectual Gramsci provides is counterintuitive: the capitalist entrepreneur who organizes her subordinates and creates culture. Gramsci writes, "thus it is to be noted that the mass of the peasantry, although it performs an essential function in the world of production, does not elaborate its own 'organic' intellectual." The popular use of *organic intellectual*, like in "Acid Rhythms," elides the major claim in Gramsci's analysis: that there are classes in society who do *not* have their own intellectuals. Later in the *Prison Notebooks* it becomes apparent that for Gramsci it is structurally impossible to claim to represent the masses, or to speak in the name of a large and fractured collectivity.

To transform the phrase *organic intellectual* in this way obscures the pessimistic question that occurs to readers of the *Prison Notebooks*: Why can only capitalists produce their own intellectual class? And how can a class that, by definition, has been excluded from representation begin to represent itself? Returning to the original Gramscian meaning brings up other questions: If organic intellectuals from marginalized classes existed, what would they specialize in? How would they organize society? What does a subaltern metaphysics look like? When we use *organic intellectuals* the way Harris and many others do, we assume that Gramsci's original textual contradictions can be neatly resolved. We transform the generative impossibility of the dynamic confrontation between an organic intellectual and capital into a static descriptor.

—Deeva Gupta

ACKNOWLEDGMENTS

SUPPORTERS

Hanif Abdurraqib
Mitzi Angel
Bobby Baird
Jack Bankowsky
Jennifer Baumgardner
Rachael Bedard &
    Gideon Friedman
Avanti Birla
Peter Blackstock
Amanda & Charles Brainerd
Amanda Branson Gill
AJ Brown
Sarah Burnes
Adam Chang
Kent Cherny
Cassius Clay
Amanda Claybaugh
Jeremy Cohen
Peter & Barbara Cohen
Frederic Cornu
Christopher Cox &
    Georgia Cool
Nellie Debbeler
Rimjhim Dey
Andrew Ellner
Henry Finder
Melissa Flashman
Blake & Andrew Foote

Elizabeth Gately
DW Gibson
Jon-Jon Goulian
Jeff Gramm & Susie Heimbach
Tom Healy & Fred P. Hochberg
Ida Hempel & James Rathmell
Courtney Hodell
Eddie Joyce &
    Martine Beamon
Meredith Kaffel Simonoff
Joshua Kim & Monica Chang
Lawrence Kolodney &
    Heather Nelson
Christopher Lay
Glenn Ligon
Michael Lindgren
Susie Lopez
Allison Lorentzen
Nick Marino
Maureen Miller
Todd Moore
Jennifer Oki &
    Christien Tompkins
Conor O'Neil
Laura Owens
Richard & Mary Jo Parrino
Samuel Popkin
Nausicaa Renner

Bruce Robbins
Christian Rudder
Katrina Rudmin
Anthony Ruozzi
Jim Rutman
Rebecca Saletan &
    Marshall Messer
Daniel Schlozman
Gary Sernovitz
Akash Shah
Susie Simonson
Mona Simpson
George Sirignano
Matthew Specter &
    Marjan Mashhadi
Katherine Sugg
Astra Taylor
The Tortorici Family
Joyce Varma
Jon Vesey
Anders Widebrant
Anna Wiener
Alexander Wilson
Scott Wood-Prince
Molly Young
Lynne Zeavin

INSTITUTIONAL SUPPORTERS

Amazon Studios
The Cheney Agency
Farrar, Straus and Giroux
The Gernert Company
Hachette Book Group
HarperCollins

LitNYS
Massie & McQuilkin
NYU Creative Writing
    Program
Penguin Random House
Purslane

Simon & Schuster
Soho Press
The Spencer Foundation
W. W. Norton & Company
WME

If you'd like to become a supporter of n+1, visit nplusonemag.com/donate.

FOUNDATION

The n+1 Foundation is a 501(c)(3) non-profit literary organization committed to publishing and promoting work by new and diverse writers whose style, subject matter, and intellectual ambition are underrepresented in mainstream publications.

STAFF	BOARD OF DIRECTORS	ADVISORY BOARD
Publisher MARK KROTOV	Ronald Barusch Carla Blumenkranz (emerita) Jynne Dilling	Carla Blumenkranz Kate Bolick AJ Brown
Executive Director DAYNA TORTORICI	Thomas Gebremedhin Keith Gessen	Georgia Cool Christopher Cox
Managing Editor TESS EDMONSON	Jeremy Glick Mark Greif Alia Hanna Habib	Jynne Dilling Eddie Joyce Katy Lederer
Development Director DANI OLIVER	Chad Harbach Mark Krotov	Allison Lorentzen Chris Parris-Lamb
Web Editor LISA BORST	Katy Lederer Lulu Martinez Chris Parris-Lamb (emeritus)	Whitney Parris-Lamb Henry Moynahan Rich Sarah Whitman-Salkin
Operations Manager NICOLE LIPMAN	Dushko Petrovich Nikil Saval (emeritus)	Thai-Son Vu
Circulation Assistant ALAN DEAN	Dayna Tortorici Zhao Yang	

Interns
Jesica Bak
Arman Deendar
Sheena Meng

Special thanks to
Adi Gandhi
Wick Hallos
Corinne Leong
Simone Liu
Eden Weinstein
Angela Yin

The n+1 Foundation's programs are made possible in part by the New York State Council on the Arts with the support of the Office of the Governor and the New York State Legislature, as well as by public funds from the New York City Department of Cultural Affairs, in partnership with the City Council. n+1 is also supported in part by the National Endowment for the Arts and is a proud recipient of a Whiting Literary Magazine Prize.

"Properly making sense of [Hudson's] legacy will require a full-dress survey at the National Gallery of Art or the Museum of Modern Art, but until then, we have this remarkable book…"
Andrew Russeth, **Artnet**

EDITED BY STEVE LAFRENIERE

"Biographies of contemporary art dealers are rarer than funny painters… Now they have some company—an utterly human telling realized through group authorship, voices guided by love for a singular character and, it is hard not to feel, a vanished civilization as well."
David Robbins, **Artbook**

"[*Hello We Were Talking About Hudson*] restores life—to the extent that it's possible—to the singular tone of the seminal gallery and its still mysterious founder, in all their unknowable complexity."
Bianca Bova, **Chicago Reader**

SOBERSCOVE PRESS

"A bold comparative model... Surprising connections and insights."

—**Adriana X. Jacobs,**
University of Oxford

Yael Segalovitz's *How Close Reading Made Us* shows that close reading exerted a far-reaching influence, impacting writers such as Clarice Lispector, Yehuda Amichai, William Faulkner, A. B. Yehoshua, and João Guimarães Rosa.

COMING SOON FROM
SUNY Press | sunypress.edu

"THIS BOOK IS A MUST-READ FOR ANYONE WHO WANTS TO UNDERSTAND WHAT AILS U.S. HEALTH CARE AND HOW TO FIX IT."

—I. GLENN COHEN,
HARVARD LAW SCHOOL

"Remarkable... meticulous historical context and examination of the strengths and weaknesses of our system of divided government... from the impact of evolving technology to consideration of current moral and cultural debates about end-of-life decisions, reproductive justice, gender identity, healthcare, and abortion, profound questions are deftly articulated and explored."

—CHRISTINE DURHAM,
CHIEF JUSTICE UTAH SUPREME COURT (RET.)

AVAILABLE NOW FROM
OXFORD UNIVERSITY PRESS

STANFORD UNIVERSITY PRESS

The Arts of Logistics
Artistic Production in Supply Chain Capitalism
Michael Shane Boyle
POST*45

A new map of supply chain capitalism that demonstrates how art and logistics are linked by the infrastructures and violence that keep supply chains moving

NOW IN PAPERBACK
Nothing Happened
A History
Susan A. Crane

"Nothing" is often a catch-all for everything uninteresting or simply not there. Discover how "Nothing" can also be something—histories we have known and can remember

The Cancel Culture Panic
How an American Obsession Went Global
Adrian Daub

A clever analysis of the global spread of cancel culture discourse and its hold on readers around the world

Totalitarianism
A Borderline Idea in Political Philosophy
Simona Forti
SQUARE ONE: FIRST-ORDER QUESTIONS IN THE HUMANITIES

A precise, compact discussion of the motives, misunderstandings, and controversies that have animated totalitarianism's current resurgence

New Sincerity
American Fiction in the Neoliberal Age
Adam Kelly
POST*45

A field-defining account of a period both recent and historically bound, and of a generation of writers who continue to shape the present literary landscape

Reading Typographically
Immersed in Print in Early Modern France
Geoffrey Turnovsky
STANFORD TEXT TECHNOLOGIES

An analysis of typographical developments in early modern France as the dominant paradigm of our contemporary age

sup.org
stanfordpress.typepad.com